The First Book of
DrawPerfect®

The First Book of
DrawPerfect®

Susan Baake Kelly and James Kevin Kelly

HOWARD W. SAMS & COMPANY
Macmillan Computer Publishing

*To our mothers,
for their love and support*

©1990 by Susan Baake Kelly and James Kevin Kelly

FIRST EDITION
FIRST PRINTING—1990

All rights reserved. No part of this book shall be reproduced, stored in a retrieval system, or transmitted by any means, electronic, mechanical, photocopying, recording, or otherwise, without written permission from the publisher. No patent liability is assumed with respect to the use of the information contained herein. While every precaution has been taken in the preparation of this book, the publisher and authors assume no responsibility for errors or omissions. Neither is any liability assumed for damages resulting from the use of the information contained herein.

International Standard Book Number: 0-672-27315-2
Library of Congress Catalog Card Number: 90-70768

Acquisitions and Development Editor: *Scott Arant*
Manuscript Editor: *Linda Hawkins*
Production Coordinator: *Becky Imel*
Cover Design: *Held & Diedrich Design*
Production: *Brad Chinn, Sally Copenhaver, Denny Hager, Tami Hughes, William Hurley, Charles Hutchinson, Lori Lyons, Jennifer Matthews, Dennis Sheehan, Bruce Steed, Mary Beth Wakefield, Nora Westlake*
Indexer: *Joelynn Gifford*
Technical Reviewer: *Damon Darais*

Printed in the United States of America

Contents

Introduction, *xiii*

How to Use This Book, *xv*
DrawPerfect Requirements, *xvii*
Conventions Used in This Book, *xvii*
Trademark Acknowledgments, *xviii*
Acknowledgments, *xix*

1 Getting Started, *1*

Starting DrawPerfect, *2*
    Starting DrawPerfect If You Have Installed the Shell, *2*
    Starting DrawPerfect If You Have Not Installed the Shell, *3*
The Main DrawPerfect Screen, *4*
    The Pull-Down menus, *5*
    The Icon Menu, *6*
    The Prompt and Status Line, *8*
    The Drawing Window, *8*

Cursor Movement, *10*
    Using the Mouse, *10*
    Using the Keyboard, *10*
Moving Through the Pull-Down Menus, *12*
    Using the Mouse, *12*
    Using the Keyboard, *12*
Using the Function Keys, *13*
Getting Help, *14*
    Alphabetical Help on DrawPerfect Features, *16*
    Function Key Help Screens, *17*
    The Topical Guide, *18*
    The Function Key Template, *20*
    Exiting Help, *21*
Clearing the Screen, *22*
Exiting DrawPerfect, *25*
What You Have Learned, *26*

2 *Your First Business Chart, 29*

Creating a Bar Chart, *31*
    The Graph Edit Screen, *32*
    Using the Graph Data Screen to Enter Your Data, *34*
Saving Your Chart, *39*
Printing Your Chart, *43*
Retrieving and Editing the Chart, *46*
    Using the Move Option, *47*
    Modifying Data in the Chart, *52*
    Changing the Bars to Lines, *54*
    Typing a Subtitle and Y-Axis Label, *56*
    Using the Rotate Option, *58*
    Using the Move Option on the Graph Edit Screen, *58*
    Replacing the Graph Description and WPG File, *59*
    Using the Graph Description File with New Data, *60*

Enhancing Your Chart with an Image from
   the DrawPerfect Figure Library, *62*
What You Have Learned, *66*

3 *Your First Text Chart,* *69*

Creating a Text Chart, *70*
    Saving Your Text Chart, *81*
Previewing and Printing Your Chart, *82*
Editing Your Text Chart, *84*
    Returning to the Text Chart Screen to Modify
      the Title, *84*
    Retrieving the Globe Figure, *86*
    Erasing the Bullets, *89*
    Retrieving a Clip-Art Figure for the Bullets, *90*
    Copying the Figure, *92*
    Creating the Horizontal Line, *94*
    Typing a Text Line, *96*
Using DrawPerfect's Built-in Text Chart Formats, *99*
What You Have Learned, *101*

4 *Your First Drawing,* *103*

Using the Grid, *104*
Drawing Rectangles and Triangles, *105*
    Drawing with the Box Tool, *106*
    Drawing with the Polygon Tool, *108*
    Deleting and Undeleting an Object, *110*
Clearing the Drawing from Your Screen Without
   Clearing the Options, *113*
Drawing the Three Rectangles That Form the Foundation
   of the Cupola, *113*
    Drawing the Roof, *117*
    Drawing the Windows, *120*

Creating the Wind Vane, *122*
What You Have Learned, *126*

5 More About the Drawing Tools and Options, *129*

How to Draw Arrows, Ellipses, Arcs, and Curves, *130*
    Drawing an Arrow, *130*
    Drawing an Ellipse, *132*
    Drawing an Arc, *134*
    Drawing a Curve, *136*
Using the Size and Stretch Tools, *137*
    Using Size, *137*
    Using Stretch, *139*
Constrain, *141*
Zoom and Pan, *142*
    Using Zoom, *142*
    Using Pan, *146*
Drawing with Freehand, *147*
What You Have Learned, *148*

6 More About DrawPerfect's Editing Tools, *151*

Selecting an Item or Area, *152*
Delete, *156*
    Restoring Deleted Items, *157*
Copy, *157*
Move, *159*
Size, *161*
The Front and Back Options on the Edit Menu, *163*
Rotate and Mirror, *165*
Modify, *166*
    Using Modify to Edit Text, *167*

Modify Drawing Objects, *168*
Modify Figure, *169*
What You Have Learned, *171*

7 *Printer Control,* *173*

Printing Your Work, *173*
    Printing the Entire Chart or Drawing in Your Drawing Window, *174*
    Printing a Section of a Chart or Drawing, *176*
    Printing Without Retrieving, *178*
Controlling the Printer, *180*
Previewing the Printed Drawing, *183*
Print Options, *184*
What You Have Learned, *185*

8 *More About Business Graphs*, *187*

Pie Charts, *188*
    Using the Options Menu to Add a 3-Dimensional Effect and Data Values, *191*
    Exploding a Slice of the Pie, *193*
Line Charts, *194*
    Grid Lines, *197*
    Formatting the Numbers on the Y-Axis, *198*
    Adding Markers for the Data Points, *200*
Stacked Bar Charts, *201*
    Changing the Fill Style and Colors for the Bars, *202*
Area Charts, *203*
Creating a Chart Using Data in a Spreadsheet, *204*
What You Have Learned, *207*

9 File Management, 211

The List Files Screen, 212
  Using Look to View the Contents of a Directory, 218
  Using Look to View the Contents of a File, 220
  Name Search: Navigating Through the List Files Screen, 222
Using List Files to Retrieve a File, 223
Making Backup Copies, 226
  Copying One File to Another Drive or Directory, 227
  Selecting a Group of Files to Copy Simultaneously, 228
Deleting Files, 230
  Deleting One File, 231
  Deleting a Group of Files, 231
Moving Files, 232
  Moving One File, 232
  Moving a Group of Files, 233
Renaming a File, 234
Printing Disk Files, 234
Creating and Changing Directories, 235
  Creating a New Directory, 236
  Changing the Default Directory, 237
  Deleting a Directory, 238
What You Have Learned, 239

10 Using the Shell to Integrate DrawPerfect and WordPerfect, 241

Starting the Shell, 242
Switching Between WordPerfect 5.1 and DrawPerfect, 243
Using the Shell to Transfer Files Between DrawPerfect and WordPerfect 5.1, 247
  Transferring a DrawPerfect Chart into WordPerfect, 249

Transferring a Graphic Image from WordPerfect to DrawPerfect, *253*

Retrieving WordPerfect Text into DrawPerfect, *254*

Spell Checking DrawPerfect Text in WordPerfect, *256*

Creating a Bar Chart from a WordPerfect Table, *257*

What You Have Learned, *259*

11 *Presentations and Slides, 263*

Creating and Viewing a Slide Show, *264*
- Using the Presentation: Edit Screen, *265*
- Viewing Your Slide Show, *269*

Editing a Slide Show, *271*

Page Options, *274*
- Margins, *274*
- Shading Top to Bottom in View, *275*
- Selecting a Top Color and Bottom Color, *276*

Producing 35mm Slides from Your DrawPerfect Files, *277*
- Preparing Your DrawPerfect Files for a Slide Service, *278*

What You Have Learned, *279*

12 *An Introduction to Macros, 281*

Creating Your First Macro, *282*
- A Drawing Macro, *285*

Editing a Macro, *287*

Designating a Default Directory for Your Macros, *290*

Using the Macros That Are Included with DrawPerfect, *291*

What You Have Learned, *294*

A Installation, *295*

Program Installation on a Hard Disk, *295*
    Basic Installation, *297*
    Printer Installation, *301*
    Custom Installation, *303*
Installing the Shell Files, *306*
    How to Set Up Your Computer So That the Shell Menu Appears As Soon As You Turn on Your Computer, *308*
Installing the Keyboard Definition Files and/or Help Files, *309*
Installing the Figure Library Files, *310*
    Custom Figure Library Installation, *311*
    Basic Figure Library Installation, *311*

B Changing DrawPerfect's Defaults, *313*

Installing Your Mouse, *313*
Display, *315*
Environment, *317*
    The Backup Options, *318*
Initial Settings, *319*
Location of Files, *321*

Index, *323*

Introduction

If it's true that a "picture is worth a thousand words," why did the vast majority of people decide to quit drawing after the third grade? Obviously, they felt that mastering the written word was the easier path to pursue, so the visual arts were left to a "gifted" few.

Technology and personal computers have changed all that by creating a new generation of artists. Graphic art is now available to anyone who can press a key and retrieve a clip-art file, and in homes and offices across the country instant illustrators are being born every day. As a result, graphic programs have proliferated in the marketplace, and choosing one can be a staggering decision. However, if you're a WordPerfect user, DrawPerfect is the obvious choice for your business graphics. Even if all you want to do is create a few bar graphs to enhance your WordPerfect reports, we think you'll love it.

But what is DrawPerfect? WordPerfect Corporation, the company that gave us that wonderful word processing program of the same name, defines their new software as a presentation graphics program that you can use to enhance all your documents and presentations. Indeed, DrawPerfect lets you create impressive business graphs, text charts, drawings, and self-running "slide show" presentations on your monitor.

You'll find that DrawPerfect is easy to learn, especially if you are already familiar with WordPerfect, and you don't have to be artistically inclined at all. In fact, the program includes an extensive figure library of over 500 clip-art drawings, such as flags, maps, arrows, computers, animals, people, and many other business, military, sports, and transportation symbols. You can use these figures to add flair to your charts and graphs, and modify them to your heart's content. Like WordPerfect, DrawPerfect is very forgiving, providing a variety of tools that you can use to edit and correct the inevitable mistakes that accompany creative endeavors. This should lay to waste all your old anxieties about artwork, even if all you could ever draw were Mommy and Daddy stick figures!

Your DrawPerfect creations can be produced in several mediums: color or black-and-white laser printouts, overhead transparencies, and even 35mm slides. To print them, you can use a dot matrix printer, laser printer, film recorder, or plotter. You can export DrawPerfect files into several other formats, including CGM (Computer Graphics Metafile), VideoShow (General Parametrics modified NAPLPS file), SCODL (Matrix Instruments Slide format file), and HPGL (Hewlet-Packard Graphics Language Plotter File). You can also import files from many other formats, including TIFF, PCX, CGM, HPGL, Lotus PIC, GEM, and DXF.

If you use a spreadsheet like PlanPerfect, Lotus, or Excel, you'll be pleased to know that DrawPerfect can easily create business graphs, such as bar charts and pie charts, using data from a spreadsheet file. As you would expect, DrawPerfect makes it very easy to exchange data with WordPerfect, especially if you are using the Shell utility that comes with the program. You can create attractive graphics in DrawPerfect, then press three keys to transfer them into WordPerfect for use in newsletters, reports, or similar documents.

Throughout this book we've provided many examples of business charts, graphs, and drawings that we've created with DrawPerfect, so do some browsing and then don your beret and start drawing!

How to Use This Book

We have organized this book so that you can use the first four chapters as a hands-on tutorial, and the remaining chapters as guides to specific features and utilities. As with all computer software, the best way to learn DrawPerfect is to sit down with your computer and use it, so please don't hide in a library and try to read our book!

If you've never used DrawPerfect, be sure to read the first chapter, *Getting Started,* to learn all the basics. You'll learn how to start DrawPerfect, and how to use the main DrawPerfect screen, menu system, function keys, on-line help screens, and various cursor movement methods. To wrap it up, we'll teach you how to clear the screen and exit DrawPerfect.

Bar charts are widely used in business applications because they provide a quick visual overview of numeric information such as sales data and population growth. In the second chapter, *Your First Business Chart,* you'll learn how easy it is to create a bar chart in DrawPerfect. We'll also teach you how to save and print your chart, and how to make modifications, such as moving the title, changing the data, rotating a label, and changing the bars to lines, so that your bar chart becomes a line graph. To add flourish, we'll show you how to combine it with a clip-art drawing from DrawPerfect's Figure Library.

Text charts are often used as slides, transparencies, and handouts in oral presentations to list important goals or other key points, so we'll teach you how to create one in the third chapter, *Your First Text Chart.* We'll also show you some of the text formatting options, such as center, indent, bold, underline, and flush right, and a variety of fonts that you can use to change the size and appearance of the type. To complete the chapter, we'll teach you how to use DrawPerfect's templates, twenty-four attractive charts that you can retrieve and modify with your own data.

Even if you don't have a background in art, you'll probably want to try the program's drawing tools. In the fourth chapter, *Your First Drawing,* we'll teach you how. As you'll see, it's easy to draw objects that incorporate geometric shapes such as lines, rectangles, triangles, and circles, and we think you'll have fun with this chapter. In the fifth chapter, *More About the Drawing*

Tools and Options, you'll study more drawing tools, including Arrow, Ellipse, Arc, and Curve, and options like Zoom, Pan, Constrain, Stretch, and Freehand.

In the sixth chapter, *More About DrawPerfect's Editing Tools,* we'll teach you how to use editing tools such as Delete and Restore, Move, Copy, Size, Rotate, Mirror, and Modify. In the seventh chapter, *Printer Control,* you'll study all of DrawPerfect's printing methods, including a method you can use to print one or more DrawPerfect files without retrieving them. You'll also learn how to print an enlarged section of a chart or drawing, how to control the printer, and how to use several of the print options, including Binding, Number of Copies, and Graphics Quality.

By the time you reach the eighth chapter, *More About Business Graphs,* you'll already know how to create a bar chart and use some of the chart options. This chapter will add to your knowledge by teaching you several other types of business charts that you can create with DrawPerfect: pie charts, line charts, area charts, and stacked bar charts. You'll also learn about graph options such as grid lines, fill styles, data values, markers, and 3-D, and we'll show you how to create graphs from data saved in a spreadsheet such as PlanPerfect, Excel, or Lotus 1-2-3.

If you are using a hard disk, we strongly suggest you invest some time studying the ninth chapter, *File Management.* There you'll learn how to use DrawPerfect's List Files menu to create directories, change the default directory, move a group of files to another directory, copy several files from a hard disk to a floppy disk, and retrieve, print, copy, rename, or delete files. If you master these tools, you won't have to use the equivalent DOS commands, which are much harder!

The Shell is a utility program that is included with DrawPerfect, so why not take advantage of it? In Chapter 10, *Using the Shell to Integrate DrawPerfect and WordPerfect,* we'll show you how to use the Shell to run DrawPerfect and WordPerfect simultaneously, and exchange files between them. You'll learn how to transfer a completed chart or drawing from DrawPerfect into WordPerfect, retrieve WordPerfect text into DrawPerfect, spell check DrawPerfect text, create a bar graph from a WordPerfect table, and more.

In Chapter 11, *Presentations and Slides,* we'll teach you how to use DrawPerfect's Presentation feature to display a series of charts and drawings on your monitor. You can view them in any order, for any length of time, and change them automatically or manually. Since the effect is like viewing a series of slides, this feature is often called a *slide show.* We'll also show you how to use a variety of fancy screen wipes, such as fade and overlay, to make the transition between slides, and how to change the background colors and margins for your slides. This chapter also includes a section on producing 35mm slides from your DrawPerfect graphics.

Macros are convenient shortcuts to any task that you perform frequently. In Chapter 12, *An Introduction to Macros,* you'll learn all about them. We will teach you how to create, save, and edit macros, and how to use several of DrawPerfect's built-in macros.

To complete the book, we've included two appendices. Appendix A covers DrawPerfect and Shell installation. Appendix B teaches you how to use several options on the Setup menu to change defaults such as fonts, colors, the default directory, and text quality while editing, and to perform tasks like installing your mouse.

DrawPerfect Requirements

DrawPerfect requires 384K of memory, and a computer that includes either a hard disk or two 720K floppy disk drives. Also, you must be using DOS 2.0 or any later version (3.0, 3.1, etc.).

Conventions Used in This Book

We have used several typographical elements in this book to distinguish different types of information. A prompt or menu that appears on the DrawPerfect screen is set off from the body of the text in this manner:

`This is a sample screen prompt.`

When we ask you to type text at the keyboard, the text will be set off from the instructions like this:

Type this text.

In many DrawPerfect menus, you can select options by typing a number or letter. For example, you can select the Print Drawing option from the Print menu by typing **1** or **P**. Since these numbers and letters are boldfaced in the DrawPerfect screen, we have followed that convention in this book and printed them in boldface.

When we ask you to press function key combinations such as Shift and F7 (the Print key), we will hyphenate them as follows: Shift-F7. This means that you press the Shift key and hold it down while pressing F7 once, then release both keys.

DOS file names and commands such as FORMAT are printed in uppercase letters in this book.

In addition, we have used several icons to make learning DrawPerfect easier:

Quick Steps appear throughout the book to give you a quick outline of what you have just learned. The Quick Steps in this book are listed on the inside front cover.

Tips give you extra advice in an easy-to-read form.

The caution icon is followed by a warning that will help you avoid disaster.

This icon precedes keyboard directions.

Instructions for using the mouse appear after this icon.

Trademark Acknowledgments

All terms mentioned in this book that are known to be trademarks or service marks are listed below. In addition, terms suspected of being trademarks or service marks have been appropriately capitalized. Howard W. Sams & Company cannot attest to the accuracy of this information. Use of a term in this book should not be regarded as affecting the validity of any trademark or service mark.

EPSON is a registered trademark of Epson Corporation.

Excel is a registered trademark of Microsoft Corporation.

Hercules InColor is a trademark of Hercules Computer Technology.

HP and LaserJet are registered trademarks of Hewlett-Packard Company.

IBM is a registered trademark and IBM PC/XT is a trademark of International Business Machines Corporation.

Lotus 1-2-3 is a registered trademark of Lotus Development Corporation.

Paradise VGA Plus Card and Paradise AutoSwitch EGA Card are trademarks of Western Digital Imaging.

Video 7 VGA is a trademark of Video Seven Inc.

WordPerfect, DrawPerfect, and PlanPerfect are registered trademarks of WordPerfect Corporation.

Acknowledgments

We are very grateful to Scott Arant of Howard W. Sams for getting us started and providing constant support and encouragement. We'd also like to thank our editor, Linda Hawkins, and all the hard-working staff at Howard W. Sams, whose help has been invaluable.

We are indebted to many people at WordPerfect Corporation, including Paul Eddington for his cheerful assistance, Rourke Mace, Jeff Acerson, and all of the wonderful people on the customer support line.

Our thanks to Karl Lautman of MAGICorp for his quick response to our request for the MAGIComm software.

Finally, we'd like to thank a few other friends and associates who have provided valuable advice on this project, including Greg Harvey, Rich Jantz, and Brad Bunin.

Chapter 1

Getting Started

In This Chapter

- ▶ *Starting DrawPerfect*
- ▶ *The main DrawPerfect screen*
- ▶ *Cursor movement*
- ▶ *Moving through the pull-down menus*
- ▶ *The function keys*
- ▶ *Getting help*
- ▶ *Clearing the screen and exiting DrawPerfect*

Now that you know a little about DrawPerfect's capabilities, let's start using it! In this chapter we will teach you how to start the program and how to work with the main DrawPerfect screen. In the process you will learn about cursor movement, the drawing window, the pull-down menus, the function keys, and Draw-Perfect's excellent on-line help. To wrap it up, we will teach you how to clear the screen and exit DrawPerfect.

Starting DrawPerfect

If you have not yet installed DrawPerfect on your computer, turn to Appendix A for complete instructions. DrawPerfect comes with an automatic installation program, so you should find it easy to install.

The method that you use to start DrawPerfect will vary according to whether or not you have installed the Shell program, a menu utility that comes with DrawPerfect. The Shell is especially useful if you plan to retrieve any of your DrawPerfect drawings or charts into WordPerfect 5.1 or move back and forth between the two programs. If you have installed the Shell, you will start DrawPerfect through the Shell menu. If you have not, you will type a DOS command to switch to the correct directory and then type the startup command, **DR**. We will explain both methods separately.

Begin by turning on the computer. After a few minutes, you should see a C prompt, similar to the one shown below:

C>

This tells you that the operating system, DOS, is started and that you can now proceed to start DrawPerfect.

If you installed DrawPerfect on a different drive, such as D or E, switch to that drive now by typing the drive name, followed by a colon (such as D:), and then pressing the Enter key.

Starting DrawPerfect If You Have Installed the Shell

If you are using the Shell program, your next step will be to switch to the subdirectory containing the Shell files. Usually, the subdirectory will be on drive C and will be named DR10. Determine the subdirectory name where you copied the Shell files. If it is DR10, type **CD\DR10** (otherwise, type **CD**, followed by your subdirectory name); then press the Enter key. Next, start the Shell program by typing **Shell** and pressing Enter. The Shell menu should appear, as shown in Figure 1.1.

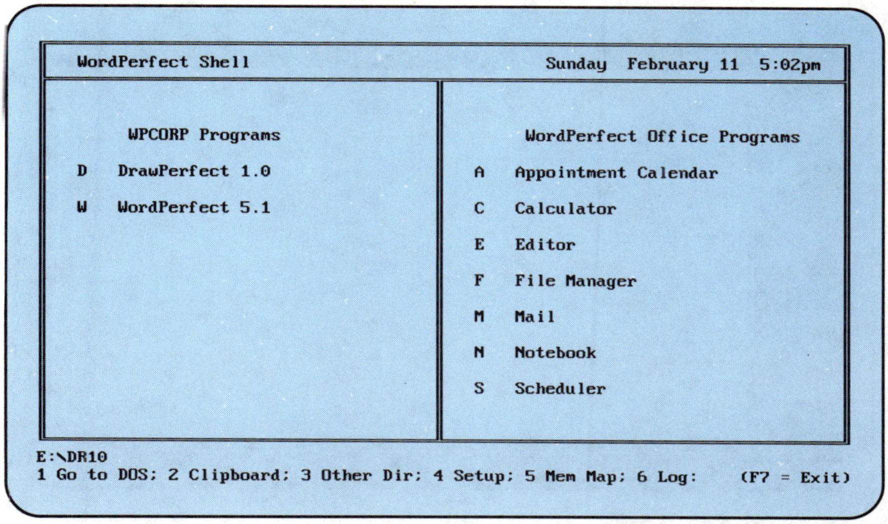

```
┌─────────────────────────────────────────────────────────────┐
│ WordPerfect Shell                    Sunday  February 11  5:02pm │
│                                                             │
│         WPCORP Programs              WordPerfect Office Programs │
│                                                             │
│     D   DrawPerfect 1.0          A   Appointment Calendar   │
│                                                             │
│     W   WordPerfect 5.1          C   Calculator             │
│                                                             │
│                                  E   Editor                 │
│                                                             │
│                                  F   File Manager           │
│                                                             │
│                                  M   Mail                   │
│                                                             │
│                                  N   Notebook               │
│                                                             │
│                                  S   Scheduler              │
│                                                             │
│ E:\DR10                                                     │
│ 1 Go to DOS; 2 Clipboard; 3 Other Dir; 4 Setup; 5 Mem Map; 6 Log:    (F7 = Exit) │
└─────────────────────────────────────────────────────────────┘
```

Figure 1.1   The Shell menu

DrawPerfect should appear as one of the options on the left side of the menu. Notice the highlighted letter that appears next to the DrawPerfect option. As shown in Figure 1.1, it is usually D. At this point there are two methods you can use to start DrawPerfect: Either press the highlighted letter (D) or use the Arrow keys to place the cursor bar onto DrawPerfect and then press the Enter key. In a few minutes, you will see the main DrawPerfect screen, as shown in Figure 1.2.

Starting DrawPerfect If You Have Not Installed the Shell

Your first step will be to switch to the subdirectory containing the DrawPerfect files. Usually, the subdirectory will be on drive C and will be called DR10. Determine the subdirectory name where you copied the DrawPerfect files. If it is DR10, type **CD\DR10** (otherwise, type **CD**, followed by your subdirectory name); then press Enter. Next, type **DR** and press Enter. In a few seconds, you will see the main DrawPerfect screen, as shown in Figure 1.2.

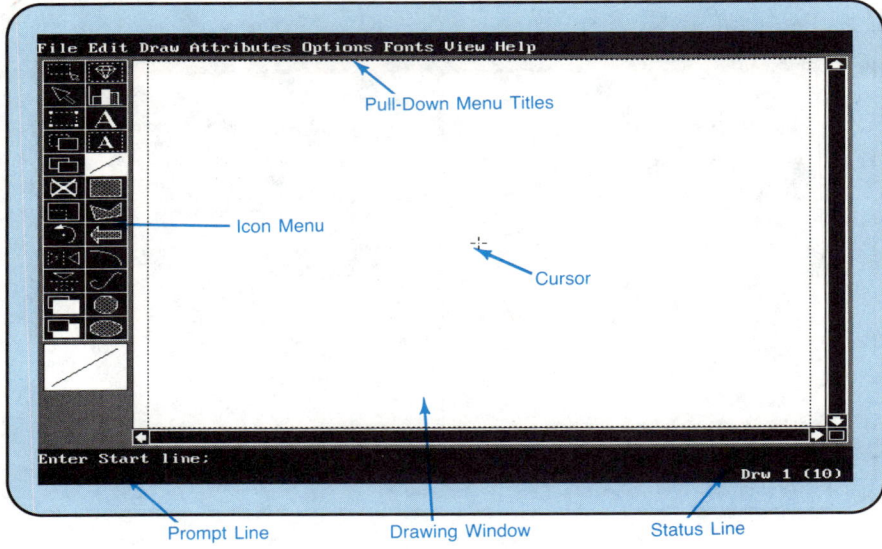

Figure 1.2 The main DrawPerfect screen

The Main DrawPerfect Screen

As you can see from Figure 1.2, the main DrawPerfect screen is divided into several sections:

- The pull-down menu titles at the top
- The icon menu at the left
- The prompt line and status line at the bottom
- The large, empty drawing window

When you start DrawPerfect, the cursor, which indicates your current position, is a large plus sign (+) that appears in the middle of the drawing window. However, it becomes a pointing arrow when you move it out of the drawing window, or when you activate one of the pull-down menus.

The Pull-Down Menus

The titles for DrawPerfect's pull-down menus appear on the first line of the screen: **F**ile, **E**dit, **D**raw, **A**ttributes, **O**ptions, **F**onts, **V**iew, and **H**elp. If you type the highlighted letter in one of the titles, a pull-down menu appears listing the options that are available from that menu. For example, if you type D, the Draw menu shown in Figure 1.3 appears, featuring these selections: Figure, Chart, Text Line, Window Text, Line, Box, Polygon, Arrow, Arc, Curve, Circle, and Ellipse. Go ahead and try it.

 Type **D**.

 Drag the cursor onto the **Draw** menu title and click the left button once.

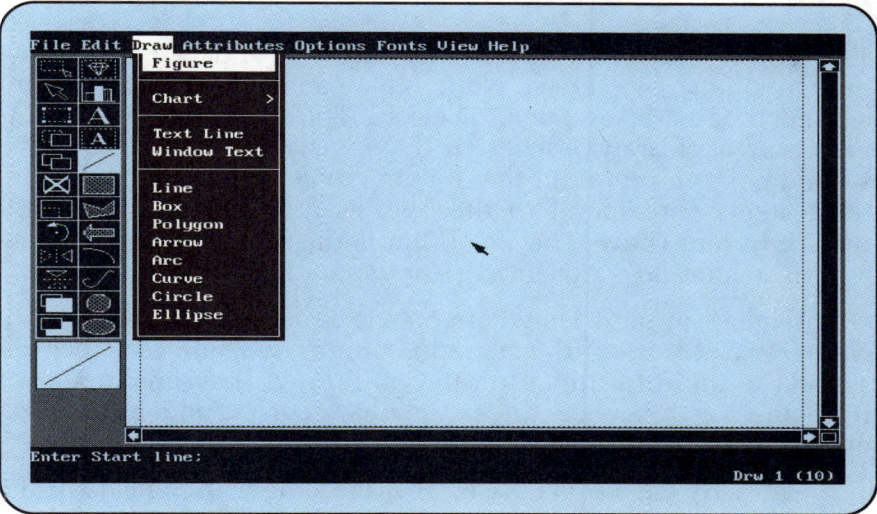

Figure 1.3   The Draw menu

Notice the > symbol next to the Chart option. This symbol tells you that Chart has a submenu. If you select Chart, another pull-down menu will appear to the right of the main Draw menu. This submenu offers eleven options: Bullet, Simple, Freeform, Bar, Line, Pie, Area, Stacked Bar, HiLo, Scatter, and Mixed.

Since you selected one of the pull-down menus, the cursor now appears as a pointing arrow. Even though the arrow remains in the drawing window, the fact that it is an arrow instead of a plus sign tells you that the drawing window has been temporarily inactivated so that you can select a menu option or icon. To return to the drawing window without making a selection:

🗝 Press the Exit key (F7).

🖱 Drag the cursor into the drawing window and click the left mouse button once.

Now the cursor should be a plus sign again.

The Icon Menu

The *icon menu* is the panel of twenty-four square boxes along the left side of the screen. Notice that each box contains a symbol, such as an arrow, box, or circle. The icons in the first column represent DrawPerfect's editing tools, while the icons in the second column represent the drawing tools. With one exception, these icons correspond to the options found under the menu titles Edit and Draw. The exception is the Edit menu's Undelete option, which does not have a corresponding icon.

When you start DrawPerfect, the Line icon is highlighted. Notice that it is the fifth square in column two, and that it corresponds to the fifth option on the pull-down Draw menu shown in Figure 1.3. Likewise, the sixth square corresponds to the Box option, the seventh one to the Polygon option, etc.

You may have also noticed that the Line icon appears in the large Status box below the two columns of icons. The purpose of this box is to tell you which object is currently selected.

You've already seen the Draw menu, so let's take a look at the Edit menu. To do this,

🗝 Type **E**.

🖱 Drag the cursor onto the **Edit** menu title and click the left mouse button once.

Your screen should now resemble Figure 1.4, which shows the pull-down Edit menu.

Getting Started

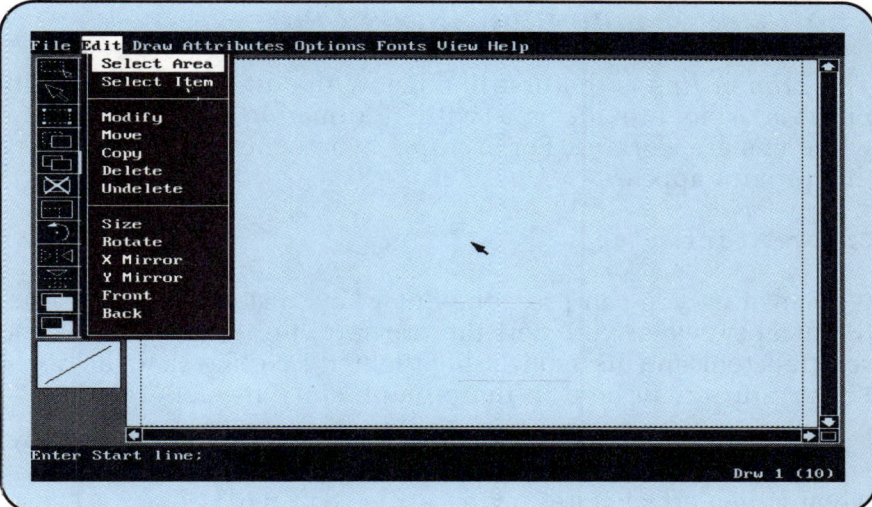

Figure 1.4   The Edit menu

The Edit menu appears to the immediate right of the icon panel. Although it includes thirteen options, there are only twelve icons. As we mentioned, Undelete does not have an icon. Therefore, the sixth icon represents Delete, and the seventh is Size.

When you have finished examining the icons and their corresponding menu options, return to the drawing mode.

 Press Exit (F7).

Drag the cursor into the drawing window and click the left mouse button once.

The icon panel provides you with an alternative method of selecting an Edit or Draw option, so that once you have learned what each icon represents you don't have to use the pull-down menus. Instead, you can select one of the options by pointing to it with the cursor. Here's how:

Use the Arrow keys to move the pointer onto an icon; then press the Enter key.

Drag the cursor onto an icon and click the left mouse button.

The Prompt Line and Status Line

The *prompt line* is the first line below the drawing window. Its purpose is to provide you with information and instructions while you are working. For example, when you start DrawPerfect this prompt appears:

Enter Start line;

It means that you can press the Enter key to start drawing a line. (Remember, when you start the program, the Line option is the selected tool and its icon is highlighted.) Notice that the word Enter appears in bold in the prompt, since it refers to a key.

The *status line* is just below the prompt line. Occasionally, you will see warnings and messages on this line. For example, when DrawPerfect is retrieving a file, you will see a * Please wait * prompt warning you not to do anything until it completes the retrieve action. When you retrieve a file from the disk, its name will appear on the status line. Also, after you have saved a drawing on your screen, the new file name will appear there.

The Drw 1 notation on the right side of the status line in Figure 1.4 tells you which of the two drawing windows you are currently using, 1 or 2. DrawPerfect provides you with two windows so that you can work with two separate drawings and switch back and forth between them to copy or move objects. The number that appears in parenthesis next to it is called the *Cursor Step,* and it is usually 10 when you start DrawPerfect. This tells you how far the cursor will move when you press an Arrow key once. By pressing the Insert key, you can change it to 1 so that the cursor will move in smaller increments per keystroke, or increase the step to 25 so that the cursor will move farther in a single keystroke.

The Drawing Window

The large, empty box that occupies the rest of the screen is called the *drawing window,* and this is your work area. In other words, if you select a drawing tool, such as Line, Circle, or Box, this is where the object will appear as you are creating it.

If you are impatient to try drawing an object, make sure that the Line icon is highlighted and that the cursor is in the drawing window. To begin drawing a line:

⌨ Press the Enter key once.

🖱 Click the left mouse button once.

Notice that the prompt line has changed to

`Enter` Continue line; `Space` end line;

The words `Enter` and `Space` appear in bold (or in a different color if you have a color monitor) to signify that they refer to key names. To draw a line, move the cursor in one direction, press Enter, and then press the Spacebar. Try it:

⌨ Press the Left Arrow key several times.

🖱 Drag the mouse to the left on the mouse pad.

As you move the cursor, you will see a line forming in the drawing window. When the line is about one inch long, stop drawing. To complete the process:

⌨ Press the Enter key and then the Spacebar.

🖱 Press the left mouse button and then the right mouse button.

Now you can use the Arrow keys or mouse to move the cursor around without drawing a line.

> ▶ **Tip:** Don't worry about the line you just drew. At the end of this chapter, we will teach you how to clear the screen so that you can begin a new drawing or exit Draw-Perfect.

Chapter 1

Cursor Movement

As we mentioned earlier, the cursor is represented by a large plus sign (+) in the drawing window and is changed into a pointing arrow when you move it out of the drawing window or when you activate one of the pull-down menus. The fastest and most efficient way to move the cursor is to use a mouse. If you don't have one, you can use the Arrow keys and certain other special keys on the keyboard.

Using the Mouse

To use a mouse for cursor movement, just move it around on your mouse pad. As you will see, the cursor follows the mouse movement.

> ▶ **Tip:** If the cursor does not move as you move your mouse, you did not install the mouse correctly. Turn to Appendix B for more information.

    In the drawing window, the left button on the mouse functions like the Enter key and the right button functions like the Spacebar (except that the right button does not insert a blank space when you are typing text). If your mouse has three buttons, the middle button functions like the Cancel key (F1). If your mouse has only two buttons, pressing both buttons simultaneously functions like the Cancel key.

Using the Keyboard

The Up, Down, Right, and Left Arrow keys move the cursor in their respective directions: up, down, right, and left. The distance the cursor will move each time you press one of these keys depends on the Cursor Step number (the number appearing in parenthesis in the lower right corner of the screen). By pressing the Insert key, you can change this number from 10 to 1 or 25. The higher the number, the farther the cursor will move in a single keystroke.

> **Tip:** If the Num Lock key is engaged, you cannot use the Arrow keys on the numeric keypad to move the cursor. If nothing happens when you press an Arrow key, press Num Lock once and try again.

You can also speed up cursor movement by pressing and continuing to hold down an Arrow key, since these keys have an auto-repeat feature.

The Home key works in combination with the Arrow keys to move to the extreme edge of the drawing window. For example, pressing Home followed by the Right Arrow key moves the cursor to the right side of the window, maintaining the horizontal position that the cursor was in when you pressed the combination. Pressing Home then the Down Arrow key moves the cursor to the bottom, maintaining the vertical position.

> **Tip:** To use a Home and Arrow key combination for cursor movement, press Home first and then release it before pressing the Arrow key.

DrawPerfect has one other key combination, called the *Go to* key, which you can use to move the cursor to an exact location along the X- and Y-axes of the drawing window. Note that X represents a horizontal location (along the X-axis) and Y represents a vertical location (on the Y-axis). For example, if you type 1 for both X and Y, the cursor will move to the lower left corner of the screen (since the default left and right margins are 1″ each).

Go to is the combination of the Ctrl and Home keys. To use it, you press Ctrl first and hold it down while you press Home. The prompt `Go to X:` will appear on the prompt line, followed by a number measured in inches, such as 5.5″. After you type a number and press Enter, DrawPerfect prompts you to type a number for Y.

Chapter 1

Moving Through the Pull-Down Menus

We've already discussed the pull-down menus briefly and have shown you one of them, the Draw menu. Now let's learn a little more about how to select pull-down menus and move the cursor around in them.

Using the Mouse

Selecting a menu option with the mouse is easy. First, move the mouse until the pointing cursor is on the menu title and then click the left button once. Next, use the mouse to move the cursor onto the option that you want to select. Once the cursor is there, just press the left mouse button.

Another way to use the mouse in pull-down menus is to drag the pointing cursor onto the menu title, press the left button, and continue holding it down while dragging the pointing cursor onto the desired option. To select the option, release the left button.

If you change your mind and want to exit a menu without selecting an option, press the right mouse button. The cursor can be anywhere when you do this.

Using the Keyboard

You've already learned that you can select a pull-down menu by typing the highlighted letter in one of the titles, such as **D** for Draw or **A** for Attributes. Another way to select a menu title is to press the Alt key, which moves the cursor onto the first option in the title line, `File`. From there you can press the Right Arrow key until you've highlighted the title you want to use and then the Down Arrow key or Enter to pull down the menu. After pulling down one menu using this method, you can just press the Right or Left Arrow key to pull down an adjacent menu.

To select an option from one of the pull-down menus, either type its highlighted letter or use the Arrow keys to move the cursor bar onto the option and then press Enter.

To exit a pull-down menu and return to the drawing window without making a selection, press the Exit key, F7. If you want to close a pull-down menu but leave the cursor on the title line, press the Cancel key, F1.

Using the Function Keys

DrawPerfect makes use of the function keys, F1 through F10, to duplicate several options on the pull-down menus. For instance, to save a drawing or chart, you can either press the Save key (F10) or you can pull down the File menu and select the Save option. To access DrawPerfect's on-line help, you can either press the Help key (F3) or select the Help title and pull down the Help menu. Note that DrawPerfect does not use F2.

Experienced WordPerfect users will probably be quite comfortable with the function keys, since many duplicate the meanings of the WordPerfect function keys. Examples include the following keys:

Cancel (F1)	Macro Define (Ctrl-F10)
Help (F3)	Flush Right (Alt-F6)
Indent (F4)	Macro (Alt-F10)
List Files (F5)	Setup (Shift-F1)
Bold (F6)	Switch (Shift-F3)
Exit (F7)	Date Text (Shift-F5)
Underline (F8)	Center (Shift-F6)
Save (F10)	Print (Shift-F7)
Shell (Ctrl-F1)	Format (Shift-F8)
Font (Ctrl-F8)	Retrieve (Shift-F10)

If you aren't a WordPerfect user or prefer using a mouse for everything, you'll be relieved to know that there is nothing you can do with the function keys that cannot be done through a pull-down menu. Therefore, learning them is entirely optional.

DrawPerfect includes a keyboard template that you can place over the function keys to help you learn their features. If you examine it, you will see that most of the keys have several

Chapter 1

meanings. For instance, these words appear next to F7: *Grid Snap, Grid Display, Print,* and *Exit.* Notice that they are printed in four colors, black, red, blue, and green. The colors correspond to these keys: black is the function key alone, red is the function key with Ctrl, blue is the function key with Alt, and green is the function key with Shift.

Let's see how the color scheme applies to the F7 function key. Since Exit is printed in black, to use this feature you would press F7 once. Grid Snap is printed in red, so pressing Ctrl-F7 would turn on the Grid Snap feature (or turn it off if it is already turned on). Grid Display is printed in blue, so you would press Alt-F7 to use it (you will learn all about Grid Snap and Grid Display later in this book). Print appears in green, so pressing Shift-F7 would bring up DrawPerfect's Print menu.

> **Tip:** To use a function key in combination with Shift, Alt, or Ctrl, press the Shift, Alt, or Ctrl key and continue holding it down while pressing the function key once. Since the function keys have an auto-repeat feature, a function key won't work properly if you continue holding it down. Instead, it will turn the function on and off.

Table 1.1 lists all the function key features. Some may be Greek to you now, but by the time you've finished this book, you should be familiar with all of them. In the next section, we'll teach you where to find an on-line copy of the function key template.

Getting Help

DrawPerfect provides an excellent on-line help feature that you can use almost anytime. There are two ways to access the Help screens, either through the pull-down menus or through the Help key, F3. Let's see how they work. To bring up the main Help screen:

 Press F3 once or type **H** and then press Enter.

Table 1.1 Function keys

Key	Alone	With Ctrl (red)	With Alt (blue)	With Shift (green)
F1	Cancel	Shell		Setup
F3	Help		Pos Display	Switch
F4	Indent			
F5	List Files	Export	Zoom Area	Date Text
F6	Bold		Flush Right	Center
F7	Exit	Grid Snap	Grid Display	Print
F8	Underline	Font		Format
F9	ReDraw	Stretch	Constrain	Freehand
F10	Save	Macro Define	Macro	Retrieve
F11	POS Display			

 Drag the cursor onto the **Help** menu title, click the left button and hold it down while moving the cursor onto the Help option, then release the button.

Next, you should see the initial Help screen shown in Figure 1.5. Notice that the DrawPerfect version number (such as DR 1.0) and date appear in the upper right corner of the screen. If you call WordPerfect Corporation's technical support line for help with DrawPerfect, they will probably ask you for this information.

Once you are in this screen, there are four different ways to get information about DrawPerfect. The four paragraphs on this screen describe them briefly. To begin with, you can type the first letter of a feature, such as **S** for Save. This brings up an alphabetical list of features that start with that letter, and shows their corresponding pull-down menus and function keys. The second way is to press any function key, which brings up a screen of information about that key. The third is to type a question mark, which displays a menu of eight topics, such as *Create Text Charts and Graphs* and *Drawing Tools and Procedures*. From there, you can go directly to one or more screens of information about a topic. Last, by pressing the Help key (F3) again, you can view a copy of the function key template. Let's try each method.

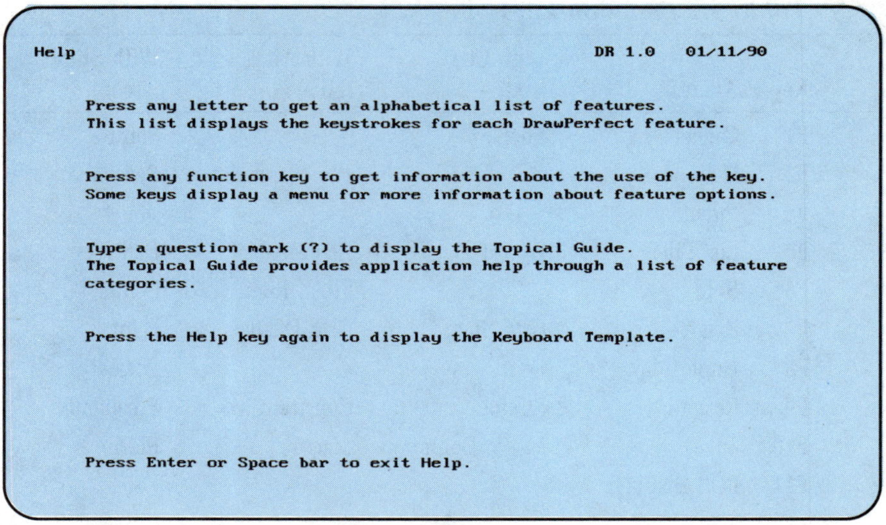

Chapter 1

```
Help                                            DR 1.0    01/11/90

     Press any letter to get an alphabetical list of features.
     This list displays the keystrokes for each DrawPerfect feature.

     Press any function key to get information about the use of the key.
     Some keys display a menu for more information about feature options.

     Type a question mark (?) to display the Topical Guide.
     The Topical Guide provides application help through a list of feature
     categories.

     Press the Help key again to display the Keyboard Template.



     Press Enter or Space bar to exit Help.
```

16

Figure 1.5   DrawPerfect's initial Help screen

> ▶ **Tip:** If you did not install the help files on your computer, when you press F3 or select Help from the menu, you will see this prompt at the bottom of the initial Help screen:
>
> `DrHelp.Fil not found. Insert the diskette and press drive letter.`
>
> If this happens, turn to Appendix A for information about how to install the help files.

Alphabetical Help on DrawPerfect Features

First, let's look at the alphabetical features list. To determine which keys to press to save a drawing, type **S** (but don't press Enter). The screen shown in Figure 1.6 should appear. Look at the top of column one, under the heading `Feature [S]`. Notice that `Save` is the first item in the list. If you prefer using pull-down menus, look on the first line of the middle column, Pull-

Getting Started

Down Menu Selection, to find out which menu to use: `File, Save`. If you use function keys, look on the first line of the third column and you'll see that F10 is the function key. Note the prompt on the last line of the screen, `MORE... Press 1 to continue`. This tells you that there is not enough room on this screen for all of the features that begin with the letter S. By pressing 1, you can see additional features, such as Size, Snap, and Switch.

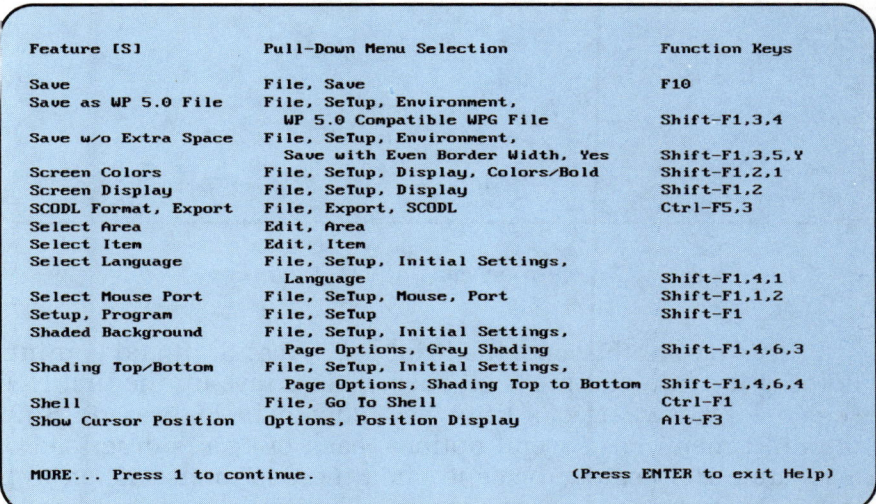

Figure 1.6 *The Help screen for the letter S*

Function Key Help Screens

Now let's look at one of the function key Help screens. Say you don't remember how to save a drawing. Just press F10, and you'll see the screen shown in Figure 1.7. Notice that the key name `Save` appears in the upper left corner of the screen. The function key `[F10]` appears in the upper right corner. The first paragraph describes exactly how to use this key, and the second paragraph tells you that you can also use the Exit key to save a drawing. You may want to press F7 to find out more about the Exit key.

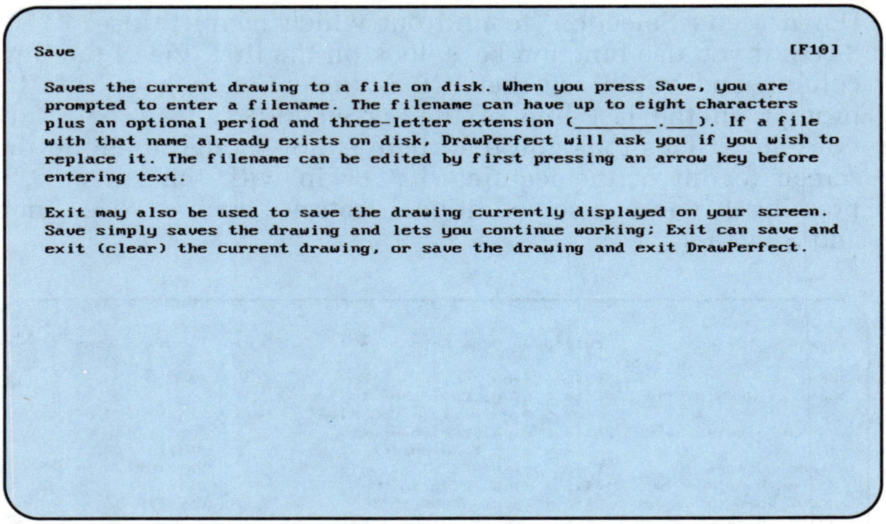

```
Save                                                            [F10]

Saves the current drawing to a file on disk. When you press Save, you are
prompted to enter a filename. The filename can have up to eight characters
plus an optional period and three-letter extension (_____.___). If a file
with that name already exists on disk, DrawPerfect will ask you if you wish to
replace it. The filename can be edited by first pressing an arrow key before
entering text.

Exit may also be used to save the drawing currently displayed on your screen.
Save simply saves the drawing and lets you continue working; Exit can save and
exit (clear) the current drawing, or save the drawing and exit DrawPerfect.
```

Figure 1.7   The Help screen for the Save key

Let's try another one, the Print key. Press Shift and continue holding it while you press F7 once. This brings up the first Help screen for DrawPerfect's Print key, shown in Figure 1.8. Since the Print menu has several options, each option is described on a separate Help screen (except when there is room enough to fit two or more options on one screen). To view one, you press the number or letter next to the option, such as **1** or **P** for Print Drawing, **6** or **V** for View Drawing, or **N** for Number of Copies. Once you select one, you can return to the initial Print key Help screen only by pressing Shift-F7 again.

The Topical Guide

Let's move on and view the topical guide. Type **?** (question mark) to bring up the menu shown in Figure 1.9. From there you can type the corresponding letter to get more information about a topic, such as **P** for Printing and Previewing or **U** for Using the DrawPerfect Menus.

Type **U** to view the Using the DrawPerfect Menus screen. As you can see, this screen leads to three more: Function Keys, Icon Menu, and Pull-Down Menus.

Getting Started

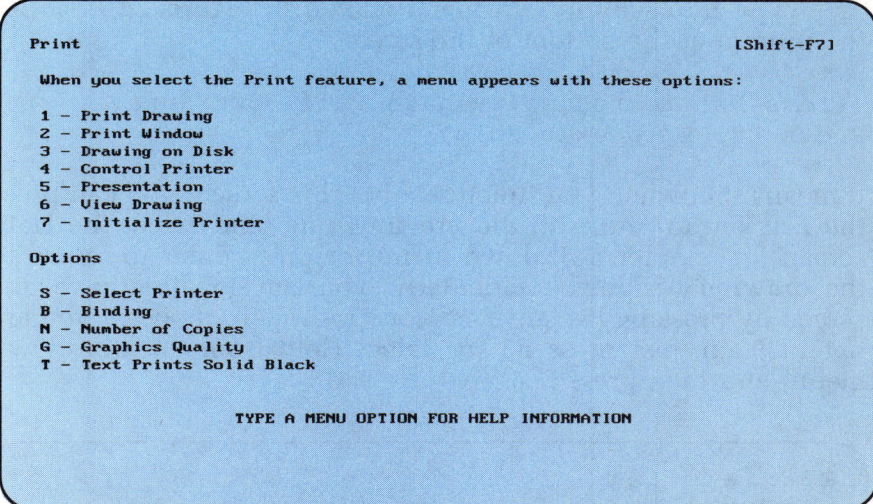

Figure 1.8   The Help screen for the Print key

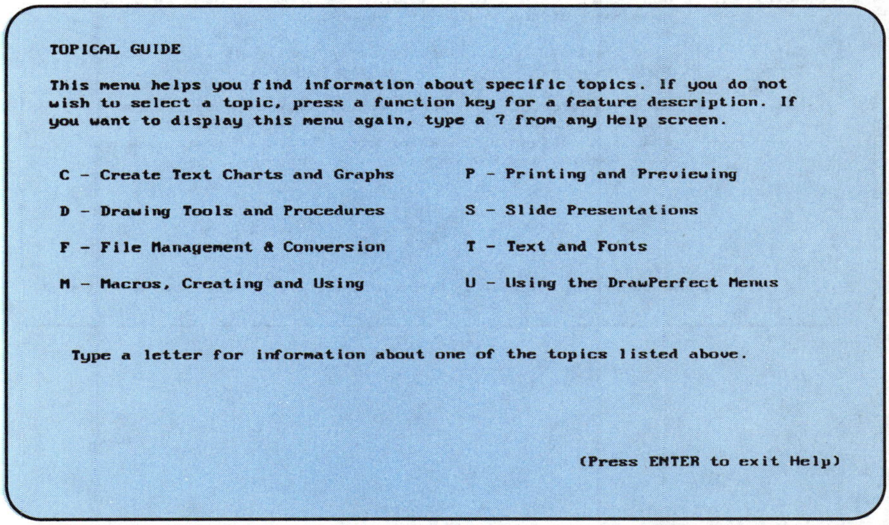

Figure 1.9   The topical guide

Type **3** (or P) for Pull-Down Menus. Now you can find out more about any of the pull-down menus by typing the menu letter.

Chapter 1

Type **E** to see the Edit menu shown in Figure 1.10. Notice the prompt at the bottom of the screen:

```
(Press Esc to redisplay main Pull-Down Menu.
Press ENTER to exit Help)
```

It means that when you finish reading this screen, you can press the Esc key to return to the previous one (and select the Help screen for another pull-down menu) or press Enter to return to the drawing window. Incidentally, you can go directly to this screen by pressing Esc anytime you are in help mode. If you are not in Help, just press F3 (or select Help from the pull-down menu) and then press Esc.

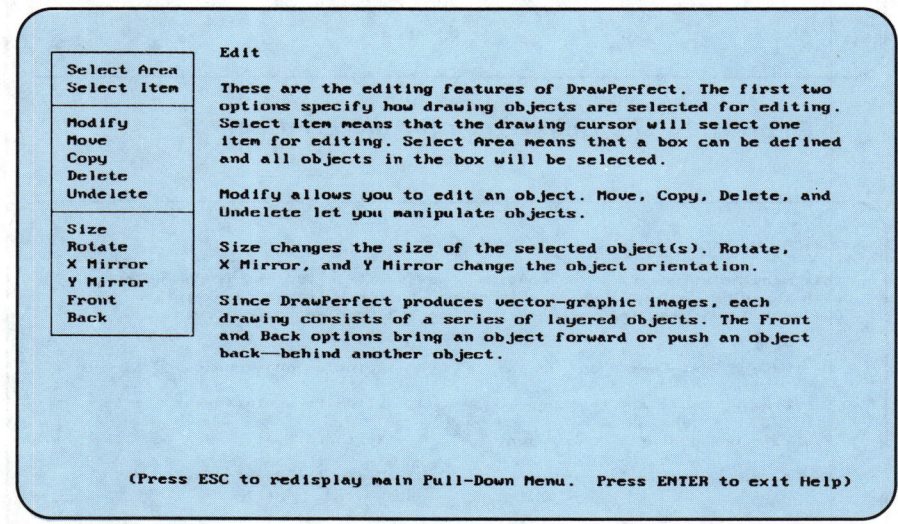

Figure 1.10   The Edit Help screen

The Function Key Template

The last major feature of the Help key is the function key template. To see it, press F3 (if you were not in help mode, you could view it by pressing F3 twice or by selecting H for the Help menu title, then T for Template). This displays a replica of the

DrawPerfect function key template for the enhanced style keyboard (those with the function keys on the top row), shown in Figure 1.11. If the function keys are on the left side of your keyboard, press **1** to view the template in PC/XT format.

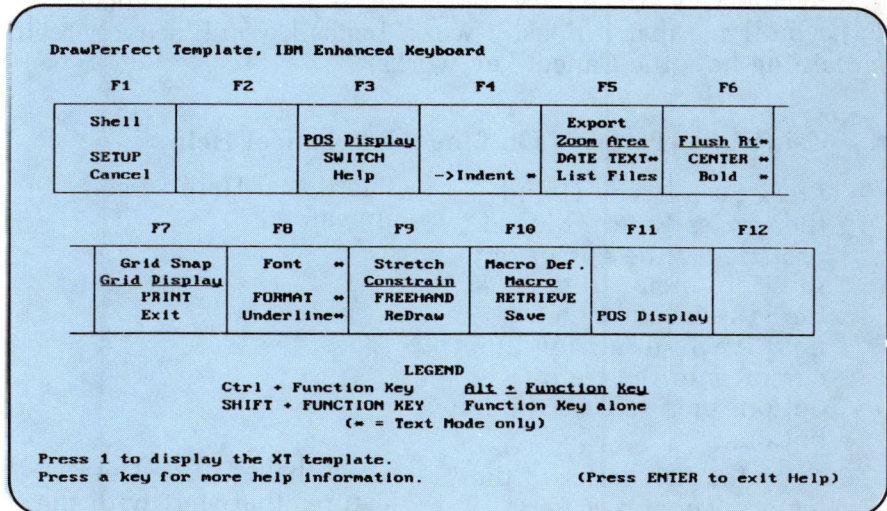

Figure 1.11   The Help screen's function key template

> **Tip:** See a previous section, *Using the Function Keys,* for more information about DrawPerfect's function keys.

Exiting Help

Exiting DrawPerfect's help area is easy: Press either the Enter key or the Spacebar. Fortunately, the Help screens constantly remind you how to do this. For instance, you may have noticed this prompt on the last line of the initial Help screen in Figure 1.5:

```
Press Enter or Space bar to exit Help
```

Also, nearly all of the submenus include this prompt in the lower right corner:

(Press ENTER to exit Help)

By the way, if you try to exit by pressing the Cancel key (F1), you'll see that it doesn't work. Instead, you'll see a screen explaining how the Cancel key works!

Using DrawPerfect's On-Line Alphabetical Help

1. Press F3 (or type H and then press Enter). Mouse users: Drag the cursor onto the Help menu title, click the left button once and hold it while moving the cursor onto the Help option, then release the left button.

   The initial Help screen appears.

2. Type the first letter of the feature, such as R for Retrieve or P for Print.

   An alphabetical list of features that start with the letter you typed appears. The first column shows the feature names, the middle column shows the corresponding pull-down menus to use, and the third column shows the function keys you can use (if any).

3. When you're finished using Help, press Enter or the Spacebar.

   The drawing window reappears.

Clearing the Screen

If you've read straight through this chapter and performed the exercises, the line that you drew earlier is probably still on your screen. In this section, we'll show you how to clear it so that you can move on to the next chapter and learn how to create your first chart.

To clear the screen, you can either use the Exit option on the pull-down File menu or press the Exit key (F7) once.

 Press Exit (F7) or type **F X**.

 Drag the cursor onto the **File** menu title, click the left button, and hold it down while dragging the cursor onto **Exit**. Release the button.

You will then see this prompt:

Save Drawing? Yes (No).

The cursor will be under the Y in the word Yes. If you press any key other than N, you will see this prompt asking for a file name:

Drawing to be Saved:

DrawPerfect assumes that you always want to save your work upon exiting, a safety feature to help remind you to save your drawings since it is not done automatically. If you see this prompt, press the Cancel key (F1) and then start over by pressing F7 or selecting File Exit again.

> **Caution:** Unlike some programs, DrawPerfect does not save automatically, so you have to tell it to do so. As a safety feature, whenever you exit DrawPerfect a prompt appears asking if you want to save the drawing.

Since you do not need to save the line that you drew, select the (**No**) option.

 Type **N**.

 Drag the cursor onto **No** and click the left mouse button once.

Chapter 1

Note that you can use either uppercase or lowercase when typing N. When you are responding to prompts like this, DrawPerfect does not differentiate. Next, you will see this prompt:

`Exit DrawPerfect? No (Yes).`

This time the cursor is under the N in `No`, and the assumption is that you do not want to exit the program. Since the assumption is true:

Type **N** (or press any other key except Y).

Drag the cursor onto the **No** option and click the left mouse button once.

This leaves you with a clear screen, ready to start a new drawing.

Clearing the Screen to Start a New Drawing

1. Press the Exit key (F7) once or type F X. Mouse users: Drag the cursor onto the File menu title, click the left mouse button once, and hold it. Drag the cursor onto Exit and release the button.

   This prompt appears: `Save Drawing? Yes (No).`

2. Assuming you do not want to save the file, type N. Mouse users: Drag the cursor onto No and click the left mouse button once.

   This prompt appears: `Exit DrawPerfect? No (Yes).`

3. Type N. Mouse users: Drag the cursor onto No and click the left mouse button once.

   The screen is cleared and you can create a new drawing.

Exiting DrawPerfect

If you want to exit DrawPerfect altogether, either press the Exit key (F7) once or select the Exit option on the pull-down File menu.

 Press F7 or type **F X**.

 Drag the cursor onto the **File** menu title, click the left button, and hold it down while dragging the cursor onto **Exit**. Release the button.

In response to the Save Drawing? prompt that appears,

 Type **N** (don't press Enter).

 Drag the cursor onto **No** and click the left button.

Next, you will see the Exit DrawPerfect? prompt.

 Type **Y**.

 Drag the cursor onto **Yes** and click the left button.

That's all there is to it! If you started DrawPerfect through the Shell, you will be back in the Shell menu. To exit back to DOS, press F7 once. You should now be back at the C prompt and can either turn off your computer or start another program.

 Exiting DrawPerfect (Without Saving)

1. Press the Exit key (F7) once or type F X. Mouse users: Drag the cursor onto the File menu title, click the left mouse button once, and hold it. Drag the cursor onto Exit and release the button.

    This prompt appears: Save Drawing? Yes (No).

2. Type N. Mouse users: Drag the cursor onto No and click the left mouse button once.

    This prompt appears: Exit DrawPerfect? No (Yes).

Chapter 1

3. Type Y. Mouse users: Drag the cursor onto Yes and click the left mouse button once.

A DOS prompt such as C:\ appears.

☐

What You Have Learned

In this chapter, you've learned how to start DrawPerfect, use the pull-down menus and other features on the main DrawPerfect screen, obtain on-line information about the program, and exit DrawPerfect. You should now be familiar with the following:

▶ The main DrawPerfect screen includes pull-down menu titles at the top, an icon menu at the left, a prompt line and status line at the bottom, and a large, empty drawing window.

▶ The large, empty box that occupies most of the screen is called the drawing window, and this is your work area. If you select a drawing tool, such as Line, Circle, or Box, the object will appear inside this window as you are creating it.

▶ The DrawPerfect cursor is a large plus sign (+) that appears in the middle of the drawing window. When you move it out of the drawing window or select one of the pull-down menus, the cursor becomes a pointing arrow.

▶ DrawPerfect has eight pull-down menus. Their titles appear on the first line of the screen: File, Edit, Draw, Attributes, Options, Fonts, View, and Help. If you type the highlighted letter in one of the titles, a pull-down menu appears listing the options that are available from that menu. You can also use the mouse to display a menu by moving the mouse until the cursor is on the menu title and then clicking the left button once.

▶ The icon menu is the panel of twenty-four boxes at the left side of the screen. They contain symbols such as an arrow, box, and circle. The icons correspond to the options found under the menu titles Edit and Draw, and provide an alternative method of selecting one of these options: pointing to the icon with the cursor.

- ▶ The prompt line is the first line below the drawing window. It provides information and instructions while you are working.
- ▶ The status line is just below the prompt line, and it displays warnings and messages as necessary.
- ▶ To use a mouse for cursor movement, just move it around on your mouse pad. The cursor follows the mouse movement. You can also move the cursor with the up, down, right, and left Arrow keys.
- ▶ DrawPerfect uses the function keys, F1 through F10, to duplicate several options on the pull-down menus.
- ▶ DrawPerfect provides on-line help, which you can use by pressing the Help key (F3) or selecting the Help menu title.
- ▶ To clear the screen and start a new drawing, you can either select Exit from the pull-down File menu or press the Exit key (F7). DrawPerfect assumes that you always want to save your work upon exiting. When you see the prompt asking if you want to exit DrawPerfect, select No.
- ▶ To exit DrawPerfect, you also use the Exit option on the File menu or the Exit key (F7). When you see the prompt asking if you want to exit DrawPerfect, select Yes.

Chapter 2

Your First Business Chart

In This Chapter

- ▶ *Creating a bar chart*
- ▶ *Saving your chart*
- ▶ *Printing your chart*
- ▶ *Editing your chart*
- ▶ *Changing the bars to lines*
- ▶ *Enhancing your chart with an image from the DrawPerfect Figure Library*

Now that you know how to start DrawPerfect and are familiar with DrawPerfect's drawing window, pull-down menus, icon panels, cursor movement, and function keys, let's get to work! In this chapter, we will teach you how to create, save, and print the bar chart shown in Figure 2.1. After saving it, we will modify it by changing it to a line graph, and learn about some of the other graph options. Next, we will make the chart more interesting by combining it with an image from the DrawPerfect Figure Library. When we finish, it will resemble Figure 2.2. Are you ready?

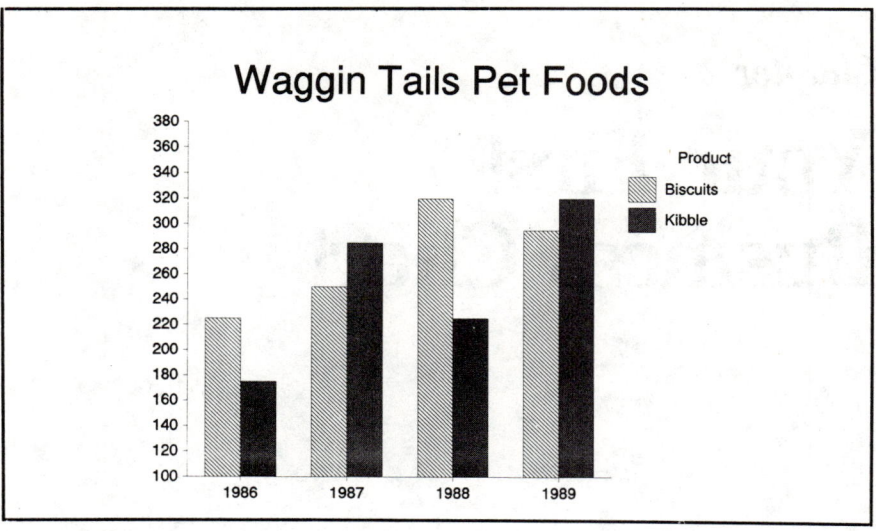

Figure 2.1   The bar chart

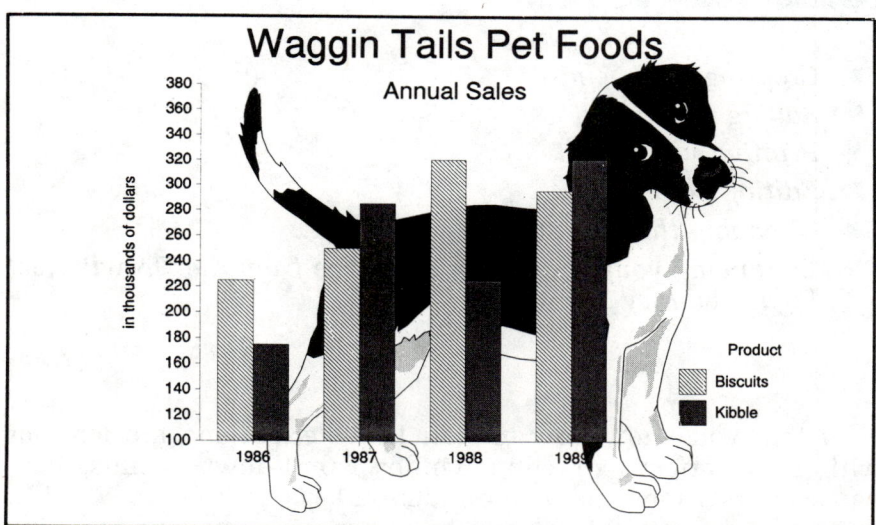

Figure 2.2   The enhanced bar chart

Creating a Bar Chart

Bar charts are among the most popular methods of conveying numeric data and are widely used in business applications. As you'll soon see, they are easy to create. DrawPerfect provides many options that you can use to enhance them, including grid lines, labels for the X- and Y-axes, a variety of fill patterns and colors for the bars, several different fonts for the text, and even a 3-D effect.

Start DrawPerfect and make sure that your drawing window is clear. (As you probably remember from the previous chapter, you can clear the drawing window using the File menu's Exit option or the Exit key, F7.) You'll begin by displaying the pull-down Draw menu and then selecting the Chart option.

> ▶ **Tip:** If you don't know how to start DrawPerfect, refer to the *Starting DrawPerfect* section at the beginning of Chapter 1.

 Type **D C**.

 Drag the cursor onto the **Draw** title, click the left mouse button, and continue holding it while dragging the cursor onto the **Chart** option. Release the left button.

The Chart submenu should pop up to the right of the main Draw menu, as shown in Figure 2.3. Your next step is to choose the Bar graph format from among the eleven options on this submenu. Notice that the first three, Bullet, Simple, and Freeform, are separated from the others by a single line. These are text chart formats, while the others are numeric. You'll study text charts in Chapter 3. For now, let's select the Bar option.

 Type **R**.

 Drag the cursor onto the **Bar** option and then click the left button.

You should see this prompt at the bottom of the screen:

`Enter Set corner of chart area (twice for full page);`

Chapter 2

DrawPerfect is asking you to designate where you want to place the chart on the page, and how large it should be. If you want it to fill the entire page, all you have to do is press Enter twice (or the equivalent on the mouse, click the left button twice). Otherwise, you would move the cursor to the position where you want the upper left corner to begin, press Enter, then move the cursor to the lower right corner and press Enter again. Let's do it the easy way the first time. Since this chart will span the entire page:

Press Enter twice.

Click the left button twice (make sure that the cursor is in the drawing window when you do this!).

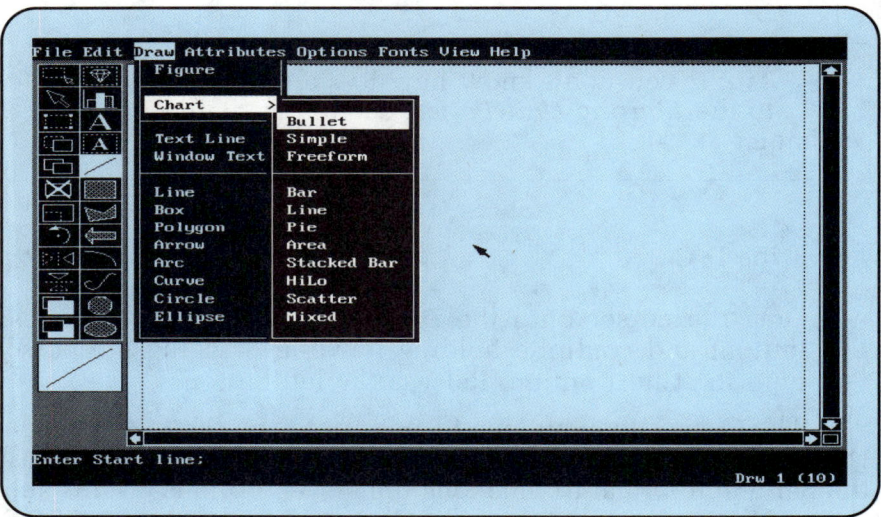

Figure 2.3   The Chart submenu

The Graph Edit Screen

The screen changes, and now you see a bar graph with *Sample Chart* as the title! What happened? Simple: You have entered DrawPerfect's Graph Edit screen, shown in Figure 2.4, and Draw-Perfect has provided sample data and titles to make it easier for you to learn how to create charts. After you become comfortable with them, you can change the default settings so that the sample data does not appear each time you start a new chart. For now, let's learn a little about the chart title, axes, legend, and data, and how to change them for our chart.

> **Tip:** For more information about how to change Draw-Perfect's default settings, see the *Initial Settings* section in Appendix B.

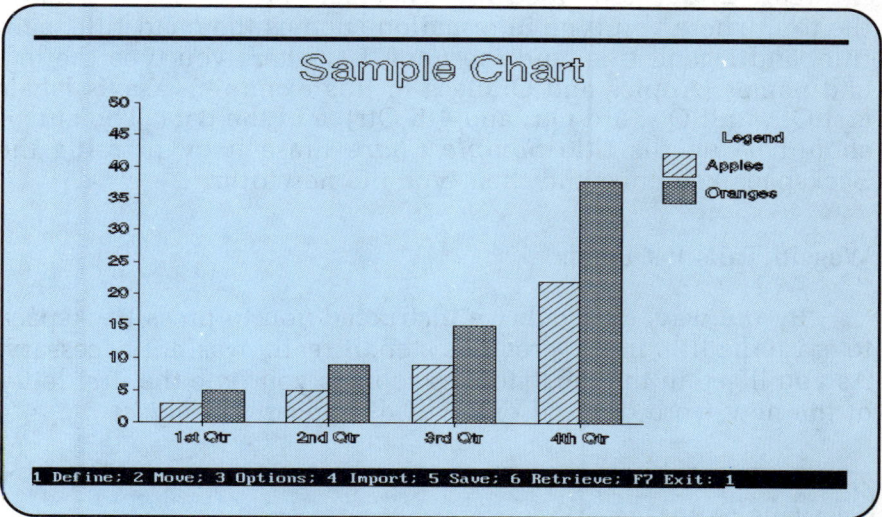

Figure 2.4   The Graph Edit screen

As we mentioned in the previous paragraph, the *chart title* is the heading at the top. In Figure 2.4 it is *Sample Chart* (not very imaginative!). The *X-axis* is the horizontal line that the bars sit on, labeled with the words *1st Qtr, 2nd Qtr, 3rd Qtr,* and *4th Qtr.* The *Y-axis* is the vertical line, labeled with the numbers 0 through 50. The *legend* at the right side of the screen is the key that identifies the bars by their patterns and colors. In this chart, the legend tells you that the bars with the diagonal line pattern represent apples, while the ones with the criss-cross pattern represent oranges. The *data* is the actual numbers that DrawPerfect used to generate the bars. You'll see these numbers as soon as you select the Define option, so do that now.

Type **D** (or 1).

 Drag the cursor onto the **Define** option and click the left button.

Using the Graph Data Screen to Enter Your Data

You should now be in DrawPerfect's Graph Data screen, shown in Figure 2.5. It is divided into two main areas: The *title list* at the top, where you type information such as the chart title, subtitle, and legend title; and the *item list,* where you type the legend names (Apples and Oranges in this example), X-axis labels (1st Qtr, 2nd Qtr, 3rd Qtr, and 4th Qtr), and the data. The cursor should be on the title *Sample Chart.* Erase it by pressing the Backspace key once and then type the new title:

Waggin Tails Pet Foods

By the way, although we instructed you to press Backspace to erase the title in the previous step, it really was not necessary. As you'll see in the next step, as soon as you type the first letter of the new word, the old one will disappear entirely.

```
Define: Graph Data

Title    : Sample Chart
Subtitle :
Legend   : Legend
X-Label  :
Y-Label L:
Y-Label R:
                  1         2         3         4
    Legend     1st Qtr   2nd Qtr   3rd Qtr   4th Qtr

  Apples          3         5         9        22
  Oranges         5         9        15        38









Arrows Move; Enter Edit; F1 Clear; F4 Data Options; Ctrl-F5 Import; F7 View;
```

Figure 2.5   The Graph Data screen

Your First Business Chart

🖮 Press the Down Arrow key twice.

🖱 Click the right button, then drag the cursor onto **Legend**, and click the left button.

Type **Product**.

Your next step will be to move the cursor into the first column, under the heading *Legend,* and change the legend names from *Apples* and *Oranges* to *Biscuits* and *Kibble.* To move the cursor onto *Apples:*

🖮 Press the Down Arrow key four times. Incidentally, Table 2.1 summarizes the keys you can use to move the cursor and delete text while in the Graph Data screen.

🖱 Click the right button, then drag the cursor onto **Apples**, and click the left button.

Once the cursor is on *Apples,* type **Biscuits** and then:

🖮 Press Enter.

🖱 Click the right button, then drag the cursor onto **Oranges**, and click the left button.

Type **Kibble**.

Now let's change the data. Begin by moving the cursor into the first data column in the Biscuits row, placing it on the number 3.

🖮 Press the Up Arrow key, then the Right Arrow.

🖱 Click the right button, then drag the cursor onto the **3**, and click the left button.

Type **200**.

Next, move the cursor into the second numeric column, under the heading *2nd Qtr.*

🖮 Press Tab.

🖱 Click the right button, then drag the cursor onto the **5** in the next column, and click the left button.

Type **235**.

Chapter 2

Repeat the previous step, using the keyboard or mouse to move the cursor into the third column, under the heading *3rd Qtr*. Type **310**. Next, move the cursor into the fourth column and type **275**.

Then:

🔹 Press Enter and then press the Left Arrow key three times.

🖱 Click the right button. Drag the cursor onto the number **5** in the first numeric column in the Kibble row and click the left button.

Type **175** and then:

🔹 Press Tab.

🖱 Click the right button, drag the cursor into the second numeric column, and then click the left button.

Type **285**.

Repeat the previous step, using the keyboard or mouse to move the cursor into the third column. Type **225**.

Move the cursor into the fourth column. Type **320**. Next:

🔹 Press Enter.

🖱 Click the right button.

Your screen should now resemble Figure 2.6. Are you eager to see your revised bar chart? The menu line at the bottom of the screen provides a clue about how to do this: `F7 View`. Go ahead and try it.

🔹 Press F7.

🖱 Drag the cursor onto **View** and click the left button.

There's your chart! However, one task remains: We forgot to change the labels on the X-axis. Our data is for the years 1986, 1987, 1988, and 1989, but the labels say 1st Qtr, 2nd Qtr, 3rd Qtr, and 4th Qtr. To change them, we'll select Define to return to the Graph Data menu.

🔹 Type **D** (or 1).

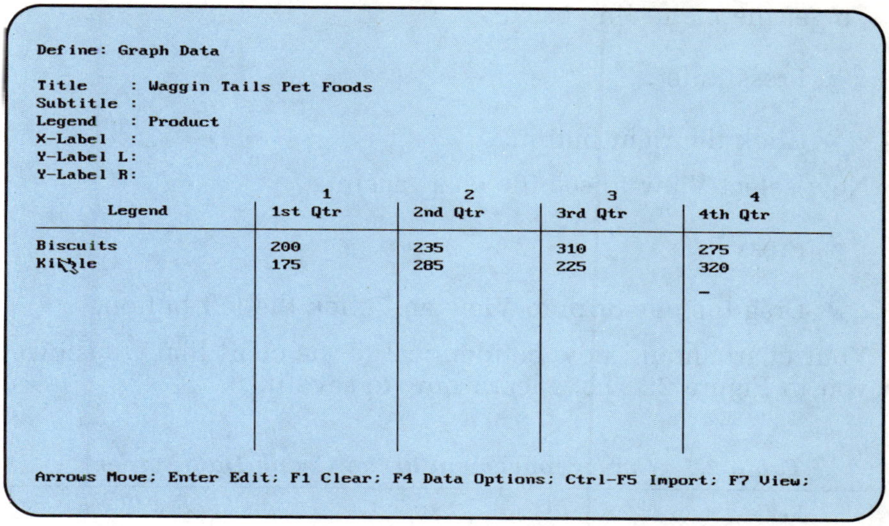

```
Define: Graph Data

Title    : Waggin Tails Pet Foods
Subtitle :
Legend   : Product
X-Label  :
Y-Label L:
Y-Label R:
                    1           2           3           4
       Legend     1st Qtr     2nd Qtr     3rd Qtr     4th Qtr

Biscuits          200         235         310         275
Kibble            175         285         225         320


Arrows Move; Enter Edit; F1 Clear; F4 Data Options; Ctrl-F5 Import; F7 View;
```

Figure 2.6   The Graph Data screen after changing the data

🖱 Drag the cursor onto **Define** and click the left button.

The Graph Data menu reappears, with the cursor in the same position it was in before you switched to the other screen. To change the labels, begin by moving the cursor onto the first one, 1st Qtr.

⌨ Press the Up Arrow key three times, then the Left Arrow key three times.

🖱 Drag the cursor onto **1st Qtr** and click the left button.

Type **1986** and then move the cursor into the next column.

⌨ Press Tab.

🖱 Click the right button, drag the cursor onto **2nd Qtr**, and click the left button.

Type **1987**.

Repeat the previous step to move the cursor into the next column and then type **1988**. Move the cursor into the last column and type **1989**.

Chapter 2

To get the menu line back:

⌨ Press Enter.

🖱 Click the right button.

Now select View to see the chart again.

⌨ Press F7.

🖱 Drag the cursor onto **View** and click the left button.

Your chart should now be identical to the chart that we showed you in Figure 2.1. Let's learn how to save it.

Table 2.1 Cursor movement in the Graph Data screen

Key	Effect
Enter	In the title list: If the menu line is displayed, pressing Enter switches to edit mode for typing or editing text. If the menu line is not displayed, pressing Enter brings it back. Pressing Enter after typing text moves the cursor down to the next option. In the item list: If the menu line is displayed, pressing Enter switches to edit mode. If the menu line is not displayed, pressing Enter moves the cursor down to the next option in the column.
Arrow Keys	If the menu line is displayed, the Arrow keys move the cursor up, down, left, or right to the next option. Otherwise, they move the cursor through existing text (if there is any) so that you can edit it.
Home Right Arrow	If the menu line is displayed and the cursor is in the item area (to type data), pressing Home followed by Right Arrow moves the cursor to the last column visible on the screen (in the same row).
End	Same as Home Right Arrow.
Home Left Arrow	If the menu line is displayed and the cursor is in the item area, Home Left Arrow moves the cursor to the first data column on the screen (in the same row).

Continued

Key	Effect
Backspace	Deletes text.
Tab	In the item list, moves the cursor to the right one option. In the title list, moves the cursor down one option.
Shift-Tab	In the item list, moves the cursor to the left one option. In the title list, moves the cursor up one option.
Page Up	Moves the cursor to the top left of the screen, placing it on the first option, *Title*.
Page Down	Moves the cursor to the last row on the screen.

Saving Your Chart

Since DrawPerfect does not save as you are working, it is important that you learn how to save your charts and do it frequently. Right now the chart you just finished creating is only in the computer's on-line memory (RAM). If the power fails or for some other reason the computer shuts down before you get a chance to save your Waggin Tails chart, you'll lose it and will have to do all that work again (horrors!). Since this has happened to us more than once, we save our work every few minutes. To save:

 Type **S** (or 5).

 Drag the cursor onto the **Save** option and click the left button.

You should see this menu line at the bottom of the screen:

`Save: 1 Description; 2 Chart as WPG file: 0`

As you can see, the menu provides two different methods of saving a chart. We'll confuse you further by telling you that there is one additional method that you select in the main DrawPerfect screen. You'll use all three, saving each as a separate file so that by the end of this chapter you will be sure to understand the differences.

The first option, *Description,* saves the graph format but does not save the data. In other words, it only saves the information in the title list, including the title, subtitle, legends, X-label, Y-labels. It also saves information about the font, font colors, graph colors and styles, and graph type (which you will study later). By saving the Graph Description, you can easily retrieve the format and use it repeatedly with new sets of data.

The second option, *Chart as WPG File,* saves both the data and the format of the graph so that you can retrieve it again later. However, when you do retrieve it you will find that DrawPerfect won't allow you back into the Graph Edit screen to change the data or formatting. The trade-off is that you will be able to modify individual items in the chart, using the Edit and Draw tools in the drawing window. For example, you could move the title, change its size, delete one of the bars, or type another line of text. Note that *WPG* stands for *WordPerfect Graphics.* You can retrieve any WPG file into WordPerfect, including the ones in the Figure Library, using WordPerfect's Graphics key (see Chapter 10 for specifics).

The third way to save the chart is through the *Save* option in the drawing window. When you use this method, you can later retrieve it and come back into this screen to edit the data and formatting. Like the previous save method, DrawPerfect automatically adds the extension WPG to your file name.

Select the first option, Description:

Type **D** (or 1).

Drag the cursor onto **Description** and then click the left button.

You should see this prompt at the bottom of the screen:

`Graph Description to be Saved:`

We will assign the name *Wagtail1* to this file, so type **wagtail1** and then press Enter or click the right mouse button. DrawPerfect automatically adds a period and these three characters to your file name: GDF. Therefore, the actual file name is *wagtail1.gdf.* As you may have guessed, *GDF* stands for *Graph Description file.*

> **Tip:** DrawPerfect file names must follow the rules imposed by the operating system, DOS. You can type as many as eleven characters for a file name, split into two parts: a first part consisting of one to eight characters, and an optional second part, called a file extension, which can contain from one to three characters. You must separate the first part from the second by a period, as in *chart1.wpg* or *chart1.gdf*. You can use letters, numbers, or a combination of the two in your file names. However, you can never use a space in a file name, as in *chart 1.wpg*.

Next, let's save the chart as a WPG file (WordPerfect Graphics file), using the name *wagtail2*. Remember, DrawPerfect will automatically add a period and the extension WPG to your file name, so the actual name will be *wagtail2.wpg*. Select the Save option again.

Type **S** (or 5).

Drag the cursor onto the **Save** option and click the left button.

Select the Chart as WPG File option:

Type **C** (or 2).

Drag the cursor onto **Chart as WPG File** and click the left button.

In response to the `Drawing to be Saved` prompt, type this file name: **wagtail2**. Press Enter or click the right mouse button.

Next, let's learn how to save the chart using the third method. The first step is to exit from the Graph Edit screen and return to the main DrawPerfect screen. To do this:

Press Exit (F7).

Drag the cursor onto **Exit** and then click the left button.

You should see this prompt:

`Insert chart in current drawing? Yes (No)`

The cursor will be under `Yes`, since DrawPerfect assumes that yes will be your response. To accept this assumption:

☞ Type **Y** or press the Enter key.

☞ Click the right button.

After a few seconds you will see the main DrawPerfect screen, with the Waggin Tails chart in the drawing window. It should be similar to Figure 2.7.

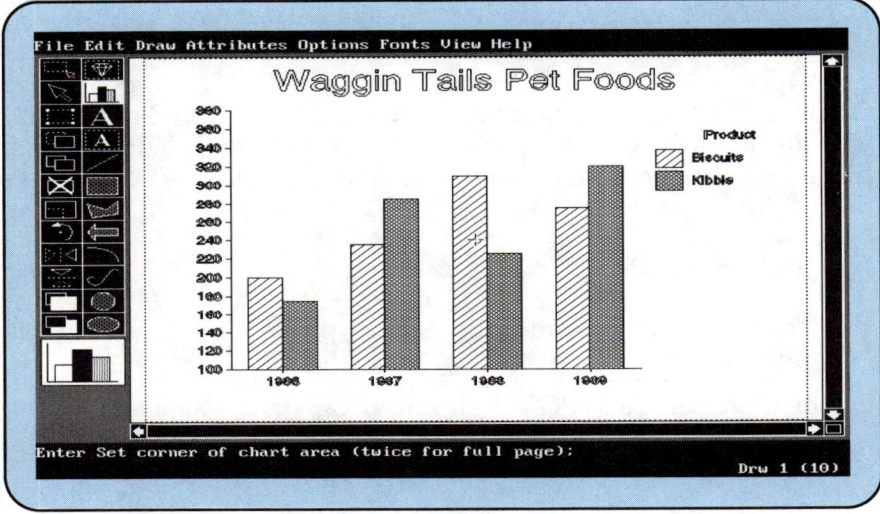

Figure 2.7 The main DrawPerfect screen with bar chart

To save the chart:

☞ Either type **F S** or press the Save key (F10).

☞ Drag the cursor onto **File**, click the left button and hold it while dragging the cursor onto **Save**, then release the button.

You should see this prompt at the bottom of the screen:

`Drawing to be Saved:`

Let's use the name *wagtail3* for this version. Type **wagtail3** and then press Enter or click the right mouse button. Now that the file has been saved, look in the lower left corner of the screen for a new prompt showing your file name and the name of the drive and directory where it is stored. Since we save our DrawPerfect files on the E drive, in the DRAWINGS directory, which is a sub-directory of DR10, the file name appears as follows on our screen:

`E:\DR10\DRAWINGS\WAGTAIL3.WPG`

> ▶ **Tip:** If you try to save a chart using the same name as another file on your disk, DrawPerfect will warn you with a prompt asking if you want to replace the file. For instance, if you enter the name *PETBAR.WPG* for a new file, before saving it DrawPerfect will check to see if a file with the same name exists. If it finds one, you will see a prompt similar to this one: `Replace C:\DR10\PETBAR.WPG? No (Yes)`. If you select Yes, DrawPerfect will erase the disk file and replace it with the drawing now appearing on your screen. To be safe, always select No when you see the Replace prompt. DrawPerfect will then let you type a new name for the chart.

Printing Your Chart

Printing the bar chart is easy. You can either use the Print option on the File menu, or DrawPerfect's Print key. Either way, you end up in the main Print menu.

 Type **F P** or press the Print key (Shift-F7).

 Drag the cursor onto **File**, click the left button and hold it down while dragging the cursor onto the **Print** option, then release the button.

The Print menu shown in Figure 2.8 should appear.

Chapter 2

```
Print
     1 - Print Drawing
     2 - Print Window
     3 - Drawing on Disk
     4 - Control Printer
     5 - Presentation
     6 - View Drawing
     7 - Initialize Printer

Options
     S - Select Printer           HP LaserJet Series II
     B - Binding                  0"
     N - Number of Copies         1
     G - Graphics Quality         Medium
     T - Text Prints Solid Black  No




Selection: 0
```

Figure 2.8 The Print menu

Your printer's name should appear next to the `Select Printer` option in the middle of the screen (note the arrow pointing at our printer's name in Figure 2.8). For instance, if you were using a Hewlett-Packard LaserJet II, you would see `HP LaserJet Series II`. If you don't see your printer's name, your printer is not installed correctly, so you probably won't be able to print the chart. If this happens, turn to Appendix A and follow the instructions for installing your printer; then go on to the next paragraph.

To print your chart, you'll use the Print Drawing option. First, make sure that your printer is turned on. Next:

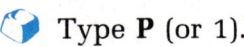 Type **P** (or 1).

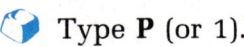 Drag the cursor onto the **Print Drawing** option and click the left button.

After a minute or two (depending on the speed of your printer), your chart will emerge from the printer.

Now that you've created, saved, and printed the bar chart, use Exit to clear the screen.

 Press the Exit key (F7) or type **F X**.

Drag the cursor onto **File**, click the left button and hold it while dragging the cursor onto **Exit**, then release the button.

You should see a `Save Drawing?` prompt at the bottom of the screen. Since you have already saved it and have not made any changes to the chart since saving, it is not necessary to save it again. The `Drawing was not modified` prompt in the lower right corner of your screen confirms this.

 Type **N**.

 Drag the cursor onto **No** and click the left button.

Next, you'll see the `Exit DrawPerfect?` prompt. Since you'll want to continue using DrawPerfect (we assume!), select No.

 Type **N**.

 Drag the cursor onto **No** and click the left button.

This clears the drawing window so that you can begin creating a new drawing or chart, or retrieve an existing one.

Printing a Chart

1. Press the Print key (Shift-F7) or type F P. Mouse users: Drag the cursor onto the File menu title, click the left mouse button once and hold it while dragging the cursor onto Print, then release the button.

   The Print menu appears.

2. Type 1 or P to select Print Drawing. Mouse users: Drag the cursor onto Print Drawing and click the left mouse button once.

   The printer starts printing your chart, and you return to the main DrawPerfect screen.

Retrieving and Editing the Chart

Do you remember that you saved the Waggin Tails bar chart using three different methods? When you were in the Graph Edit screen, you used the Description option to create a file named wagtail1.gdf. Next, you used the Chart as WPG File option to create a file named wagtail2.wpg. Finally, you exited back to the drawing window and used the File Save option to create a file named wagtail3.wpg. In this section, you'll learn how the three files differ.

Let's begin by retrieving the wagtail2.wpg file and making some changes to it.

 Press the Retrieve key (Shift-F10) or type **F R**.

 Drag the cursor onto **File**, click the left button and hold it while dragging the cursor onto **Retrieve**, then release it.

You will then see this prompt at the bottom of the screen, asking for the file name:

`Drawing to be Retrieved:`

Type the name **wagtail2** and then press Enter. (You do not have to type the file extension, WPG, because DrawPerfect assumes it.)

You'll see a `* Please wait *` message on the status line, and soon your chart will materialize inside the drawing window. Let's experiment with some of the options on DrawPerfect's Edit menu. You'll begin by moving the title, *Waggin Tails Pet Foods*.

Retrieving a Chart from the Disk

1. Press the Retrieve key (Shift-F10) or type F R. Mouse users can drag the cursor onto File, click the left button and hold it, highlight Retrieve, and then release the button.

   The `Drawing to be Retrieved:` prompt appears at the bottom of the screen.

2. Type the file name and then press Enter or click the left mouse button.

A Please Wait prompt appears briefly; then the chart appears on your screen.

Using the Move Option

Display the Edit menu and then select the Move option.

 Type **E O**.

 Drag the cursor onto **Edit**, click the left button and hold it while dragging the cursor onto **Move**, then release the button. Alternatively, you can drag the cursor onto the Move icon, the fourth icon in the first column, and click the left button.

This prompt should appear above the file name at the bottom of the screen:

`Enter` Select/Unselect objects;

It means that you can select an object to move by placing the cursor on it and then pressing Enter (or the mouse equivalent, clicking the left button). *Unselect* means that if you have already selected an object, pressing Enter turns off the selection.

Your next step is to move the cursor back into the drawing window and place it anywhere on the title (Waggin Tails Pet Foods); then select the title.

 Use the Arrow Keys to place the cursor on the title and then press the Enter key.

 Drag the cursor onto the title and click the left button.

Notice the changes: Several small boxes surround the title, showing that you have selected it, and the prompt at the bottom of the screen has changed to:

`Enter` Select/Unselect objects; `Space` Move;

You now have two options: Unselect the title (since it is already selected) or move it. Let's move it.

Press the Spacebar.

Click the right button.

Now you should see a dashed box surrounding the title, and your screen should resemble Figure 2.9.

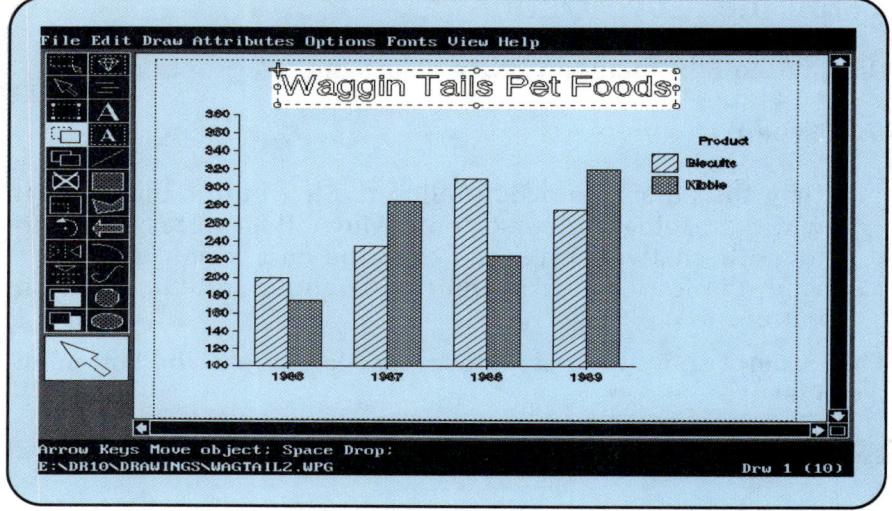

Figure 2.9 Selecting an object to move

Notice that the prompt has changed to:

`Arrow Keys` Move object; `Space` Drop;

Press the Down Arrow key a few times.

Drag the cursor down about an inch.

As you move the cursor, it will appear as though you are only moving an empty box. However, as soon as you press the Spacebar or click the right button, the title will reappear.

Continue moving the box until its right corner is covering the words *Product* and *Biscuits* and then set it down.

Press the Spacebar.

Click the right button.

The entire title will reappear in the new position. Whoops! You've just covered part of the Biscuits section of the legend. Move the title up just a little.

🖱 Press the Spacebar.

🖱 Click the right button.

The box should reappear. Move the box until the right corner of the box is just above *Biscuits* and to the left of *Product*. Next, drop it and unselect it.

🖱 Press the Spacebar and then press Enter.

🖱 Click the right button, then the left button.

The results appear in Figure 2.10. What a mess! It looks as though we've erased part of the legend (the Biscuits title and box). However, did you notice the Redraw message in the lower right corner of the screen? DrawPerfect displays this message whenever it senses a change that might affect other sections of the drawing. In this case, it appears as though parts of the legend have disappeared, but that is only temporary. They will reappear as soon as you select ReDraw.

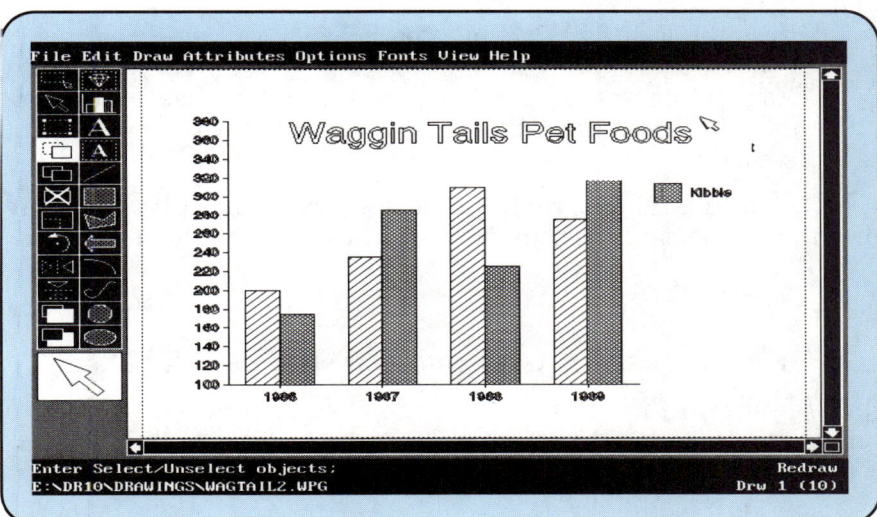

Figure 2.10 The screen before using ReDraw

There are three ways to redraw the screen:

1. Press the ReDraw key, F9.
2. Use the keyboard or mouse to display the View menu and then select the ReDraw option.
3. Place the cursor on the box in the lower right corner of the screen (just above the word `Redraw`, with two arrows pointing at it). Press Enter or click the left button.

Go ahead and use one of these methods to redraw the screen. Isn't that better?

That was just one example of how you can modify an object in your chart. Other objects you could have selected and moved include one of the bars, a legend box or legend title, or a number on the X- or Y-axis. Note that you can move more than one object simultaneously. For instance, you could have selected all five of the objects in the legend (the two boxes, the words *Biscuits* and *Kibble,* and the title *Product*). You'll learn more about these useful editing tools in Chapter 6.

Let's see what happens if we try to move items in our other chart, wagtail3.wpg. Begin by clearing the drawing screen, because if you don't, you'll end up with two charts. To clear it:

 Press the Exit key (F7) or type **F X**.

 Drag the cursor onto **File**, click the left mouse button and hold it, then drag the cursor onto the **Exit** option and release it.

The `Save Drawing?` prompt appears. Since you will not be saving the changes we just made to the wagtail2 chart, select No.

 Type **N**.

 Drag the cursor onto **No** and then click the left button.

In response to the `Exit DrawPerfect?` prompt, repeat the previous step to select No.

Now retrieve the wagtail3 file.

 Type **F R** or press Shift-F10.

Drag the cursor onto **File**, click the left mouse button and hold it, highlight **Retrieve**, then release the button.

In response to the `Drawing to be Retrieved:` prompt, type **wagtail3** and press Enter (you do not have to type the file extension WPG).

To start the move:

 Type **E O**.

 Drag the cursor onto **Edit**, click the left button, highlight **Move**, then release the button. Alternatively, you can drag the cursor onto the Move icon (the fourth icon in column one) and click the left button.

Next, place the cursor onto the title (Waggin Tails Pet Foods) and select it.

 Press Enter.

 Click the left button.

What happened? The tiny boxes that surround an object to signify that it has been selected appear around the edges of the chart, not around the title. In fact, instead of selecting the title, you have inadvertently selected the entire chart. Try placing the cursor on the legend name *Biscuits* and pressing Enter or clicking the left button again. Continue pressing Enter or clicking the left button a few times until you understand that you can only select the chart as a single unit, and that you are just turning the selection on and off by pressing Enter or clicking the button. Be sure to turn it off before continuing.

What we are trying to demonstrate is that you cannot select and edit individual items in this chart as you could with the wagtail2.wpg version. However, you can go back into the Graph Edit screen and modify the data or any of the options, which you could *not* do with the wagtail2 file. The next section shows you how.

Moving an Object

1. Type E O. Mouse users: Drag the cursor onto the fourth icon in the first column and click the left button once.

   The `Enter Select\Unselect objects;` prompt appears.

2. Use the Arrow Keys to move the cursor onto the item that you want to move. Press the Enter key, then the Spacebar. Mouse users: Drag the cursor into the drawing window and place it on the item you want to move. Click the left button once, then the right button once.

   A dashed box appears around the selected object and the prompt changes to include: `Space Drop;`

3. Use the Arrow Keys to reposition the object and then press the Spacebar. Mouse users: Reposition the object by dragging the cursor and then click the right mouse button once.

4. Press Cancel (F1). Mouse users: Click the two buttons simultaneously (or the center button).

   The tiny boxes disappear, signifying that the object is no longer selected. □

Modifying Data in the Chart

To make changes to the data or formatting in your chart, you begin by using the Edit menu's Modify option. To do this:

 Type **E M**.

 Drag the cursor onto **Edit**, click the left button and hold it, highlight **Modify**, then release the button. Alternatively, you can use the third icon in the first column on the panel.

Position the cursor anywhere in the drawing window, then:

🖮 Press Enter.

🖱 Click the left button.

You should see this prompt:

`Enter Select/Unselect objects; Space Modify;`

By now you should be able to guess what it means: Press the Enter key (or mouse equivalent, right button) to select or unselect, or press the Spacebar (or left mouse button) to modify. Since you will modify the drawing:

🖮 Press the Spacebar.

🖱 Click the right button.

Voilà! The Graph Edit screen appears, and there's your bar chart!

Let's use the familiar Define option to change some of the data, then learn how to change the graph type. Select Define.

🖮 Type **D**.

🖱 Drag the cursor onto **Define** and click the left button.

Change the Biscuits data to the following:

1986	225
1987	250
1988	320
1989	295

To see how this has changed the graph, use the View option.

🖮 Press F7.

🖱 Drag the cursor onto **View** and click the left button.

You should be back in the screen that shows your bar graph. Can you see the results? If not, compare the chart on your screen to Figure 2.7.

Chapter 2

Changing the Bars to Lines

Now let's learn how to change the bars in the chart to lines. To do this, you use the Graph Data Options screen, which you access through the Define option. Select Define again.

 Type **D**.

Drag the cursor onto **Define** and click the left button.

You may have noticed the Data Options selection on the menu line at the bottom. Let's find out what it has to offer.

Press F4.

Drag the cursor onto **Data Options** and click the left button.

You should now see the Graph Data Options screen shown in Figure 2.11. Note that you can switch back and forth between this screen and the Graph Data screen by pressing F4 or using the mouse to select Data from the menu line.

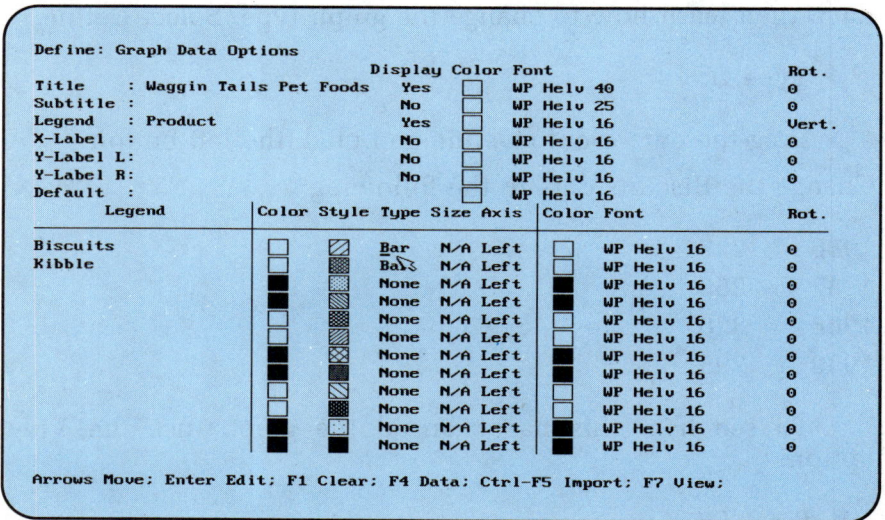

Figure 2.11 The Graph Data Options screen

There is a lot of information on this screen but it isn't hard to understand, so please don't feel intimidated. Like the Graph

Data screen, it is divided into two main areas: the title list and the item list. In the title list, you can change formatting characteristics such as the size, type, and color of the fonts used for the chart title, subtitle, legend title, and X- and Y-axis labels. In the item list below the horizontal line, you can change formatting for the legend and the graph bars. For instance, you can change the color or pattern in the bars or change their appearance from bars to lines. Let's try changing the appearance of the bars to lines. To do this, you can use the Type option.

Place the cursor on the word Bar in the Biscuits row, under the heading Type (note that in Figure 2.11 the arrow is pointing to it). To select it:

 Press Enter.

 Click the left button.

This menu line appears at the bottom of the screen:

1 Pie; 2 XPie; 3 Bar; 4 Area; 5 Line; 6 Scatter; 7 Hi-Lo; 8 None: 3

Select Line.

 Type **L**.

 Drag the cursor onto **Line** and click the left button.

Move the cursor down to the next row and repeat the previous step to select Line again. Incidentally, since you know which option you want to use, you don't even have to bring up the menu. Instead, just type **L** and it changes instantly to Line. Now let's see how our line chart looks. To return to the chart:

 Press F7.

 Drag the cursor onto **View** and click the left button.

Your chart should be similar to the one in Figure 2.12.

The chart looks quite different, doesn't it? Compared with the bar chart, we think it provides a much better understanding of how the data has changed. Biscuits increased steadily until 1988, then declined slightly, while Kibble has gone up and down. This brings up another point: The chart does not tell us

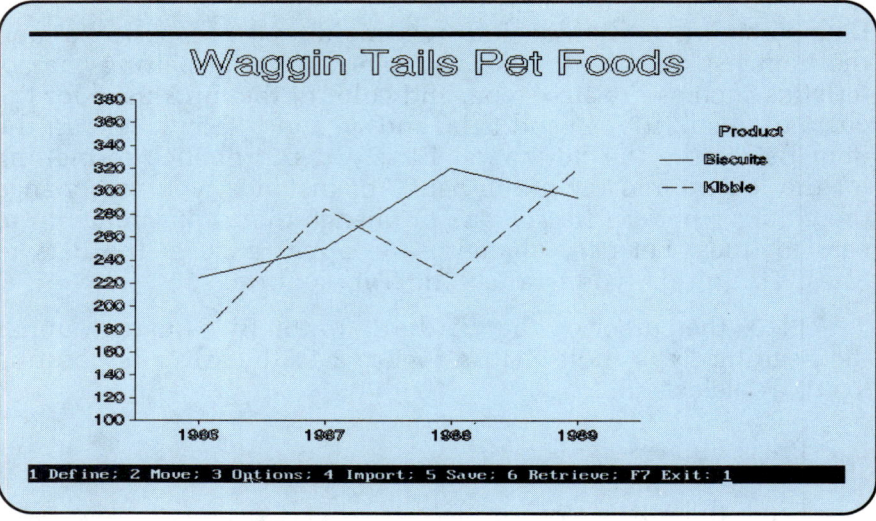

Figure 2.12   The Waggin Tails chart after using the Graph Data Options menu to convert it to a line chart

what the data represents. Is it sales, profits, volume, or something else? Let's say that it represents sales in thousands of dollars, and add a subtitle and Y-axis label to our chart to signify this to the reader.

Typing a Subtitle and Y-Axis Label

Select Define again to return to the Graph Data Options screen. Position the cursor on the subtitle line, near the top of the screen.

Press the Page Up key, then the Down Arrow key.

Drag the cursor into the subtitle area and click the left button.

Type **Annual Sales** and press Enter or click the right mouse button. Next, add a title for the Y-axis to indicate that we measure sales in thousands of dollars. To do this, move the cursor down a few lines to the title Y-Label L. You may be wondering why there are two Y-Label options on this screen, so we'll digress for a moment to explain. DrawPerfect permits you to use both a left and right Y-axis, useful when you are contrasting two sets of data that cannot be measured in the same terms. For example, Figure 2.13 graphs monthly ice cream sales and average monthly temperature, and shows an obvious relationship between them. However, the left Y-axis measures gallons sold and has nothing to do with average temperature. To show the temperatures, a right Y-axis is necessary.

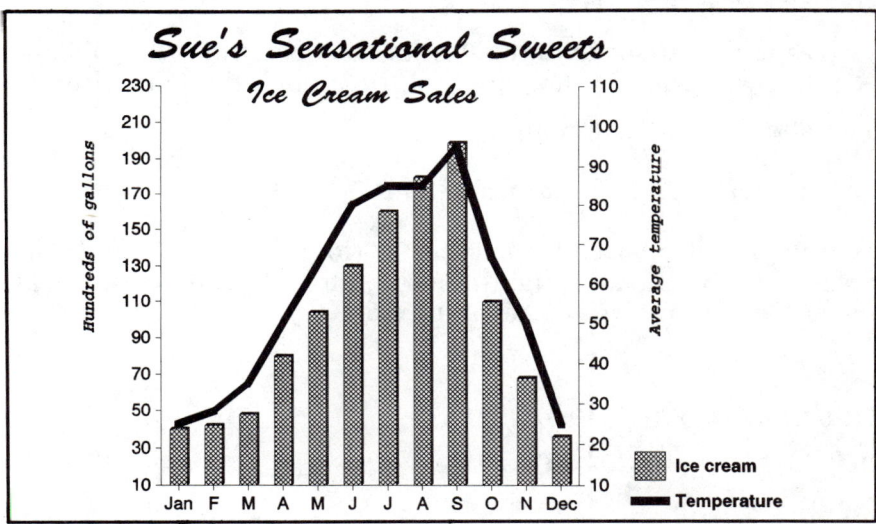

Figure 2.13   A chart with two Y-axes

To continue with our example, type this title:

in thousands of dollars

then press Enter or click the right button.

Now select the View option to see the results. The chart looks great except for one detail. The Y-axis label overlaps the word *Waggin* in the chart title. To correct it, you can rotate it and move it down so that it will be printed vertically along the Y-axis. Let's begin by rotating it.

Using the Rotate Option

To rotate the Y-Label, select Define to return to the Graph Data Options screen. Next, move the cursor to the Y-Label L row and place it in the last column, under the heading Rot.

Use the Arrow Keys to move the cursor into the Y-Label L row, press the End key, then Enter.

Drag the cursor onto the **0** in the last column of the Y-Label L row, under the heading **Rot**, then click the left button.

You should see this prompt:

Enter angle of rotation (0-360)

To rotate it a quarter turn, type **90** (for 90 degrees) and then press Enter or click the right mouse button. To see how it looks, select View to return to the Graph Edit screen.

Using the Move Option on the Graph Edit Screen

What's wrong with this picture? Part of your Y-axis label, *in thousands of dollars,* has disappeared off the top of the screen! Let's move it down so the entire label will be visible.

Select Move and you will see this prompt:

Choose Letter of Item to be Moved: 0

Notice that DrawPerfect has placed a letter next to each item that can be moved. For example, you should see the letter *e* next to the Y-axis label, the letter *a* next to the chart title, *b* next to the subtitle, and *c* in the legend area. To select the Y-axis label:

Type **e**.

Drag the cursor onto the letter **e** and click the left button.

The prompt changes to:

Arrow Keys Move Item; **Space** Drop;

Use the Down Arrow keys or mouse to move the cursor down until it is about ãeven with the number 180 on the Y-axis and then drop it.

- Press the Spacebar.

- Click the left button.

Now exit the Move option.

- Press Enter.

- Click the right button.

Doesn't that look better?

Replacing the Graph Description and WPG File

Since you have improved the graph significantly, you'll want to save it again. Use both Save options on this menu, saving the graph both as a Graph Description and as a WPG file.

You no longer need the files that you saved earlier, Wagtail1 and Wagtail2, so you can use the same file names for the revised versions. Be aware that by using the same names, you will delete the original Wagtail1 and Wagtail2 files on the disk, and replace them with the screen versions. Got that?

Select the **Save** option from the menu line and then select **Description**. In response to the Graph Description to be Saved prompt, type **wagtail1** and press Enter or click the right mouse button (if the file name already appears, you don't have to retype it; just press Enter). Next, you will see a prompt asking if you want to replace the disk file of the same name. Select Yes.

Before using the other method to save, Chart as WPG File, let's change the chart back to a bar type. Here's why: In the last section of this chapter, you will be combining this chart with the dog image shown in Figure 2.2. Once you add the dog figure, it overwhelms the lines and the chart loses its effect. If you don't make the change now, you won't be able to do it later, because when you save using the Chart as WPG File option, you cannot return to this screen to edit.

Select **Define** from the menu and then use the **Graph Data Options** menu to change the type to Bar for both products, Biscuits and Kibble. After you finish, select **View** to return to the Graph Edit screen. Now you are ready to save it again.

Select **Save** from the menu and then choose **Chart as WPG File**. In response to the prompt

```
Drawing to be Saved:
```

type **wagtail2** and select Yes when asked if you want to replace the existing file.

Now let's clear the screen and return to the drawing window. Select the **Exit** option from the File menu. In response to the prompt

```
Save edit changes to chart? Yes (No)
```

select **No**. You should be back in the main DrawPerfect screen, where the old Waggin Tails bar chart is still visible. Let's use the Exit option to clear it from the screen. Display the **File** menu and select **Exit**. In response to the Save Drawing prompt, select **No**. The next prompt will ask if you wish to exit from DrawPerfect. Again, select **No**.

Using the Graph Description File with New Data

Suppose you wanted to produce a chart that is similar to the Waggin Tails chart, but that uses data from sales of the company's other division, Pet Toys. You've already done most of the formatting work, so all you really need to do is retrieve the Graph Description file that you saved earlier and then enter the new data. Let's learn how.

Display the **Draw** menu and select the **Chart** option; then select **Bar** for the chart type. To have the chart span the entire page:

- Press Enter twice.

- Click the left button twice.

After a few seconds you will be back in the Graph Edit screen, where you will see the original sample chart (with apples and oranges). Let's begin by clearing the data.

Select the **Define** option to move to the Graph Data screen. Next, select the **Clear** option:

Press F1.

Drag the cursor onto **Clear** and click the left mouse button.

You should see this prompt:

```
Clear all current data? No (Yes)
```

Select **Yes**. Notice that this removes all of the information in the item area, but leaves the titles. Now select **View** to return to the chart. As you can see, all that remains is the title (*Sample Chart*), the legend title (*Legend*), and the lines that represent the X- and Y-axes.

Select **Retrieve** from the menu line. You should see this prompt:

```
Graph Description to be Retrieved:
```

If the wagtail1 name appears automatically, press Enter or click the right mouse button. If not, type the name of your Graph Description file,

wagtail1

then press Enter or click the right button. Your screen should now resemble Figure 2.14, with the Waggin Tails Pet Foods title, and the subtitle, legend title, and Y-axis label that you saved in the previous section. Let's fill it out with our new data.

Select **Define** and then type the legend names, X-axis labels, and data shown in the chart below.

| | 1 | 2 | 3 | 4 |
Legend	1986	1987	1988	1989
Dog Toys	100	95	102	103
Cat Toys	85	88	89	92

Chapter 2

Figure 2.14 *The Graph Edit screen after retrieving the Waggin Tails Graph Description*

Use the View option to see the new chart. Wasn't that easy? At this point, you may wish to save your chart. If not, just use the Exit option to return to the main DrawPerfect screen and then use the File menu's Exit option to clear the drawing window.

Enhancing Your Chart with an Image from the DrawPerfect Figure Library

Compare the bar chart in Figure 2.1 to the one shown in Figure 2.2. As you can see, adding the clip-art drawing of a small dog makes the chart much more interesting. DrawPerfect includes over 500 drawings of such subjects as animals, arrows, business objects, computer-related objects, flags, flow chart symbols, graphic devices, banners, borders, maps, military objects, sports, and transportation. These drawings are on the four Figure Library disks that come with the program. Let's see how easy it is to add one to our bar chart.

Make sure that your screen is clear (use File Exit if it is not) and then use the File menu's Retrieve option to retrieve the bar chart you saved earlier, Wagtail2.

Type **F R**.

Drag the cursor onto **File**, click the left button and hold it while highlighting **Retrieve**, then release the button.

Type the file name **Wagtail2** and press Enter or click the left mouse button.

Before showing you how to add the dog image, we'd like to explain the difference between retrieving it as a file and retrieving it inside a Figure box. If you retrieve the dog image as a figure, DrawPerfect considers it to be a single object. This gives you the advantage of being able to modify the entire image at once. For example, you can move, copy, reduce, enlarge, or rotate it as a single unit. However, if you retrieve the dog image as a file, you can only select and change individual sections of the dog, such as the nose or ears. You can end up with some very strange effects, like the ones we got in Figure 2.15. Since it is likely that you will want to make some changes to the dog after adding it to the bar chart, let's use the Figure method to retrieve it.

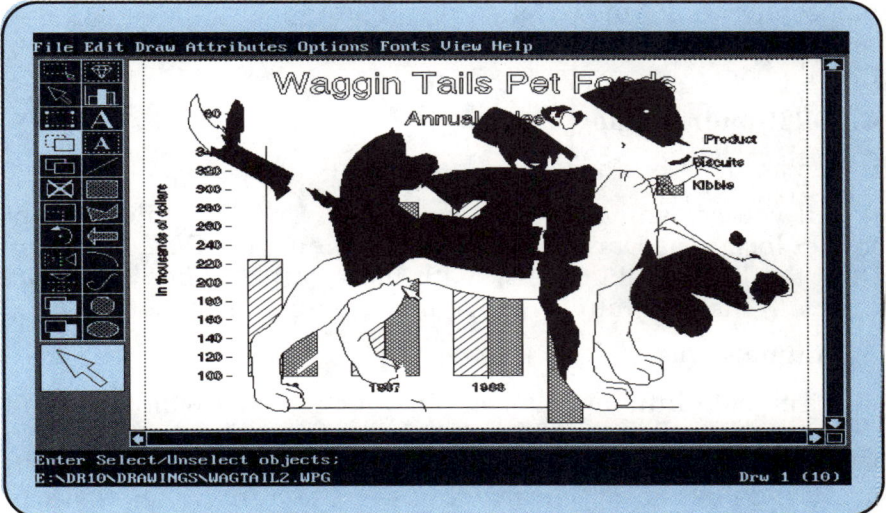

Figure 2.15   The bar chart with distorted dog figure

Chapter 2

 Type **D F**.

 Drag the cursor onto **Draw**, click the left button and hold it, highlight **Figure**, and release the button.

You should see this prompt:

`Enter` `Set corner of figure area (twice for full page);`

It may seem familiar, since this is the same prompt that you saw earlier when you selected the Chart option to create your bar chart. Essentially, DrawPerfect is asking where you want to place the figure and how large it should be. If you press Enter twice (or the mouse equivalent, clicking the left button twice), your chart will fill the entire page. Since that is what we want:

 Press Enter twice.

 Click the left button twice.

You should now see this prompt:

`Drawing to be Retrieved:`

Type the file name **Dog** and then press Enter or click the right mouse button. If you installed the Figure Library files in a separate subdirectory, you will have to include the path when typing the file name. For example,

C:\DR10\animals\dog

where animals is a subdirectory of DR10.

If you see an error message indicating that the file was not found, locate the DrawPerfect disk containing the DOG.WPG file. (It is the Figure Library disk with the subtitle *Animals, People, Special*.) Insert it into drive A, then type this name:

A:\Animals\Dog

The cute little dog appears in your drawing window (don't you love those big eyes?), but it is blocking the bar chart and legend, so we can't make sense of the data. Fortunately, the Edit menu includes an option that you can use to move an object to the front or back of another one. Since you retrieved the dog image as a figure, it is one object, so moving it to the back should be easy. Let's see how it works.

Display the Edit menu and select Back. Next, place the cursor anywhere on the dog, then select it.

⌨ Press Enter.

🖱 Click the left button.

Small boxes appear to indicate that you have selected it. You should see this prompt:

`Enter` Select/Unselect objects; `Space` Push to Back;

To change the dog's position from front to back:

⌨ Press the Spacebar.

🖱 Click the right mouse button.

The screen changes and the dog appears behind the bars. That's much better, isn't it?

All that remains now is a little clean-up work. You should probably move the dog figure down a little so that the entire chart title is visible and then move the legend area away from his muzzle. Since you have already selected the dog, it will be easy to move it. Display the Edit menu and select Move. Move the box down as far as you can and a little to the right. When it is in place, press the Spacebar or click the right mouse button. If you see the `Redraw` prompt, be sure to use one of the three methods we discussed earlier to redraw the screen.

The last step is to move the legend area. Begin by unselecting the dog. To do this:

⌨ Press Enter.

🖱 Click the left button.

Move the cursor onto the *Product* title and select it by pressing Enter or clicking the left button. Repeat until you have selected both boxes and the two legend names, *Biscuits* and *Kibble*. Each of the five objects should now be surrounded by tiny boxes to show that they are selected. Next,

⌨ Press the Spacebar.

🖱 Click the right button.

Move the cursor down until the bottom line of the box is aligned with the X-axis. To complete the move:

Press the Spacebar and then Cancel (F1).

Click the right button and then click both the left and right buttons simultaneously (or click the middle button if you have one).

Notice that the Redraw message appears in the lower right corner. Be sure to select ReDraw again.

Wasn't that fun? At this point, you may wish to save and print your drawing. If not, either exit DrawPerfect or continue on to the next chapter, where we will teach you how to create text charts.

What You Have Learned

In this chapter, you've learned how to create, save, print, and modify a bar chart. You should now be familiar with the following:

- ▶ You can use the Chart option on the Draw menu to create a variety of business graphs, including Bar, Pie, Line, Area, Scatter, HiLo, and Stacked Bar.
- ▶ DrawPerfect provides many options that you can use to enhance your business charts, including legends, grid lines, labels for the X- and Y-axes, a variety of fill patterns and colors, several different fonts for the text, and even a 3-D effect.
- ▶ The Figure Library that comes with DrawPerfect includes over 500 drawings of such subjects as animals, arrows, business objects, computer-related objects, flags, flow chart symbols, graphic devices, banners, borders, maps, military objects, sports, and transportation. You can use them to enhance your charts and graphics, or retrieve them directly and modify them as you wish.
- ▶ Since DrawPerfect does not save as you are working, it is important that you save frequently in case of a power failure or computer malfunction. To save the chart or drawing

you are working on, you can use the Save option on the File menu. To save a business chart while you are creating or editing it, you can use the Chart as WPG File option in the Graph Edit screen.

▶ If you create many similar graphs, you can use the Description option on the Graph Edit screen to save graph formatting information for the graph you are working on (but it does not save the data). This saves the title, subtitle, legends, X-Label, Y-Labels, font, font colors, graph colors and styles, and graph type into a special file called a Graph Description file. Whenever you want to use the formatting with a new set of data, you can retrieve the Graph Description file.

▶ To print a chart or drawing, you can use the Print option on the File menu or press the Print key (Shift-F7). Both bring up DrawPerfect's Print menu, where you select the Print Drawing option.

▶ To retrieve a chart or drawing that you saved earlier, you can use the Retrieve option on the File menu or press the Retrieve key (Shift-F10).

▶ DrawPerfect displays the Redraw prompt in the lower right corner of the screen whenever it senses a change that might affect other sections of the drawing. There are three ways to redraw the screen: select ReDraw from the View menu, press F9, or move the cursor onto the small box in the lower right corner of the screen (with the two arrows pointing at it); then press Enter or click the left mouse button.

▶ To edit the data or formatting of a business chart, you can use the Modify option on the Edit menu.

Chapter 3

Your First Text Chart

In This Chapter

- ▶ *Creating a text chart*
- ▶ *Previewing your chart before printing*
- ▶ *Editing the text chart*
- ▶ *Using clip-art to enliven your chart*
- ▶ *Copying a figure*
- ▶ *Drawing straight lines*
- ▶ *Typing a line of text*
- ▶ *Using DrawPerfect's built-in text charts*

Text charts are useful in presentations, both as slides and as handouts, when you want to list important goals, features, or other key points. DrawPerfect provides formats for three types of text charts: Bullet, Simple, and Freeform. All three include a title, subtitle, and one or more lines of body text. In the *Bullet* chart format, each line of body text begins with a round bullet, as shown in Figure 3.1. These bullets help stress the key points in the chart. In the *Simple* chart format, all lines are automatically centered, and none have bullets. The *Freeform* format is the least structured one, for it has no formatting at all, and all lines begin at the left margin.

Now that you know how to create, save, and print bar charts, text charts will be easy. To create one, you simply select the chart type, designate the size and position, then type your text. If you want to get fancy, you can select from among a variety of fonts to change the size and appearance of the type, and use formatting features, such as centering, indenting, boldfacing, and underlining. To add visual appeal, you can include one or more clip-art figures from the DrawPerfect Figure Library, turning a plain chart into a fascinating one.

We will begin by teaching you how to create the bullet chart shown in Figure 3.1. Next, we will enhance the chart by combining it with two images from the DrawPerfect Figure Library: a globe and a planet. Figure 3.2 shows how it will look when you are finished.

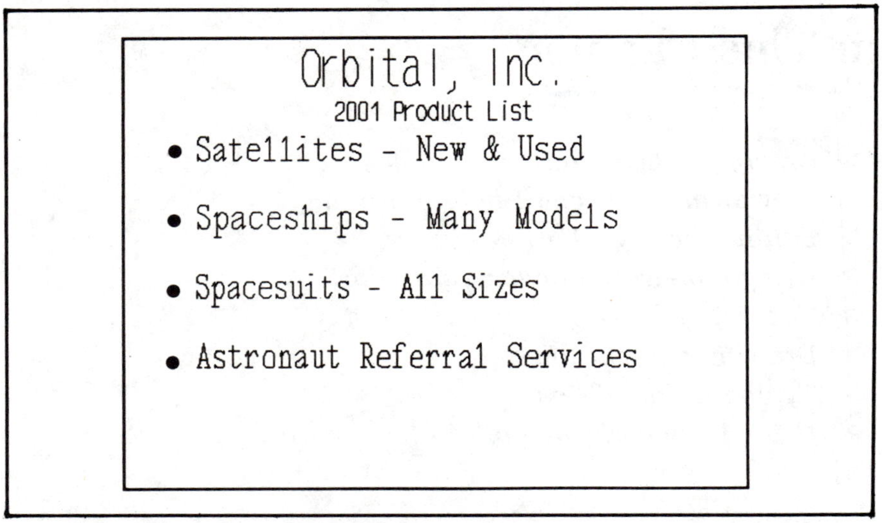

```
           Orbital, Inc.
           2001 Product List
  • Satellites - New & Used

  • Spaceships - Many Models

  • Spacesuits - All Sizes

  • Astronaut Referral Services
```

Figure 3.1   The bulleted text chart

Creating a Text Chart

Start DrawPerfect and make sure that your drawing window is clear (you can use File Exit or F7 to clear it). Since the initial steps that you use to create a text chart are similar to the ones you used

Figure 3.2   The enhanced text chart

in the last chapter to create a bar chart, you should find the procedure easy to follow. You begin by displaying the Draw menu, selecting the Chart option, and then designating the position and size of your chart.

Type **D C**.

Move the mouse until the cursor is on the **Draw** title, click the left button once and continue holding it down while dragging the pointing cursor onto the **Chart** option, then release the left button.

The Chart submenu appears to the right of the main Draw menu. Your next step is to choose the type of text chart that you want to use. There are three formats you can select from: Bullet, Simple, and Freeform. Notice that a line separates them from the other eight options: Bar, Line, Pie, Area, Stacked Bar, HiLo, Scatter, and Mixed. The first three are text chart formats, while the other eight are for graphic charts.

Select the Bullet option.

Type **B** (or press Enter).

Drag the cursor onto the **Bullet** option and click the left button once.

Note the icon that appears in the Status box under the icon panel. It symbolizes the bullet chart format, with three small boxes representing bullets and three lines representing the text lines next to them.

You should now see this prompt at the bottom of the screen:

`Enter Set corner of chart area (twice for full page);`

DrawPerfect is asking you to indicate the size and position of your chart. To create a full-page chart, you press Enter twice or click the left button twice. If you want a smaller chart, first move the cursor to the position where you want the upper left corner of the chart and press Enter or click the left button once. Next, move the cursor to the lower right corner and press Enter or click the left button again.

Since this chart will fill the entire page, your next step is to:

Press Enter twice.

Click the left mouse button twice.

You should now be in the Text Chart screen shown in Figure 3.3. The cursor has changed into a text cursor, represented by the line in the upper left corner of the window. Notice that several options on the menu appear in brackets, such as `[Edit]` and `[Draw]`. This means that you cannot use them while typing your text chart. For example, try selecting **O** for Options and you'll find that instead of bringing up a menu, you type the letter O! In fact, if you type **N** for the Fonts menu or **F** for the File menu, the only two options that are not bracketed, you will also type the letter in the text window. Why? Because you are working in text mode, and need to be able to type all the letters of the alphabet! The only way to bring up a menu is to press the Alt key or use the mouse.

Before continuing, be sure to press the Backspace key to erase the O and any other letters you may have typed.

The prompt line at the bottom of the screen gives you a clue about what you are supposed to be doing:

`Input title text;`

Your First Text Chart

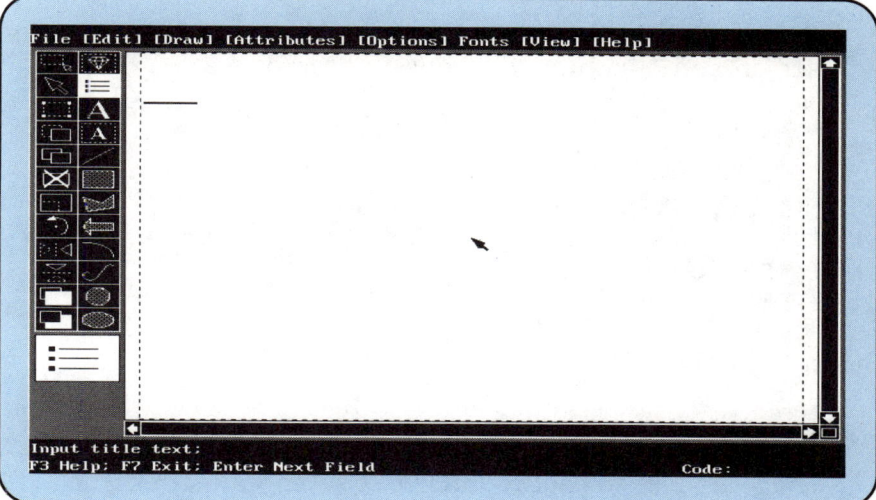

Figure 3.3   The Text Chart screen

In DrawPerfect, text charts include three sections: a title on the first line, a subtitle on the second line, and body text below the titles. In our example, the title is *Orbital, Inc.,* the subtitle is *2001 Product List,* and the body text is the four bulleted items in the list.

Before typing the title, let's turn on DrawPerfect's automatic centering. There are two ways to do this: Press the Center key (Shift-F6) or use the menu at the bottom of the screen to select it. Let's learn how to use the menu. Notice the options:

F3 Help; **F7** Exit; **Enter** Next Field

Unlike many of DrawPerfect's other menus, the first letters of the menu options do not appear in bold. This is because you cannot press a letter to use them. Instead, you have to press the key (F3 or F7 or Enter) or select an option with the mouse.

The Help menus that you studied in Chapter 1 are not available when you are typing a text chart. Instead, pressing the Help key (F3) or selecting Help from the menu at the bottom of the screen brings up a menu that lists available formatting tools, such as indent, date, bold, and center.

Press F3.

Chapter 3

 Drag the cursor onto the **F3 Help** option at the bottom of the screen and click the left mouse button once.

The prompt line changes, displaying several text formatting options:

```
F4 Indent; Shift-F5 Date; F6 Bold;
Shift-F6 Center; Alt-F6 Flush Rt.; F8 Underline;
Shift-F8 Format;
Ctrl-F8 Font; F7 Exit
```

Select the Center option.

 Press Shift-F6.

 Drag the cursor onto **Shift-F6 Center** and click the left mouse button once.

Notice that the cursor line has moved into the middle of the screen so that the title will be centered as you type it. Also, this prompt appears in the lower right corner of the screen:

```
Code: [C/Flrt]
```

If you use WordPerfect, you'll probably recognize this code as the one that ends centering (it also turns off Flush Right, symbolized by Flrt). Like WordPerfect, DrawPerfect inserts hidden codes into your text whenever you use a formatting option, such as bold, underline, center, flush right, or italics. The codes serve as commands to tell the program where to turn these features on and off, but they do not appear in the text. If they did, they would clutter up your screen and confuse you, since they do not appear in the printed version. However, they can be most helpful. For instance, if you change your mind after using a formatting feature, such as centering, you can remove it by pressing the Delete key when you see the code in the lower right corner of the screen.

To continue, type:

Orbital, Inc.

Then press Enter. Incidentally, if you move the cursor back up to the title line that you just typed (the cursor should be at the left edge), you'll see on the prompt line the code that turns centering on:

```
Code: [Cntr]
```

When you typed *Orbital, Inc.,* the cursor was positioned between the two centering codes, [Cntr] and [C/Flrt], so DrawPerfect automatically centered your title as you typed it.

> **Tip:** On most screens, text appears as an outline of the selected font. However, when you print the document or use a special preview screen called View Drawing (which you'll study later in this chapter), you will see that the text is filled in. To speed up your typing and editing, DrawPerfect displays text in a medium text quality, but prints it in high quality. If you want to change the text display to high quality, display the File menu and select Setup, then Display, and then Text Quality While Editing.

If you used the Up Arrow to see the [Cntr] code, press the Down Arrow before continuing. The prompt changes and now tells you to type your subtitle:

```
Input subtitle text;
```

Let's center the subtitle also. To select the Center option:

 Press Shift-F6.

 Drag the cursor onto the **F3 Help** option and click the left mouse button once. Drag the cursor onto **Shift-F6 Center** and click the left mouse button once.

Type:

2001 Product List

and then press Enter. A round bullet appears on the screen, as shown in Figure 3.4, and the cursor is positioned to the right of it.

You may have noticed that the text in the subtitle appears smaller than the heading. This is because DrawPerfect automatically selects the base font—the typeface, type size, and style—

Chapter 3

Figure 3.4 *The Text Chart screen with bullet*

for each section in a text chart. The default typeface is always Helvetica, as shown in the first line of Figure 3.5. As you can see, Helvetica comes in several other styles, including bold, italic, italic bold, and simplex.

Type size is measured in points. One point is 1/72 inch, so the larger the point size, the larger the type. DrawPerfect selects the type size for each section based upon the chart size. For example, if the chart occupies the entire page (as ours does), DrawPerfect selects a 60-point font for the title, a 30-point font for the subtitle, and a 39-point font for the body text. You can override the selected fonts using the Base Font option on the Fonts menu. There are thirteen typefaces to choose from, in a variety of styles, and you can select them in point sizes from 1 to 450. In text charts, you are limited to one font for each of the three sections (title, subtitle, body text).

> **Tip:** You can change the default settings for the fonts and font colors using the Initial Settings option on the File Setup menu. See Appendix B for more information.

Your next step will be to type the bulleted items. Before typing, let's change the font. To change the font,

Your First Text Chart

Helvetica, 60 point
Helvetica bold, 50 point
Helvetica italic, 40 point
Helvetica italic bold, 30 point

Helvetica simplex, 25 point

Figure 3.5   DrawPerfect's Helvetica fonts, printed on a laser printer

 Press the Font key (Ctrl-F8).

 Drag the cursor onto the **F3 Help** option and click the left mouse button once. Drag the cursor onto **Ctrl-F8 Font** and click the left mouse button once. Note that there is another way to select this option with the mouse, which we will show you the next time you change the font.

The prompt line changes to show you the names of the five submenus on the Fonts menu:

```
1 Size; 2 Appearance; 3 Normal;
4 Base Font; 5 Text Color: 0
```

Select Base Font.

 Type **F**.

 Drag the cursor onto the **Base Font** option and click the left mouse button once.

The menu shown in Figure 3.6 appears, listing DrawPerfect's base fonts. Notice the prompt at the bottom:

```
1 Select; N Name search: 1
```

Chapter 3

```
Base Font
    WP Bodoni Bold
    WP Broadway
    WP BrushScript
    WP Century Schoolbook
    WP Chelmsford Book
    WP Commercial Script
    WP Cooper Black Bold
    WP Courier
    WP Courier Bold
    WP Courier Italic
    WP Courier Italic Bold
    WP Courier Simplex
    WP Eurostile
  * WP Helv
    WP Helv Bold
    WP Helv Italic
    WP Helv Italic Bold
    WP Helv Simplex
    WP Hobo
    WP Old English
    WP Roman

1 Select; N Name search: 1
```

Figure 3.6 The Base Font menu

The default font, WP Helv, is highlighted and an asterisk appears next to it. Instead of using Helvetica, let's try one of the other fonts, WP Century Schoolbook. As soon as you select it, DrawPerfect will prompt you for the size.

 Use the Up Arrow to move the cursor bar until it is highlighting **WP Century Schoolbook** and then press Enter.

 Drag the cursor onto **WP Century Schoolbook** and click the left mouse button once. Drag the cursor to the **Select** option at the bottom of the screen and click the left mouse button once.

This prompt appears asking you to select a point size:

`Point size:`

followed by a number such as 39. Let's use the suggested point size.

 Press Enter.

 Drag the cursor onto the point size number and click the right mouse button once.

Now you are ready to enter the items in the bullet list. Type the first one:

Satellites—New & Used

Press Enter twice. Now type the second item in the list:

Spaceships—Many Models

Press Enter twice. Type the third item:

Spacesuits—All Sizes

Press Enter twice and type the last item:

Astronaut Referral Services

Then press Enter once. Now you have finished typing the text chart and are ready to exit back to the main DrawPerfect screen.

Press Exit (F7).

Drag the cursor onto the **Exit** option and click the left mouse button once.

You should now be back in the main DrawPerfect screen, and your chart should resemble Figure 3.7.

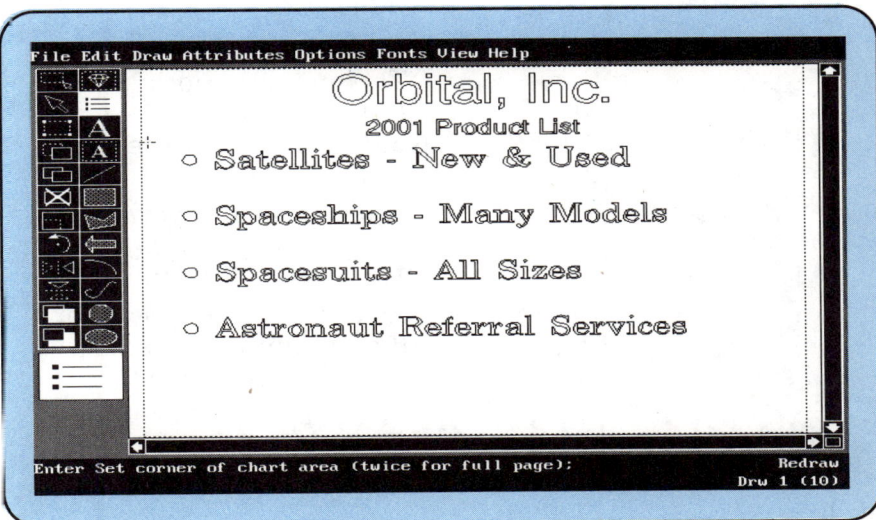

Figure 3.7 The completed bullet chart as seen in the main DrawPerfect screen

Notice the `Redraw` prompt in the lower right corner of the screen. You may remember from the last chapter that DrawPerfect displays this prompt whenever you make a change that might affect the chart in the drawing window. DrawPerfect displays this prompt whenever you exit the Text Chart screen. To redraw the screen:

- Press the ReDraw key (F9) or type **V** for View and **D** for ReDraw.

- Drag the cursor onto the **View** menu, click the left mouse button, and hold it while dragging the cursor onto the **ReDraw** option. Release the button. Another method is to drag the cursor onto the box in the lower right corner of the screen and click the left mouse button.

 Creating a Text Chart

1. Type D C. Mouse users: Drag the cursor onto the Draw menu title, click the left mouse button once and hold it down until the cursor is on the Chart option, then release the button.	The pull-down Draw menu and its Chart submenu appear.
2. Type B. Mouse users: Drag the cursor onto the Bullet option and click the left mouse button once.	This prompt appears: `Enter Set corner of chart area (twice for full page);`
3. Press Enter twice or click the left mouse button twice.	A text cursor appears and the prompt changes to: `Input title text;`
4. Type your title and press Enter. Type your subtitle and press Enter.	A round bullet appears and the prompt changes to: `Input body text;`
5. Type the first item in your list and then press Enter twice. Repeat for all items in your list. When you finish, press Exit (F7) or drag the cursor onto F7 Exit and click the left mouse button once.	The main DrawPerfect screen reappears.

Saving Your Text Chart

Let's save the text chart before continuing. Unlike the numeric chart that we created in the last chapter, there is only one format for saving a text chart. You can use either the Exit key (F7) or the Save key (F10), or their corresponding options on the File menu. Here's how to save the chart before you continue working on it:

 Press the Save key (F10) or type **F** for File and **S** for Save.

 Drag the cursor onto the **File** menu title, click the left mouse button once and hold it while dragging the cursor onto **Save**, then release the button.

The `Drawing to be Saved:` prompt appears. Type the new file name:

orbital

Next:

 Press Enter.

 Click the right mouse button.

Notice that your new file name appears in the lower left corner of the screen.

 Saving a Text Chart

1. Press the Save key (F10) or type F S. Mouse users: Drag the cursor onto File, click the left mouse button and hold it while dragging the cursor onto Save, then release the button.

2. Type the new file name and then press Enter or click the right mouse button.

This prompt appears:
`Drawing to be Saved:`

Previewing and Printing Your Chart

As we mentioned earlier, text charts often appear different on screen than in the printed version because the text appears in outline instead of solid black, as you can see in Figure 3.7. However, in the printed version the text is black (filled in), as shown in Figure 3.1. Fortunately, DrawPerfect includes a View Drawing option that you can use to preview the printed drawing. Let's see how it works.

Since it is related to printing, the View Drawing option is found on the main Print menu. To use it,

 Press the Print key (Shift-F7), or type **F** for File and then **P** for Print.

 Drag the cursor onto the **File** menu title, click the left mouse button once and hold it while dragging the cursor onto **Print**, then release the button.

The Print menu (shown in Figure 2.8 in the previous chapter) appears. Notice that View Drawing is the sixth option. To select it,

 Type **V**.

 Drag the cursor onto the **View Drawing** option and click the left mouse button once.

Figure 3.8 shows how our screen appeared when we selected the View Drawing option. Compare this to Figure 3.7, and you will see how different the text appears. When printed, it should look very similar, with the words printed in black instead of being outlined. Go ahead and print your chart now. Make sure that the printer is turned on, then:

 Press Enter once and then type **1** or **P** to select Print Drawing.

 Click both the left and right buttons simultaneously (or the center button, if you have one), drag the cursor onto **Print Drawing**, and click the left mouse button once.

You return to the main DrawPerfect screen, and the printer goes to work printing your chart.

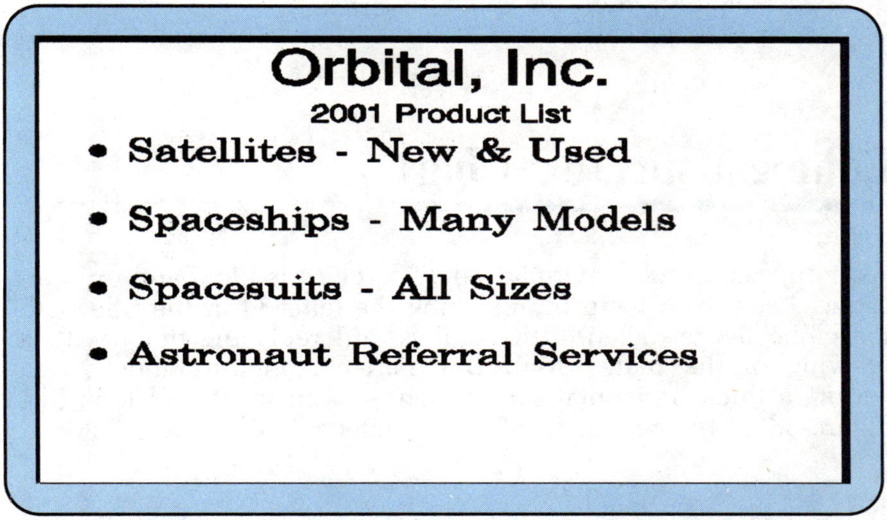

Orbital, Inc.
2001 Product List
- Satellites - New & Used
- Spaceships - Many Models
- Spacesuits - All Sizes
- Astronaut Referral Services

Figure 3.8   The text chart as seen in the View Drawing screen

Q Previewing and Printing Your Text Chart

1. Press the Print key (Shift-F7) or type F P. Mouse users: Drag the cursor onto the File menu title, click the left mouse button once and hold it while dragging the cursor onto Print, then release the button. — The Print menu appears.

2. Type V. Mouse users: Drag the cursor onto the View Drawing option and click the left mouse button once. — The drawing appears in the View Drawing screen.

3. When you finish looking at the drawing, press Enter to return to the Print menu. Mouse users: Click both buttons simultaneously (or the middle button) to return to the Print menu. — The Print menu reappears.

4. Type 1 or P to select Print Drawing. Mouse users: Drag the cursor onto Print Drawing and click the left mouse button once.

The printer starts printing your chart and you return to the main DrawPerfect screen.

Editing Your Text Chart

As it appears now, the Orbital, Inc. text chart is plain and uninteresting. Let's liven it up by replacing the letter O in the title with the globe figure, deleting the bullets and replacing them with a drawing of the planet from DrawPerfect's Figure Library, and adding a thick horizontal line. When you finish, it will look like Figure 3.2 at the beginning of this chapter.

Returning to the Text Chart Screen to Modify the Title

To make the title area of our chart look like Figure 3.2, we made several major changes. Since we couldn't move the title down a line, we had to erase the title and subtitle, then change the font and retype the title (minus the letter O) on the line reserved for the subtitle. The last step was to return to the drawing window and bring in the globe.

To modify the title, you must return to the Text Chart screen using the Edit menu's Modify option.

Type **E M** and press the Enter key, then the Spacebar.

Drag the cursor onto the **Edit** menu title, click the left mouse button, and hold it down while dragging the cursor onto the **Modify** option. Release the button. (Another method is to drag the cursor onto the Modify icon, the third one in the first column, and click the left button once.) Place the cursor in the drawing window and click the left mouse button, then the right button.

You should be back in the Text Chart screen, with the `Input title text;` prompt appearing under the window and all of the menu options except File and Fonts surrounded by brackets. Next, erase the title by pressing this combination: Ctrl-End (press and continue to hold Ctrl while pressing End once). Use the Down Arrow key to move the cursor down one line, so that the prompt changes to:

`Input subtitle text;`

Press Ctrl-End to delete the subtitle. Later, you'll retype it using another method.

Before retyping the title, let's change the font. You may remember that the default font for the subtitle is 30 points, half the size of the font used for the title.

- Press Ctrl-F8, type **F**, then use the Up Arrow key to move the cursor onto **WP Century Schoolbook**. Press Enter, then type **60** for the font size, and press Enter again.

- Earlier in this chapter you used the Help menu at the bottom of the screen to select a font. Let's try a different method. Drag the cursor onto the **Fonts** menu title, click the left button and hold it down while dragging the cursor onto the **Base Font** option, and then release the button. Drag the cursor onto **WP Century Schoolbook** and click the left button to highlight it. Drag the cursor down onto the **Select** option and click the left mouse button. Type **60** and click the right mouse button.

Now you should be back in the text chart window. Before typing the title, let's center it.

- Press Shift-F6.

- Drag the cursor onto the **Help** option and click the left mouse button once. Drag the cursor onto **Center** and click the left mouse button once.

Type:

rbital, Inc.

Note that you do not type the letter O, because it will be represented by the globe in the final drawing.

Your next step is to exit back to the main DrawPerfect screen, then retrieve the globe file.

Press Exit (F7).

Drag the cursor onto **F7 Exit** at the bottom of the screen and click the left mouse button once.

You should now be back in the main DrawPerfect screen. Notice that all of the options on the menu line are available now (none are bracketed).

Retrieving the Globe Figure

The globe figure is one of several hundred drawings that are included with your DrawPerfect package on the four Figure Library disks. During DrawPerfect's automatic installation process, you were given the opportunity to copy them onto your hard disk and we are assuming that you did.

To retrieve the globe figure, you use the Draw menu's Figure option.

Type **D F**.

Drag the cursor onto the **Draw** menu, click the left mouse button once, and hold it down while dragging the cursor onto **Figure**. Release the button. Another method you can use is to drag the cursor onto the icon, the first one in the second column.

This prompt appears under the drawing window:

`Enter Set corner of figure area (twice for full page);`

You have seen this prompt a few times before and probably remember what it means by now: DrawPerfect is asking where to place the figure and how large it should be. In the previous examples, you have always pressed Enter twice so that the figure would fill the entire page. This time it will not fill the page, so the procedure will be different.

⬢ Place the cursor in the upper left corner of the screen and press Enter. Press the Down Arrow key about eight times, then the Right Arrow key about twelve times. You should see a box forming, as shown in Figure 3.9. If the box is not positioned correctly, you can start again by pressing Cancel (F1). If it is, press Enter.

🖱 Drag the cursor to the upper left corner of the screen and then click and release the left mouse button. Drag the cursor down and to the right so that you form a box like the one shown in Figure 3.9 and click the left mouse button. If the box is not positioned correctly, you can start again by pressing the two buttons simultaneously (or the middle button if you have one).

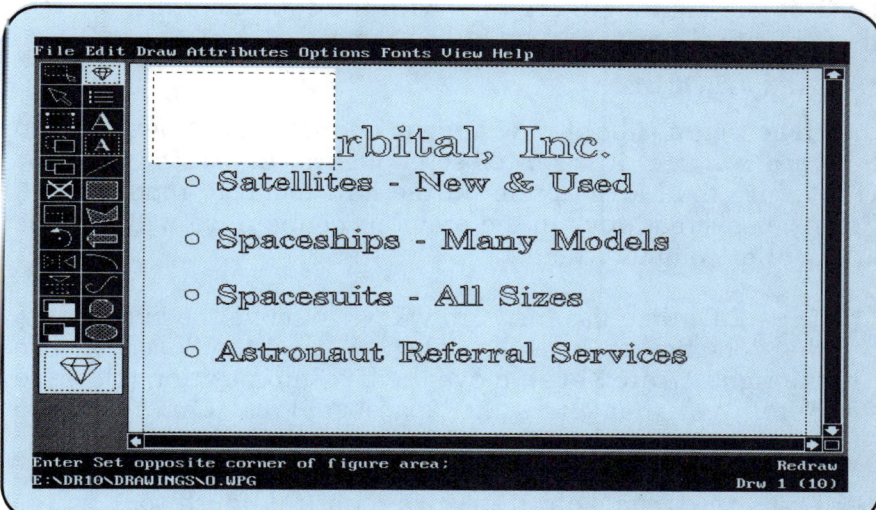

Figure 3.9 Designating the size and position of the globe figure

You should now see this prompt at the bottom of the screen:

`Drawing to be Retrieved:`

Type the file name:
GLOBE1-M

Then:

 Press Enter.

 Click the left mouse button once.

If you installed the Figure Library files in a separate subdirectory, you will have to include the path when typing the file name. For example,

C:\DR10\MAPS\GLOBE1-M

where MAPS is a subdirectory of DR10, and DR10 is a subdirectory of C. This subject is exlained in detail in Chapter 9.

If you see an error message indicating that the file was not found, locate the DrawPerfect disk containing the GLOBE1-M file (it is the Figure Library disk with the subtitle *Maps, Sports*). Insert it into drive A and type this name:

A:\MAPS\GLOBE1-M

The globe figure should now appear on the screen, right next to the word *rbital*. If it is not close enough to the word, you may wish to use the Move option on the Edit menu to reposition it. Since we covered Move in the previous chapter, we will provide only a brief summary here.

 Type **E O**; then use the Arrow keys to move the cursor onto the globe figure. Press the Enter key, then the Spacebar. Use the right Arrow Key to move the box into position (closer to *rbital*) and then press the Spacebar. Press Cancel (F1) to remove the tiny boxes.

 Drag the cursor onto the **Move** icon (the fourth one in the first column) and click the left button once. An alternative method is to drag the cursor to the **Edit** menu title, click the left button and hold it down while selecting **Move**, then release the button. Drag the cursor back into the drawing window and place it on the globe. Click the left mouse button once, then the right once. Drag the cursor into position and click the left mouse button. Click the two buttons simultaneously (or the center button) to remove the tiny boxes.

Erasing the Bullets

The next task in your editing process will be to erase the bullets and replace them with the small planet figures. You'll begin by returning to the Text Chart menu and erasing the round bullets. While there, you can insert a blank line above the first item in the list, Satellites. This will provide space for the horizontal line that spans the page.

To return to the Text Chart menu:

 Type **E M**.

 Drag the cursor onto the **Edit** menu title, click the left mouse button once and hold it while dragging the cursor onto **Modify**, then release the button. Or, you can drag the cursor onto the Modify icon (the third one in the first column) and click the left mouse button once.

This prompt appears:

`Enter Select/Unselect objects;`

asking you to select the objects that you want to modify by pressing the Enter key. Remember, while working in the main DrawPerfect window, you cannot select individual items in the chart, such as the bullets or title. Instead, you select the entire chart as one object, then return to the Text Chart screen to edit it.

Place the cursor anywhere in the drawing window, except on the globe figure.

 Press Enter.

 Click the left mouse button once.

The prompt changes to:

`Enter Select/Unselect objects; Space Modify;`

to let you know that your next step is to press the Spacebar.

 Press the Spacebar once.

 Click the right mouse button once.

You should now be back in the Text Chart screen. Your next step, erasing the bullets, is easy. All you have to do is place the cursor onto a bullet and press the Delete key.

- Use the Arrow keys to position the text cursor onto the first bullet.

- Drag the cursor onto the **Enter Next Field** option at the bottom of the screen and click the left mouse button twice. The cursor should move onto the first bullet.

To erase the bullet, press the Delete key once. To erase the second bullet, press the Down Arrow key twice and then press Delete again. Repeat until you have deleted all four of the bullets. Note that you cannot use the mouse to move the cursor to the other bullets inside this window, since they all are part of the same field, body text. In the Text Chart screen, you can only use the mouse to make menu selections.

Next, let's insert the blank lines above the first item, Satellites. Use the Up Arrow key to move the cursor onto the Satellites line and press Enter once.

Now exit back to the drawing window, where you will retrieve the planet figure to use in place of the bullets.

- Press Exit (F7).

- Drag the cursor onto **F7 Exit** at the bottom of the screen and click the left mouse button once.

You should now be back in the main DrawPerfect screen. You should see the Redraw prompt, so:

- Press F9.

- Drag the cursor onto **View**, click the left button and hold it down while dragging the cursor onto **ReDraw**, then release the button.

Retrieving a Clip-Art Figure for the Bullets

To retrieve the Planet figure, we will use the Draw menu's Figure option.

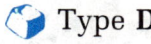 Type **D F**.

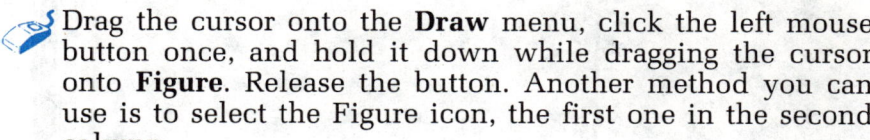 Drag the cursor onto the **Draw** menu, click the left mouse button once, and hold it down while dragging the cursor onto **Figure**. Release the button. Another method you can use is to select the Figure icon, the first one in the second column.

This prompt appears under the drawing window:

`Enter` Set corner of figure area (twice for full page);

Next, designate the size and position of the first planet figure.

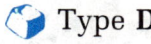 Place the cursor in the line above the S in the word Satellites, move it as far to the left as you can, then press Enter. Now press the Down Arrow key three times, then the Right Arrow key three or four times. You should see a box forming. If it is similar to Figure 3.10, press Enter. If not, start again by pressing Cancel (F1).

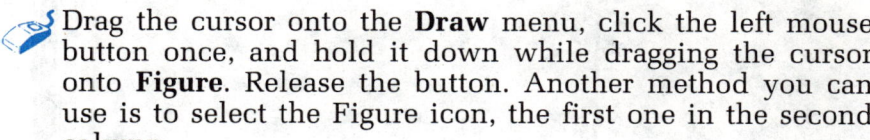 Drag the cursor to the line above the S in the word Satellites, moving it as far to the left as you can, then click and release the left mouse button. Drag the cursor down so that it is about even with the bottom of the S and then move it to the right. You should see a box forming. If it resembles Figure 3.10, click the left mouse button. If not, start again by pressing the two buttons simultaneously (or the middle button if you have one).

You should now see this prompt at the bottom of the screen:

`Drawing to be Retrieved:`

Type the file name:

Planet

then press Enter or click the left mouse button. If you installed the Figure Library files in a separate subdirectory, you will have to include the path when typing the file name. For example,

C:\DR10\SYMBOLS\PLANET

Figure 3.10 *Designating the size and position of the planet figure*

> **Tip:** If you see an `ERROR: file not found` prompt, the file is not in the current directory (you will probably find it in the Symbols subdirectory). Locate the DrawPerfect disk containing the Planet.wpg file (with the subtitle *Business, Flags, Military, Symbols, Transportation*). Insert it into drive A, type **A:\SYMBOLS\PLANET**, and press Enter.

The planet figure should now appear in your text chart, next to the word *Satellites.* Rather than going through this procedure three more times to create the remaining bullets, you can copy them. In the next section, we'll teach you how.

Copying the Figure

To copy the bullets, you can use the Copy option on the Edit menu. As you will see, this procedure is faster and easier than creating figure boxes and retrieving the planet three more times. The real advantage is that when you use this method, your planet bullets will all be the same size.

Type **E C**.

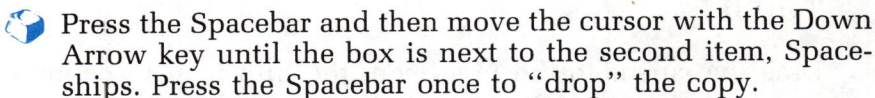 Drag the cursor onto the **Copy** icon (the fifth one in the first column) and click the left mouse button once. Another method is to drag the cursor to **Edit**, click the left mouse button and hold it while dragging it to **Copy**, then release the button.

This prompt appears:

`Enter` Select/Unselect objects;

Your next task is to mark the object that you want to copy.

 Move the cursor onto the planet figure and press the Enter key once.

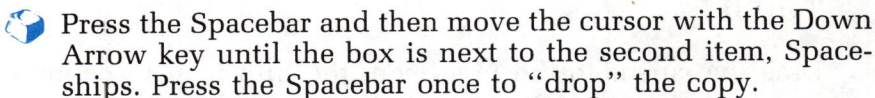 Drag the cursor onto the planet figure and click the left mouse button once.

Tiny boxes surround the figure, signifying that it has been selected. Notice the prompt now includes this instruction:

`Space` Copy;

and it means that you can press the Spacebar (or click the right mouse button) to begin the copy process.

 Press the Spacebar and then move the cursor with the Down Arrow key until the box is next to the second item, Spaceships. Press the Spacebar once to "drop" the copy.

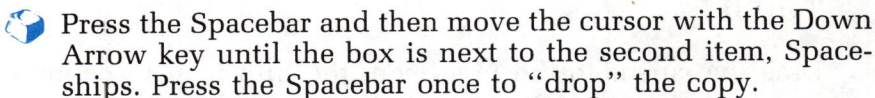 Click the right mouse button once and then drag the cursor down until the box is next to the second item, Spaceships. Click the right mouse button once to "drop" the copy.

Wasn't that easy? Since the planet is still selected, you can repeat the previous step to copy it twice more. When you finish, turn off the selection.

 Press Cancel (F1).

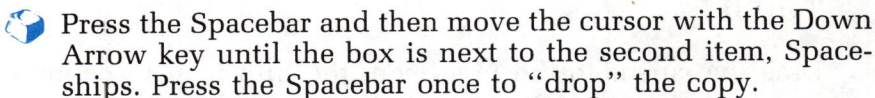 Click both buttons simultaneously (or the middle button, if you have one).

Be sure to check for the Redraw prompt and, if necessary, select the ReDraw option from the View menu (or press F9). Next, we will show you how to create the horizontal line separating the title section from the items in the bullet list.

Creating the Horizontal Line

Since it isn't easy to draw a straight line, DrawPerfect has two tools that can help you, *Grid Display* and *Grid Snap.* The Grid is a set of points that serve as a guide while you draw. When you draw with Grid Snap on, DrawPerfect forces the line to begin and end on a grid point, since the cursor can only move from grid point to point. You can use Grid Display and Grid Snap with or without the Grid displayed, but it's easier to understand when it is on.

Type **O G**, then **O R**.

Drag the cursor onto **Options**, click the left mouse button, and hold it down while dragging the cursor onto **Grid Display**. Release the button. Repeat to select **Grid Snap** from the Options menu.

Your screen should now resemble Figure 3.11. Notice the Snp prompt under the drawing window to let you know Grid Snap is currently on. Your next step is to select the Line tool.

Type **D L**.

Drag the cursor to the **Line** icon, the fifth icon in column two, and click the left mouse button once. Another method is to drag the cursor onto **Draw**, click the left mouse button and hold it down while dragging the cursor onto **Line**, then release the button.

Next, use the Attributes menu to change the line width. There are 16 different line widths to choose from, and the default is the thinnest one. Appendix D of the DrawPerfect manual shows each line width (as well as the other attributes).

Type **A W**.

Drag the cursor onto **Attributes**, click the left mouse button, and hold it down while dragging the cursor onto **Line Width**. Release the button.

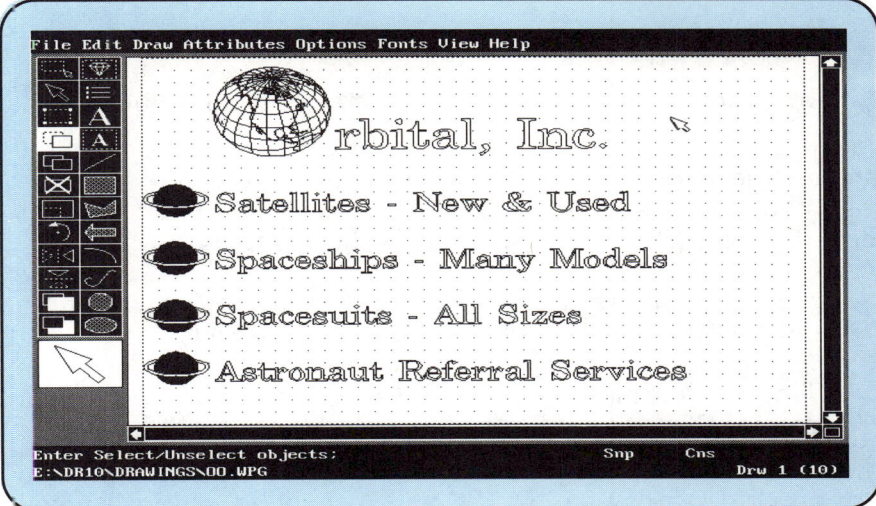

Figure 3.11   The screen after turning on the Grid Display

The menu shown in Figure 3.12 appears at the bottom of the screen, displaying the 16 line widths. Let's use one of the thickest ones, option 14.

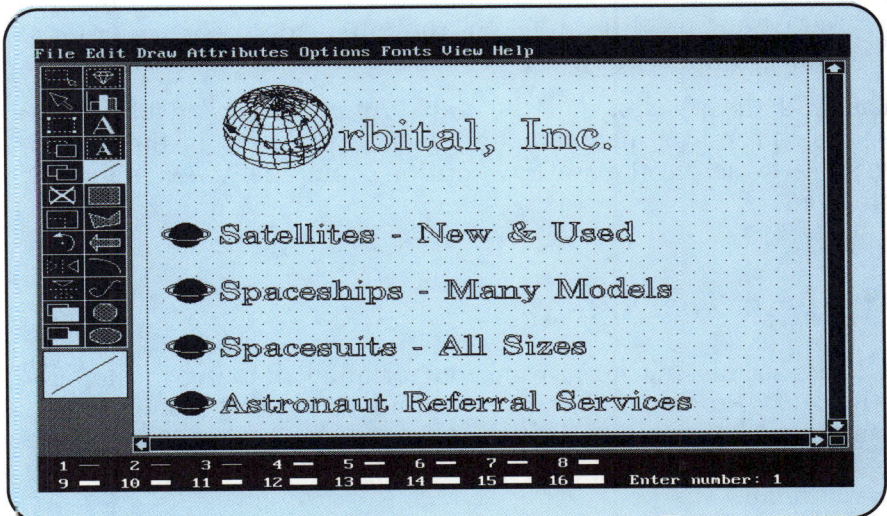

Figure 3.12   The Line Width menu

Chapter 3

 Type **14** and press Enter.

 Drag the cursor onto **14** and click the left mouse button.

Notice that the line in the Status box has changed to display the thicker line width that you just selected. Now you're ready to draw the thick horizontal line. Move the cursor a few lines above the Satellites line, placing it at the left margin.

 Press Enter, press Home, then press the Right Arrow key. To end the line, press Enter and then the Spacebar.

 Click the left mouse button and drag the cursor to the right margin. Click the left button once, then the right button.

Before saving and printing, let's use the Options menu to turn off Grid Display and Grid Snap. Although the grid is never printed, you won't be using it anymore. Note that if you were to use Exit now to clear the screen and start a new drawing, this step would not be necessary since DrawPerfect would turn Grid Display and Grid Snap off automatically.

 Type **O O**.

 Drag the cursor onto **Options**, click the left mouse button, and hold it while dragging the cursor onto **Clear Options**. Release the button.

The grid disappears, and the `Snp` prompt is turned off. If the `Redraw` prompt appears in the lower right corner of the screen, be sure to select the ReDraw option from the View menu (or press F9).

Typing a Text Line

All that is missing now from your original drawing is the subtitle, *2001 Product List,* since we had to erase it from the text chart to make room for the title. Fortunately, you can type a line of text anywhere you want using the Text Line option on the Draw menu.

 Type **D T**.

Drag the cursor onto **Draw**, click the left mouse button, and hold it down while dragging the cursor onto **Text Line**. Release the button.

Notice the prompt that appears in the lower left corner of the screen:

`Enter Set start of text line;`

Also, the icon in the Status box is now a large letter A, representing Text Line.

> ▶ **Tip:** If you want to type more than one line of text at once, use the Window Text option instead of Text Line. Window Text lets you create a window of any size and type text inside it. Your text word-wraps within the window, just like a word processor. You can also retrieve a WordPerfect text file into the window.

Your next step is to place the cursor where you want the text line to start, under the letter *r* in the title (Orbital), and then change the font so that it will match the one you used for the title, WP Century Schoolbook. Here's how:

 Use the Arrow keys to position the cursor under the letter **r** and press Enter.

 Drag the cursor into position under the letter **r** and click the left button.

Notice that the cursor has changed to an underline character, to represent the text cursor. Also, the prompt changes to:

`Input text;`

and this menu appears:

`F3 Help; F7 Exit`

The Help option brings up the menu of text formatting options that you used earlier to center the title. You can also use it to change the font.

Chapter 3

 Press F3, then Ctrl-F8. Type **4**.

 Drag the cursor onto the **Help** option at the bottom of the screen, click the left button, and drag the cursor onto **Fonts** and click the left button. Drag the cursor onto **Base Font** and click the left button again.

The Base Font list that you saw earlier (in Figure 3.6) appears. Let's use it to select a size 30 WP Century Schoolbook font, so the subtitle will be slightly smaller than the title.

 Use the Arrow keys to place the cursor onto **WP Century Schoolbook**, press Enter to select it, then type **30** and press Enter.

 Drag the cursor onto **WP Century Schoolbook** and click the left mouse button. Drag the cursor to the **Select** option at the bottom of the screen and click the left mouse button. Type **30** and click the right mouse button.

Now type the subtitle:

2001 Product List

To complete the process, use the Exit option.

 Press F7.

 Drag the cursor onto the **Exit** option in the menu at the bottom of the screen and click the left button.

If you see the `Redraw` prompt, select the ReDraw option from the View menu (or press F9).

Your text chart should now resemble Figure 3.2. If you wish to print it, do that now (use the Print option on the File menu). Next, follow these steps to save your final drawing and clear the screen:

 Press Exit (F7) or type **F X**.

 Drag the cursor onto **File** and click the left mouse button once. Drag the cursor onto **Exit** and release the button.

In response to the `Save Drawing` prompt:

 Type **Y** and then press Enter.

Drag the cursor onto **Yes**, click the left mouse button once, then click the right button once.

Next, DrawPerfect asks if you want to erase the disk file named Orbital.wpg and replace it with the chart now on your screen. Remember, you saved the first version of the chart before enhancing it with the figures and horizontal lines. If you wanted to save both versions, you would answer No and type a new file name. We'll assume that you only want the enhanced version.

 Type **Y**.

 Drag the cursor onto **Yes** and click the left mouse button.

The next prompt asks if you want to exit DrawPerfect. If you are finished using DrawPerfect, your answer should be Yes. If you wish to remain in DrawPerfect, answer No.

Using DrawPerfect's Built-in Text Chart Formats

DrawPerfect comes with twenty-four charts that you can modify and use for your own work. Their file names are TEMPLATE.1 through TEMPLATE.24, and they are shown in Appendix R of the DrawPerfect manual. Most of them are text charts. For example, Figure 3.13 shows TEMPLATE.5, and Figure 3.14 shows how we used it to create another version of the Orbital Inc. text chart.

To edit one of the text chart templates, retrieve it into the drawing window, then display the **Edit** menu and select **Modify**. Place the cursor on the text that you want to change and press the Enter key or left mouse button. Next, press the Spacebar or right mouse button. This places you in the text chart screen, where you can delete the existing text and retype your own. When you finish, press Exit (F7) or select the **Exit** option from the menu. Be sure to save it under a different name if you want to retain the original file.

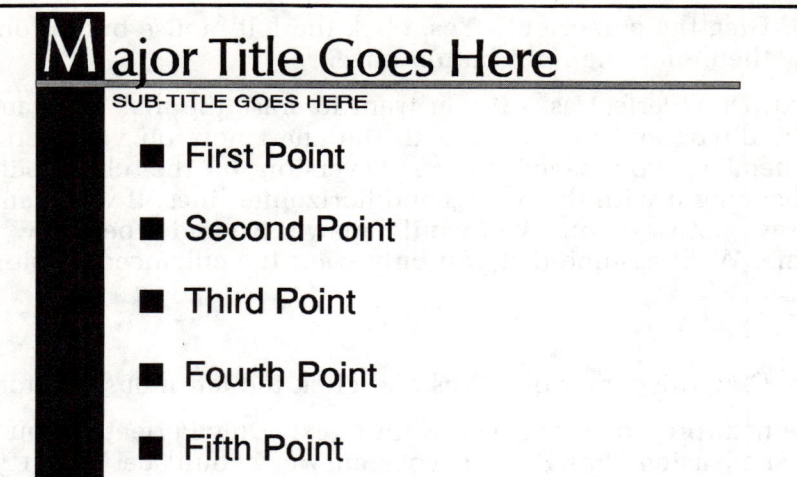

Figure 3.13   Template.5

Figure 3.14   Template.5 after modifications

What You Have Learned

In this chapter, you've learned how to create a bulleted text chart and enliven it with clip-art from DrawPerfect's Figure Library. You should now be familiar with the following:

- ▶ You can use the Chart option on the Draw menu to create three types of text charts: Bullet, Simple, and Freeform.
- ▶ DrawPerfect provides many options that you can use to enhance your text charts, including formatting features, such as center, indent, bold, underline, and flush right. Also, the program includes a variety of fonts that you can use to change the size and appearance of the type.
- ▶ You can use the Copy option on the Edit menu to copy an object in a chart or drawing.
- ▶ To draw a line, you can use the Line option on the Draw menu. DrawPerfect has two tools on the Options menu that can help you draw a straight line, Grid Display and Grid Snap. The Grid is a set of points that serve as a guide while you draw. Grid Snap forces the line to begin and end on a grid point so that it will be completely straight.
- ▶ You can use the Attributes menu to change the line width, color, or style.
- ▶ You can type a line of text anywhere in the drawing window using the Text Line option on the Draw menu.
- ▶ To type several lines of text, use the Window Text option on the Draw menu. Your text word-wraps within the window, just like a word processor. You can also retrieve a WordPerfect text file into the window.
- ▶ To speed up your typing and editing, DrawPerfect displays text in a medium text quality, but prints it in high quality. As a result, text charts often appear different on screen than in the printed version. On screen, text appears as an outline of the selected font, but in the printed version it is filled in. The Print menu includes a View Drawing option that you can use to preview the printed drawing and view the text in high quality.
- ▶ DrawPerfect comes with twenty-four charts that serve as models that you can retrieve and modify. Most of them are text charts. Their file names are TEMPLATE.1 through TEMPLATE.24.

Chapter 4

Your First Drawing

In This Chapter

▶ *How to draw rectangles, triangles, lines, and circles*
▶ *How to delete objects*
▶ *How to clear the screen and retain your grid options*
▶ *How to change an object's fill color and fill pattern*
▶ *How to change line width and color*

DrawPerfect is a drawing program, so isn't it about time you learned how to draw? Don't worry if you don't have a background in art. The drawing tools are geometrically oriented, so it's easy to create objects that incorporate rectangles, circles, triangles, and lines. For instance, Figure 4.1 shows a cupola that consists of three rectangles, three triangles, and six small boxes for the windows. Since all the shapes are simple geometric figures, the cupola is easy to draw. In this chapter, we'll teach you how.

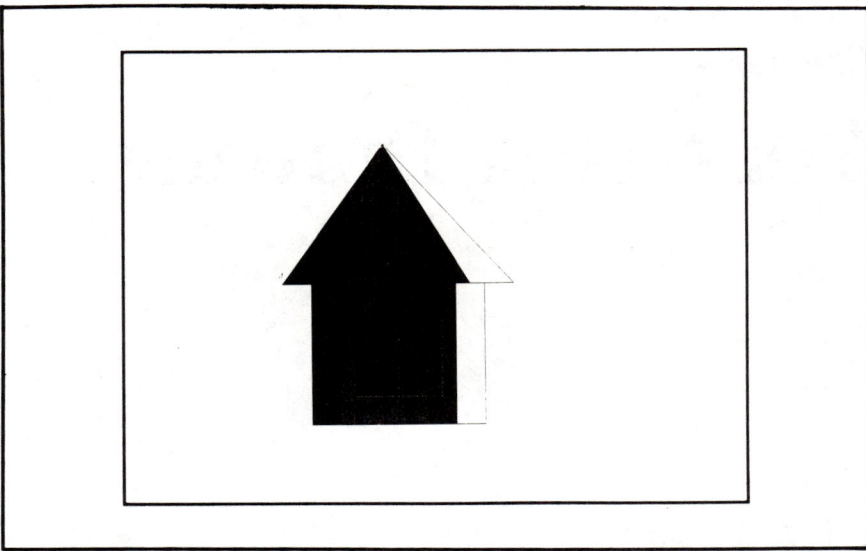

Figure 4.1   A cupola

Using the Grid

Start DrawPerfect and make sure your drawing window is clear. Before you begin drawing, we'd like you to turn on Grid Display and Grid Snap. If you read Chapter 3, you may recall using these two options. *Grid Display* provides reference points to help you while drawing, and eliminates the "blank page syndrome" that terrifies all creative minds (especially when on a deadline!). *Grid Snap* forces your lines to begin and end on a grid point, which means they will be absolutely straight.

 Type **O G**.

 Drag the cursor to the **Options** menu, click the left button and continue holding it down while dragging the cursor onto the **Grid Display** option, then release the left button. Incidentally, from now on when we want you to select an option from one of DrawPerfect's pull-down menus, we'll just ask you to display the menu and select the option. The procedure will always be identical: Drag the cursor to the menu title and click the left button to display it, hold the button down while dragging the cursor onto the option you are selecting, then release the button.

A series of evenly spaced dots appear in the drawing window, representing the grid points. By default a dot appears every 1/4 inch, but you can change this interval using the Define Grid option (you'll learn how in Chapter 5).

Your next step is to turn on the Grid Snap feature so the cursor can only move from grid point to point. As you'll see, Grid Snap is especially helpful in a drawing of this type since it forces you to draw straight lines. To activate it, you display the Options menu and select Grid Snap.

 Type **O R**.

 Display the **Options** menu and select the **Grid Snap** option.

You should now see the `Snp` prompt, which always appears when Grid Snap is on, in the lower right side of your screen.

Before drawing the cupola, let's learn how to create the individual objects that form it—rectangles and triangles—and how to erase them. That way, if you make a mistake while drawing the cupola, you'll know how to fix it.

Drawing Rectangles and Triangles

Before we teach you how to draw a rectangle, we want to be sure your version of DrawPerfect is working the same way as ours in the steps that follow. If it isn't, the steps may not work for you! In particular, we need to check an option called *Start With Mini-object* and make sure that it is set to No. If it is set to Yes (which it probably is, since Yes is the default), as soon as you start drawing a box, the cursor will move from your starting position and create a small box (the mini-object). This will interfere with our drawing instructions since we're constantly asking you to start in a certain position and move the cursor a specific number of grid points.

To change the Start With Mini-object option:

 Type **F T D**.

Display the **File** menu, select **Setup** and then **Display**.

You should see the Setup Display menu shown in Figure 4.2. You can use this menu to change display defaults, such as your screen colors. Notice that `Start With Mini-object` is the eighth option on this menu (and is highlighted in Figure 4.2). If it is set to No, just return to the drawing window by pressing Enter twice or clicking the right mouse button once. If it is set to Yes, use these steps to change it:

 Type **8 N** and then press Exit (F7) to return to the drawing window.

 Select **Start With Mini-object**, select **No**, then return to the drawing window by clicking the right mouse button once.

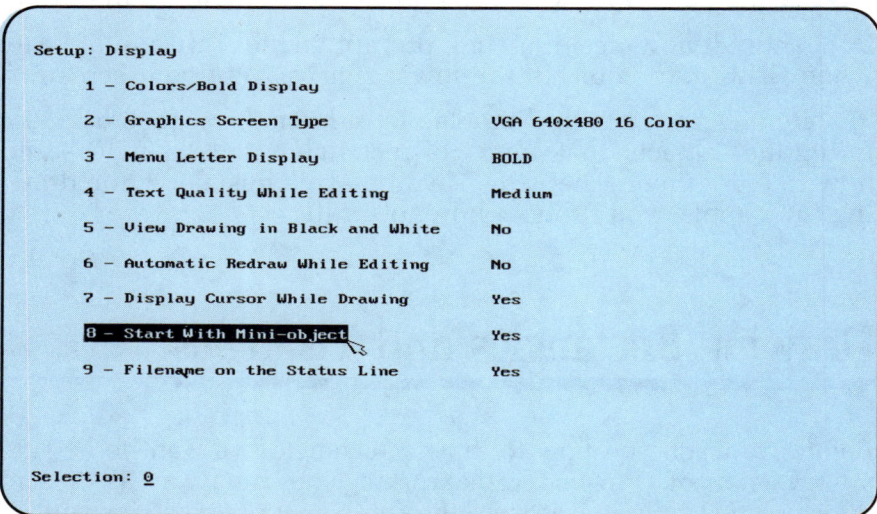

Figure 4.2   The Setup Display menu

Drawing with the Box Tool

Let's learn how to draw a rectangle. You'll begin by selecting the Box tool from the pull-down Draw menu. Here's how:

 Type **D B**.

Display the **Draw** menu, then select **Box** (or select the sixth icon in column 2).

You should see this prompt in the lower left corner of your screen:

`Enter Set corner of box;`

It means that as soon as you press Enter (or the mouse equivalent, the left button), that position will become the first corner of your box. What else happened when you selected the Box tool? The icon in the Status box (below the icon panel) changed from a line to a box. The Line tool is the default, so its icon always appears there until you select another tool, such as Box.

To start drawing your rectangle:

 Press Enter.

 Click the left mouse button.

The prompt changes to

`Enter End box;`

This means that after moving the cursor and shaping the box, you press Enter to finish drawing it. You've just created the first corner of your box, so the next step will be to move the cursor and watch as the box is created. Let's make it a big square.

 Press the Up Arrow key ten times and then press the Right Arrow key ten times.

 Drag the cursor up ten grid points, then to the right ten grid points.

As soon as you pressed the Right Arrow or dragged the cursor to the right with the mouse, an outline of your box appeared! You still aren't finished, though. Remember the `Enter End box;` prompt? To complete your square:

 Press Enter.

 Click the left button.

As you can see from Figure 4.3, pressing Enter not only completes the box, but it fills it with a pattern. DrawPerfect has 64 fill patterns you can use when drawing boxes, polygons,

Chapter 4

arrows, circles, and ellipses. Later in this chapter, we'll teach you how to select a different one.

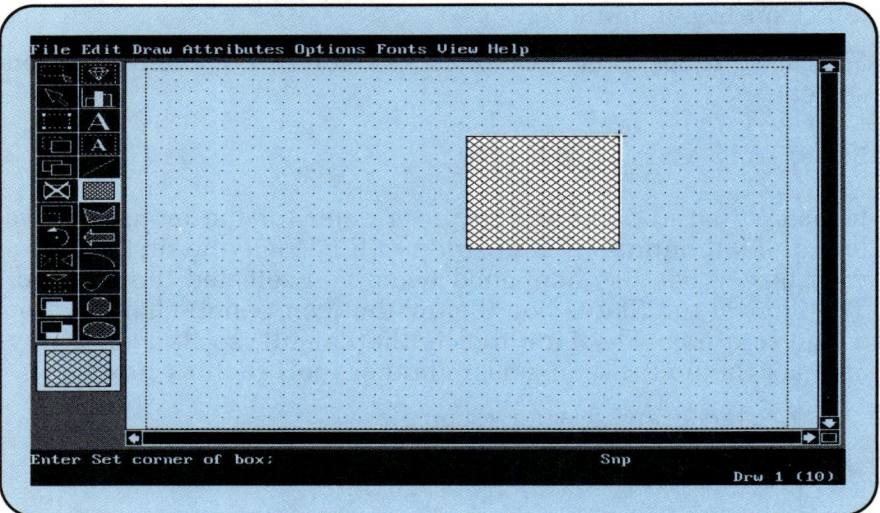

Figure 4.3 Drawing a box

Since the Box tool is still selected, the `Enter Set corner of box;` prompt reappeared after you completed the first box. This means that if you press Enter again, you'll start a new box. If you want to practice, go ahead and press Enter and draw another box. However, if you press Enter by mistake and don't want to draw one, just press the Cancel key (F1) or its mouse equivalent, the left and right buttons simultaneously (or the center button if you have one).

Drawing with the Polygon Tool

Let's select the Polygon tool and learn how to draw a triangle. First, move the cursor down to the lower left corner of the drawing window so you'll have plenty of room to draw a large triangle. Next, use these steps to select Polygon:

 Type **D P**.

 Display the **Draw** menu and select **Polygon**.

Notice that the Status Box icon has changed again to represent the polygon tool. The prompt tells you what to do next:

Enter Start polygon:

Go ahead and begin drawing:

⌨ Press Enter.

🖱 Click the left button.

　　Next, you'll use the Arrow keys or mouse to draw the base of the triangle.

⌨ Press the Right Arrow key ten times.

🖱 Drag the cursor ten grid points to the right.

That completes the first side, which you can see as you're drawing it. Notice the prompt,

Enter Continue polygon; **Space** end polygon;

　　Polygons can have many sides. Our triangle will have only three, but the sample polygon shown in the Status box has five sides. Unlike a box, DrawPerfect can't make assumptions about how many sides a polygon will have, so you must complete each side by pressing Enter or the left mouse button. When you finish drawing the polygon, you press the Spacebar or right mouse button.

⌨ Press Enter and then press the Up Arrow key ten times and the Left Arrow key five times. Press Enter to complete the second side.

🖱 Click the left button, then drag the cursor up ten grid points and to the left five. Click the left mouse button to complete the second side.

　　To finish the triangle:

⌨ Press the Down Arrow key ten times, then the Left Arrow key five times. Press the Spacebar to complete it.

🖱 Drag the cursor down ten grid points, then left five. Click the right button.

Chapter 4

Once again, DrawPerfect adds a fill pattern inside your object. It should resemble Figure 4.4. Since we didn't change the pattern, it should be the same as the one in the box.

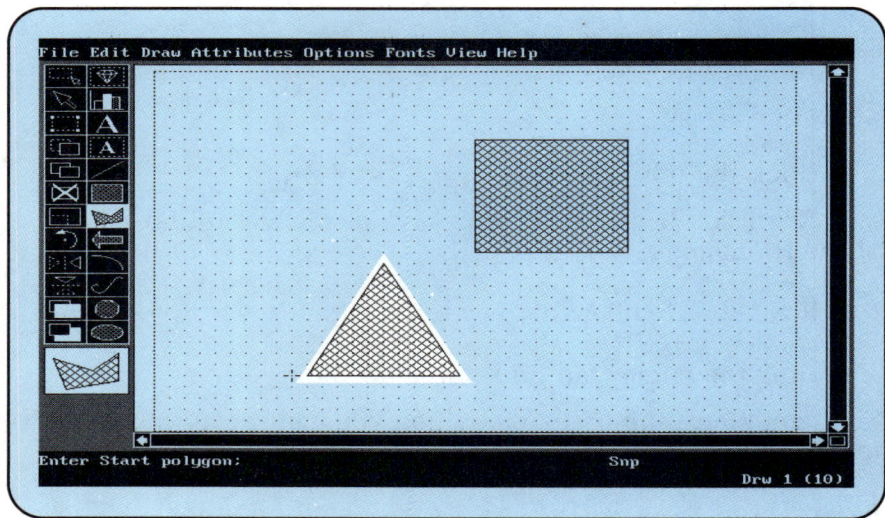

Figure 4.4 *Drawing a polygon*

Deleting and Undeleting an Object

As you learn how to use DrawPerfect, there will be countless times that you experiment with the drawing tools and find your results less than satisfactory. Fortunately, you can use the Delete tool on the Edit menu to erase individual objects like the square and triangle you just drew. If you change your mind after erasing something, you can even bring it back! Enough talk: Let's try it.

 Type **E D**.

 Display the **Edit** menu and select **Delete** or select the sixth icon in the first column.

The Status box changes and now includes an arrow, representing the Select Item tool. Also, this prompt appears:

`Enter Select/Unselect objects;`

and it means that you can select an object by placing the cursor on it and pressing Enter or the left mouse button. Let's begin by erasing the triangle. Place the cursor anywhere on the triangle, then:

 Press Enter.

 Click the left button.

You should see three small boxes around the triangle, as shown in Figure 4.5. The boxes signify that the triangle is now selected.

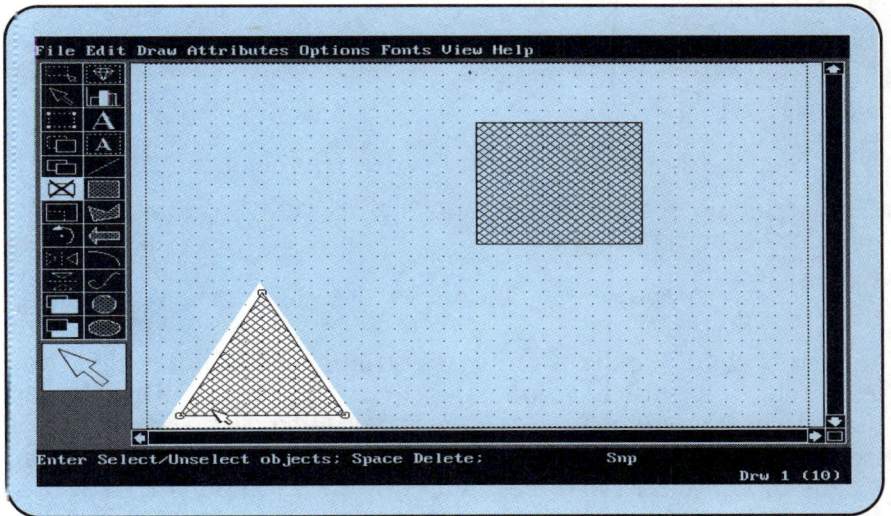

Figure 4.5 Selecting an object to delete

Notice the prompt has changed and now includes this phrase:

`Space Delete;`

By pressing the Spacebar or right mouse button, you can delete the selected object. Go ahead and try it.

 Press the Spacebar.

 Click the right mouse button.

Chapter 4

Has your triangle disappeared? Also, you should see a `Redraw` prompt in the lower right corner of the screen. You may remember from Chapter 2 that DrawPerfect displays this message whenever it senses a change that could affect other sections of the drawing. There are three methods you can use to redraw the screen: Display the View menu and select ReDraw; press the ReDraw key (F9); or place the cursor on the box in the lower right corner of the screen (just above the word `Redraw`, with two arrows pointing at it) and then press Enter or click the left mouse button. Go ahead and use one of these methods.

If you change your mind after erasing an object, use Undelete to bring it back. Here's how you can get your triangle back:

 Type **E U**.

 Display the **Edit** menu and select **Undelete**.

Your triangle reappears and looks fine, right? Wrong! Did you notice the new prompt,

`Undelete: 1 Restore; 2 Previous Deletion: 0`

and the small boxes around the triangle signifying that it is selected? You still have one step to go. Right now, DrawPerfect is just showing you the last object you deleted and asking if you want to restore it. If you had erased another object before the triangle, you could use the second option, Previous Deletion, to display that one. To bring back the triangle:

 Type **R** (or 1).

 Select **Restore**.

Now you've brought the triangle back into your drawing, and the small selection boxes disappear. Before moving to the next section, feel free to continue experimenting with these basic drawing and editing tools.

Clearing the Drawing from Your Screen Without Clearing the Options

Before you begin drawing the cupola, you'll need to clear the screen. In previous chapters you learned how to do this using the Exit option on the File menu, but if you use it now you'll also clear the Grid Snap and Grid Display options. Since we want you to continue using these options while drawing the cupola, we'll teach you a new method, the Clear option on the File menu. This method clears the screen but retains any options that are currently turned on. To use it:

 Type **F C Y**.

 Display the **File** menu, select **Clear**, then select **Yes**.

Drawing the Three Rectangles That Form the Foundation of the Cupola

The first object you'll draw is the black rectangle on the left side of the cupola. Begin by displaying the Draw menu and selecting the Box option.

 Type **D B**.

 Display the **Draw** menu and select **Box** (or select the Box icon, the sixth square in the second column).

This prompt appears in the lower left corner of your screen:

`Enter Set corner of box;`

Now you're ready to create the first rectangle in the cupola, the black one on the left. Note the icon that appears in the Status box under the icon panel, symbolizing the box format you've just selected. If yours has a pattern, use the Attributes menu to change it to black.

⌨ Type **A P 2** and press Enter.

🖱 Display the **Attributes** menu and select **Fill Pattern**. Drag the cursor onto the box representing pattern 2 and click the left mouse button.

Now the rectangle inside the Status box should be black.

To position the cursor to start drawing the lower left corner of the rectangle, you can count grid points until you are on the fifth grid point from the bottom and the twelfth horizontal grid point from the left border. An easier method is to use the Go to option on the View menu, which will move the cursor to any point on the grid. Let's try it.

⌨ Type **V G**.

🖱 Display the **View** menu and select **Go to**.

This prompt appears:

`Go to X:`

followed by a number representing the cursor's current X-axis position. To change it, type **3.5** and press Enter or click the right mouse button.

Next, DrawPerfect asks where you want to position the cursor on the Y-axis. Type **1.75** and press Enter or click the right mouse button. Now your cursor should be in the same position we were in when we began drawing the rectangle. Remember the `Enter Set corner of box;` prompt? DrawPerfect is patiently waiting for you to begin drawing the box. To start drawing:

⌨ Press Enter.

🖱 Click the left mouse button.

The prompt changes to:

`Enter end box;`

You've just created the first corner of the box. The next step is to move the cursor vertically (up) ten grid points, then horizontally (right) two grid points. The easiest way to do this is to use the Arrow keys, counting exactly how many times you press the Up Arrow key and the Right Arrow key.

> Press the Up Arrow key ten times, then press the Right Arrow key twice, and press Enter.

> Drag the cursor up ten grid points, then right two. Click the left mouse button.

You just drew your first rectangle, and it should resemble Figure 4.6. Wasn't that easy? Did you notice that each time you pressed the Arrow key or moved the mouse, the cursor only moved one grid point? This is Grid Snap at work!

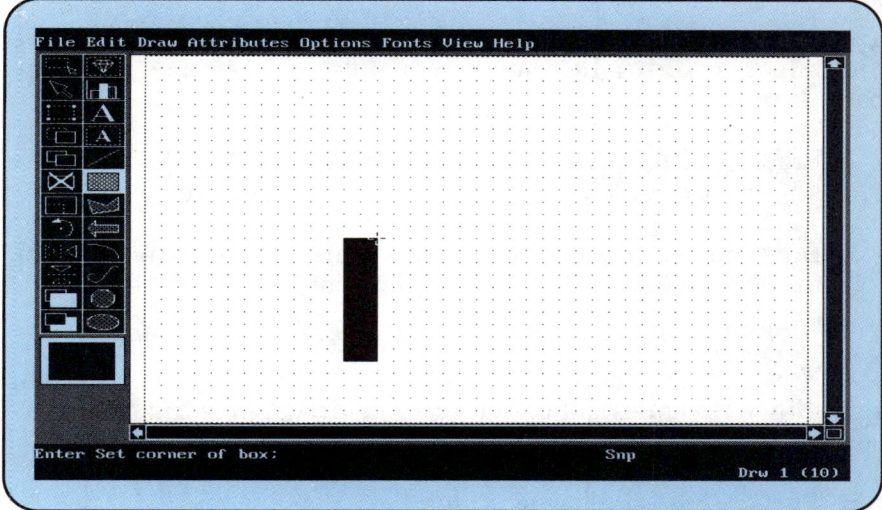

Figure 4.6 The first rectangle

Now you can begin drawing the second rectangle. Since this one will be gray, your first step will be to change the fill color.

> Type **A F**.

> Display the **Attributes** menu and select **Fill Color**.

Chapter 4

Two rows of colored boxes appear at the bottom of the screen. The gray one is number 8.

🖮 Type **8** and press Enter.

🖱 Drag the cursor onto the gray box and click the left button.

If you have a color monitor, you'll see that the icon in the Status box is now gray.

Before starting the second rectangle, make sure that the cursor is still in the upper right corner of the first box. If it is not there, use Go to on the View menu to move to 4″ on the X-axis and 4.25″ on the Y-axis. To begin drawing:

🖮 Press Enter.

🖱 Click the left mouse button.

The `Enter End box` prompt should appear. Next, you'll move the cursor to the right, then down until it is aligned with the base of the first rectangle.

🖮 Press the Right Arrow key eight times and the Down Arrow key ten times. To complete the box, press Enter.

🖱 Drag the cursor right eight grid points, then down ten. Click the left mouse button to complete the box.

Your drawing should now include the large gray rectangle.

Next, create the last rectangle, the white one on the right side. Since this one will be white, your first step is to change the color.

🖮 Type **A F 16** and press Enter.

🖱 Display the **Attributes** menu, select **Fill Color**, and then select white (#16).

If you move the cursor while doing this, you can use Go to to move it back to 6″ on the X-axis and 1.75″ on the Y-axis. Next:

🖮 Press Enter, press the Right Arrow key twice, then press the Up Arrow key ten times. To complete the rectangle, press Enter.

Your First Drawing

 Click the left button, drag the cursor right two grid points, then up ten. Click the left button.

When you finish drawing the third rectangle, it should resemble Figure 4.7.

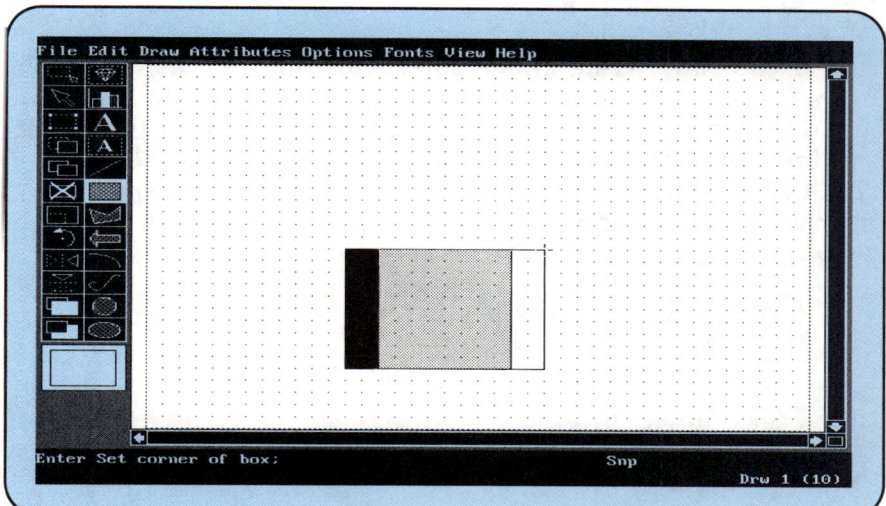

Figure 4.7 The drawing after completing the three rectangles

Drawing the Roof

To create the roof of the cupola, you'll draw three triangles using the Polygon option on the Draw menu. Begin by selecting the Polygon tool.

 Type **D P**.

 Display the **Draw** menu and select **Polygon** (or select the seventh icon in column two).

You should see this message on the prompt line:

`Enter Start polygon`

The first polygon you'll draw will be the white triangle on the right side of the drawing shown in Figure 4.1. Notice the

Chapter 4

color of the polygon icon in your Status box. Unless it's already white, you should change the color before you start drawing. Although you can change the color after drawing an object, it's easier to do it before. To change it, display the **Attributes** menu and select **Fill Color**. White is fill color #16, so you can either type 16 and press Enter or highlight it with the mouse and click the left button.

If you moved the cursor after finishing the last rectangle, move it back to the top right side of the white rectangle that you just drew. If you want to be certain the cursor is on the correct starting point, display the **View** menu and select **Go to**, then type **6.5** for the X-axis and **4.25** for the Y-axis. Next, move it to the right two grid points where the lower right side of the triangle will begin.

Press the Right Arrow key twice.

Drag the cursor two grid points to the right.

Now begin drawing:

Press Enter.

Click the left button.

You've just created the first point of your polygon. You should see this prompt:

`Enter` Continue polygon `Space` End Polygon

Next:

Press the Left Arrow key three times and then press Enter to create the second point. Press the Left Arrow six times, then the Up Arrow ten times.

Drag the cursor three grid points to the left and click the left mouse button to create the second point. Now move the cursor to the left six grid points, then up ten.

You should see the left edge of your triangle forming. To complete it:

Press Enter, then the Spacebar.

🖱 Click the left button to create the third point and then click the right button.

As soon as you pressed the Spacebar or clicked the mouse button, DrawPerfect completed the figure by connecting the last point with the first point of the object.

Did you manage to complete the first triangle? If you drew it correctly, it should look like Figure 4.8.

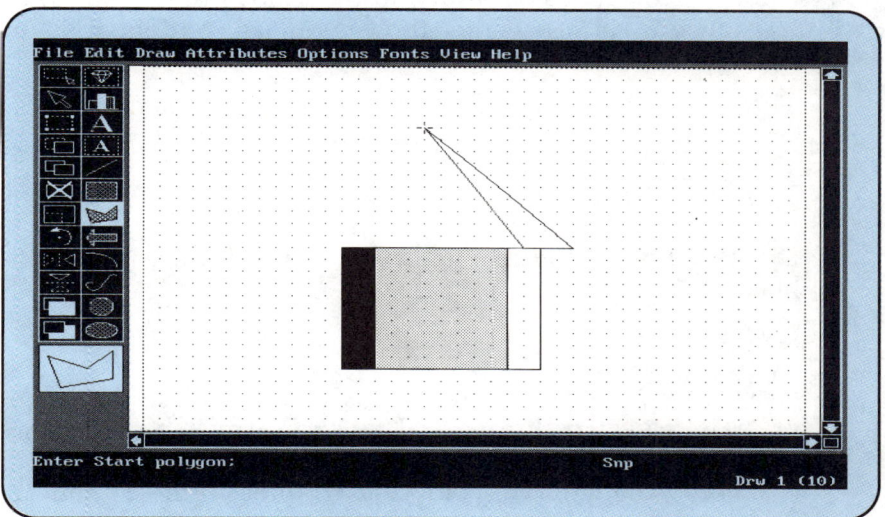

Figure 4.8 *The drawing after completing the first triangle*

Now follow these steps to draw the second triangle, the large gray one in the center. Begin by changing the fill color to gray (color #8).

⌨ Type **A F 8** and then press Enter.

🖱 Display the **Attributes** menu, select **Fill Color**, then select gray (#8).

Next, begin drawing the polygon.

⌨ Press Enter and then press the Down Arrow key ten times and the Right Arrow key six times.

Chapter 4

 Click the left button. Drag the cursor down ten grid points, then to the right six grid points.

Notice that this triangle shares a common side with the white triangle. To complete it:

 Press Enter, then the Left Arrow key ten times. Press Enter, then the Spacebar.

 Click the left mouse button and then move the cursor to the left ten grid points. Click the left mouse button, then the right mouse button.

The last polygon you'll draw is the small black triangle. Your first step is to change the fill color.

 Type **A F 1** and press Enter.

 Display the **Attributes** menu, select **Fill Color**, then select black (#1).

To draw it:

 Press Enter, then press the Left Arrow key three times, and press Enter again. Press the Up Arrow key ten times, then the Right Arrow key seven times so that it connects with the gray triangle. To complete it, press Enter, then the Spacebar.

 Click the left button. Drag the cursor to the left three grid points, then click the left mouse button. Move the cursor up ten grid points, then to the right seven grid points so that it connects with the gray triangle. To complete it, click the left, then the right button.

When you finish, your drawing should look like Figure 4.9.

Drawing the Windows

Your next task is to draw the windows, using the Box tool on the Draw menu to create six small rectangles. Begin by displaying the **Draw** menu and selecting the **Box** option.

 Type **D B**.

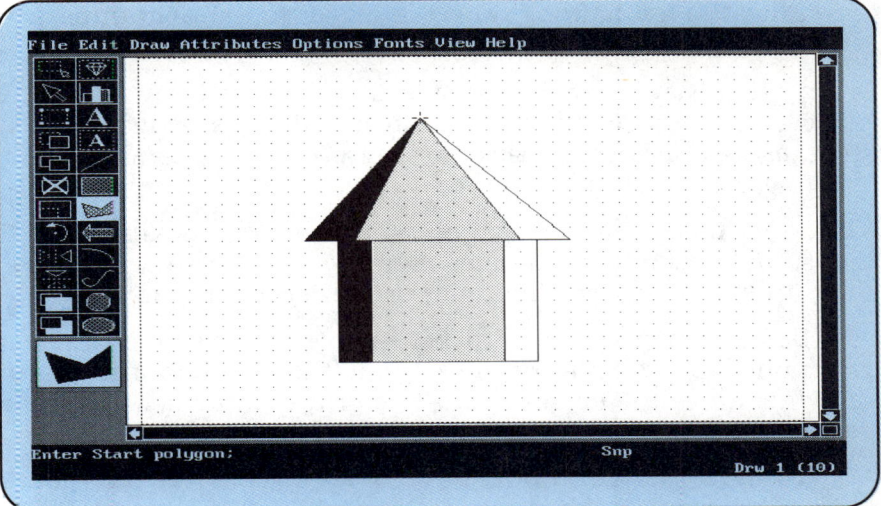

Figure 4.9 The drawing after completing all three triangles

🖱 Display the **Draw** menu and select **Box**.

Incidentally, if your box is not black (look at the icon in the Status box), use the Fill Color option on the Attributes menu to change it before continuing. Next, you should change the outside line color to white so that the lines around the window panes will be white.

🖱 Type **A C 16** and press Enter.

🖱 Display the **Attributes** menu and select **Line Color**, then highlight 16 and click the left mouse button.

Since the icon's background is white, you cannot see the white line color in the Status box. You'll have to wait until you draw the windows to see it.

Begin by drawing the first box in the left column. To position the cursor correctly, use **Go to** (on the View menu) to go directly to **4.25"** on the X-axis and **3.75"** on the Y-axis. To draw it:

🖱 Press Enter. Press the Right Arrow key three times, then the Down Arrow key twice, and then Enter to complete the box.

🖱 Click the left button. Move the cursor to the right three grid points, then down two, and then click the left button.

Wasn't that easy? Now you should be able to see the white line color around the window that you just drew. Follow the next steps closely and refer back to Figure 4.1 as necessary while drawing the remaining windows.

Draw the second box by pressing Enter or clicking the left mouse button, moving the cursor to the right three grid points, then up two, then pressing Enter or the left mouse button.

Before drawing the third box, move the cursor down two grid points. Press Enter or click the left mouse button to begin drawing. Move the cursor down two grid points, then left three grid points, and then press Enter or the left mouse button.

To draw the fourth box, press Enter or click the left mouse button. Next, move the cursor to the left three grid points, then up two. To complete it, press Enter or click the left mouse button.

To draw the fifth box, move the cursor down two grid points and press Enter or click the left mouse button. Move down two grid points, then right three, and press Enter or click the left mouse button.

To draw the last box, press Enter and move the cursor right three grid points, then up two grid points. Press Enter or click the left mouse button.

Do your windows look like the ones in Figure 4.1?

Creating the Wind Vane

Let's enhance the cupola by adding a wind vane at the top so that it will resemble Figure 4.10 when you finish. Creating the wind vane is a three-step operation that will involve drawing a line and circle, then creating a figure and retrieving one of the images from the Figure Library. It's much easier than it sounds!

You'll begin by changing the line color to black, then changing the line width so it will be thicker:

🖱 Type **A C 1** and press Enter. Type **A W 8** and press Enter.

Your First Drawing

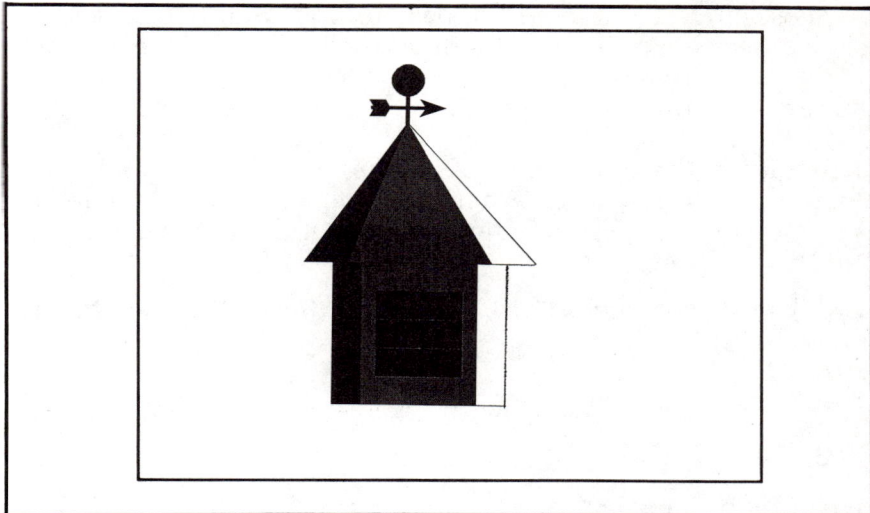

Figure 4.10 The enhanced cupola

Display the **Attributes** menu, choose **Line Color**, then select black (1). Display the **Attributes** menu, choose the **Line Width** option, then select 8.

Now move the cursor to the top of the cupola, where the three rectangles form a peak (4.75" X-axis and 6.75" Y-axis). When you get there, follow these steps to draw the line:

Type **D L** and press Enter to begin drawing. Press the Up Arrow three times. To end the line, press Enter, then the Spacebar.

Display the **Draw** menu, select **Line**, then move the cursor back to the peak of the three triangles. Click the left button to begin drawing. Next, move the cursor up three grid points. To end the line, click the left button, then the right.

To draw the black ornament at the top of the weather vane, you'll use the Circle tool on the Draw menu.

Type **D I**.

Move the cursor onto **Draw**, click the left mouse button, highlight **Circle**, then release the button. Move the cursor back to the top of the line.

Chapter 4

A black circle icon should appear in your Status box, and you should see this prompt in the lower left corner of the screen:

`Enter` Set center of circle;

This means that the center of the circle will be established as soon as you press Enter. After that, you can move the cursor in any direction and press Enter again to set the perimeter and finish the drawing.

The cursor should still be at the top of the line you just drew. To begin drawing:

🖱 Press Enter.

🖱 Click the left mouse button.

This prompt appears:

`Enter` End circle;

You now control the diameter of the circle, and moving the cursor in any direction will expand it proportionately. Since Grid Snap is on, you can only move the cursor one point at a time, either vertically or horizontally. To move the cursor one grid point:

🖱 Press the Up Arrow once and then press Enter.

🖱 Drag the cursor one grid point up, and then click the left button.

As you can see, DrawPerfect has automatically created the circle.

To complete the wind vane, all that's missing is the arrow. Instead of drawing it, you can use a clip-art file from Draw-Perfect's Figure Library. Do you remember retrieving the DOG.WPG file into the bar chart that you created in Chapter 2? The procedure is identical. Begin by displaying the Draw menu and selecting Figure.

🖱 Type **D F**.

🖱 Display the **Draw** menu and select **Figure**.

Next, use Go to (on the View menu) to move the cursor to 4" on the X-axis and 7.5" on the Y-axis:

 Type **V G 4** and press Enter. Type **7.5** and press Enter.

Display the **View** menu and select **Go to**. Type **4** and click the right button. Type **7.5** and click the right button.

Your next step will be to set the first corner of the figure, then move the cursor down four grid points and to the right six grid points to form a symmetrical box for the arrow figure.

Press Enter to set the corner, then press the Down Arrow key four times and the Right Arrow key six times, and press Enter.

Click the left mouse button to set the corner, then drag the cursor down four grid points and to the right six. Click the left mouse button.

Now you should see this prompt:

`Drawing to be Retrieved:`

In response, type the file name of the clip-art file:

ARROW-13.

If you installed the Figure Library files in a separate subdirectory, you may see an error message telling you that the file was not found. If so, you will have to include the path when typing the file name, such as

C:\DR10\ARROWS\ARROW-13

where ARROWS is a subdirectory of DR10 and the ARROW-13 file is in that subdirectory. (If you don't understand this, Chapter 9 explains directories and subdirectories in detail.)

If that doesn't work, locate the DrawPerfect disk containing the ARROW-13 file (the Figure Library disk with the subtitle *Arrows, Computer, Flow, Graphic, Objects*). Insert it into drive A and type this name:

A:\ARROWS\ARROW-13

Then press Enter.

Your drawing should now look like Figure 4.10. If so, you may wish to save and print it, but you should not feel restricted to just creating an exact duplicate of our drawing. Once you know the basic tools, the possibilities are endless, so never be afraid to experiment! For instance, Figure 4.11 shows another version of the cupola. We added a shadow around the windows, changed some of the fill patterns, and placed the cupola inside a large oval to give a cameo effect.

Figure 4.11   Another version of the cupola

What You Have Learned

In this chapter, you've learned how to use several of DrawPerfect's drawing tools, including Line, Box, Circle, and Polygon. You should now be familiar with the following:

- ▶ Using the tools on the Draw menu, it's easy to create geometrically oriented objects, such as rectangles, circles, polygons, and lines.
- ▶ To draw a rectangle or square, you can use the Box tool on the Draw menu.

- ▶ You can use the Polygon tool to draw multi-sided shapes, such as a triangle or an octagon.
- ▶ When you draw an object such as a box, polygon, arrow, circle, or ellipse, DrawPerfect automatically fills it with a pattern. The Fill Pattern option on the Attributes menu allows you to choose from 64 different patterns, or draw the object without a pattern.
- ▶ You can use the Delete tool on the Edit menu to erase individual objects. If you change your mind after erasing an object, you can use Undelete on the Edit menu to bring it back.
- ▶ To clear the drawing window without clearing options like Grid Snap and Grid Display, you can use the Clear option on the File menu.
- ▶ You can use the Go to option on the View menu to move the cursor to a specific point in the Drawing Window designated by X and Y coordinates.

Chapter 5

More About the Drawing Tools and Options

In This Chapter

- How to draw arrows, ellipses, arcs, and curves
- Using the Size tool
- How to use the Constrain and Stretch options
- Using the Zoom and Pan tools
- Drawing with Freehand

You have already studied several of DrawPerfect's drawing tools, including Line, Polygon, and Circle. Now you can complete your repertoire by learning how to draw with the Arrow, Ellipse, Arc, and Curve tools. We will also introduce two options on DrawPerfect's View menu and three on the Options menu that can be helpful when you're drawing: Zoom, Pan, Constrain, Stretch, and Freehand.

The Zoom and Pan tools do just what you think they would. You can use *Zoom* to focus in on one section of a drawing, yet still have all the drawing tools at your disposal. Once Zoom is on, you can use *Pan* to shift your perspective left, right, up, or down so you can work on other areas of the figure. *Constrain* applies to the Box, Line, and Ellipse tools and forces you

Chapter 5

to draw a square when using Box; a completely horizontal or vertical line when using Line; and a circle when using Ellipse. You can use *Stretch* along with *Size* to stretch or compress a drawing, figure, chart, or text, completely changing the proportions. The *Freehand* option, which can only be used with a mouse, may be the most creative one in DrawPerfect. Freehand changes all the rules by allowing you to draw lines and polygons of any shape or form.

How to Draw Arrows, Ellipses, Arcs, and Curves

Like the other drawing tools you've studied, the Arrow, Ellipse, Arc, and Curve are easy to use. You start by selecting the tool from the Draw menu or icon panel. While you're creating the object, prompts appear at the bottom of the screen and provide specific instructions about how to proceed. Let's begin by learning how to draw an arrow.

Drawing an Arrow

The arrow is an effective symbol that you can use in maps, presentations, diagrams, and the like. In DrawPerfect, it is considered a special type of polygon with the arrow head at the starting point and the tail at the ending point. To create one, you just select the option, press Enter or the left mouse button to position the head of the arrow, then move the cursor to size the arrow and press Enter or the left mouse button.

To try it, begin by displaying the **Draw** menu and selecting **Arrow**, or by selecting the Arrow icon from the second column in the icon panel. This prompt appears at the bottom of the screen:

`Enter Set head of arrow;`

and the arrow icon appears in the Status box. Next, position the cursor wherever you want the head of the arrow and press Enter or the left mouse button. The prompt will change to:

More About the Drawing Tools and Options

Enter End arrow;

and the outline of an arrow will appear. Incidentally, if you don't see the outline, your version of DrawPerfect is set up differently. You may remember from the last chapter that we asked you to change the Start With Mini-object option to No (on File, Setup, Display). If you left it at No, the arrow outline won't appear until you start moving the cursor.

Now move the cursor in any direction and you'll see the tail take shape. You can make it as long as you want; however, it can't extend past the border of the drawing window. To complete the drawing, press Enter or the left mouse button. DrawPerfect then sets your arrow and fills it in with the currently selected fill pattern. Unless you changed the fill pattern, your arrow should resemble the one on the left side of Figure 5.1. We drew the other one after changing the pattern to #19, using the Attributes menu's Fill Pattern option. (Note that we also changed the arrow width for both arrows, to make them wider and easier for you to see!)

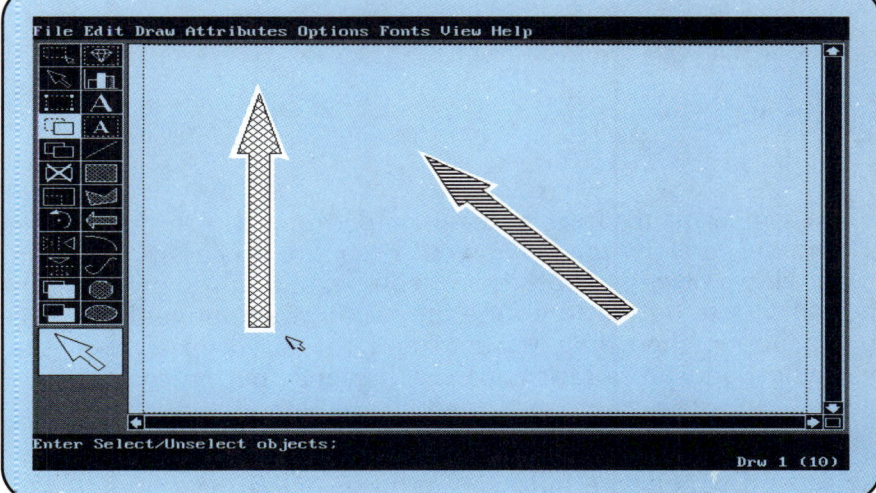

Figure 5.1 Drawing arrows

All the options on the Attributes menu are at your disposal when you draw an arrow, including Arrow Width, Fill Color and Pattern, plus Line Color, Style, and Width. Feel free to experiment with these options for different effects. For more elaborate arrows, you can retrieve one of the twenty-four clip-art arrows in the Figure Library. You may remember using one of them, ARROW-13.WPG, for the arrow on the wind vane in the previous chapter.

Q Drawing an Arrow

1. Display the Draw menu and select Arrow (or select the Arrow icon from the second column in the icon panel).

   A prompt appears telling you to press Enter to set the head of your arrow.

2. Move the cursor to the point where you want the head of the arrow and press Enter or the left mouse button.

   The prompt changes and tells you to press Enter to end the arrow.

3. Move the cursor in any direction to size the arrow and press Enter or the left mouse button to complete it.

   DrawPerfect sets your arrow and fills it in with the currently selected fill pattern.

Drawing an Ellipse

When you want to draw an oval-shaped object, use the Ellipse option on the Draw menu. As you'll see, the process is identical to drawing a circle. In both cases, you begin by pressing Enter or the left mouse button to define the center, then move the cursor to the point where you want to end the circle or ellipse (the perimeter) and press Enter or the left mouse button again.

Begin by displaying the **Draw** menu and selecting the **Ellipse** option or by selecting the Ellipse icon, the last one in the second panel. The following prompt will appear:

Enter Set center of ellipse;

and the ellipse icon will appear inside the Status box. Place the cursor where you want the center to be and press Enter or the

More About the Drawing Tools and Options

left mouse button. A dashed outline of an oval will appear, and the prompt will change to:

`Enter` End ellipse;

Next, use the Arrow keys or mouse to move the cursor in any direction. As you do this, you may see the outline of the ellipse change dramatically. When you finish drawing your oval, press Enter or the left mouse button to complete it. DrawPerfect fills in your ellipse with the currently selected fill pattern. For example, Figure 5.2 is an ellipse that we drew using pattern #42.

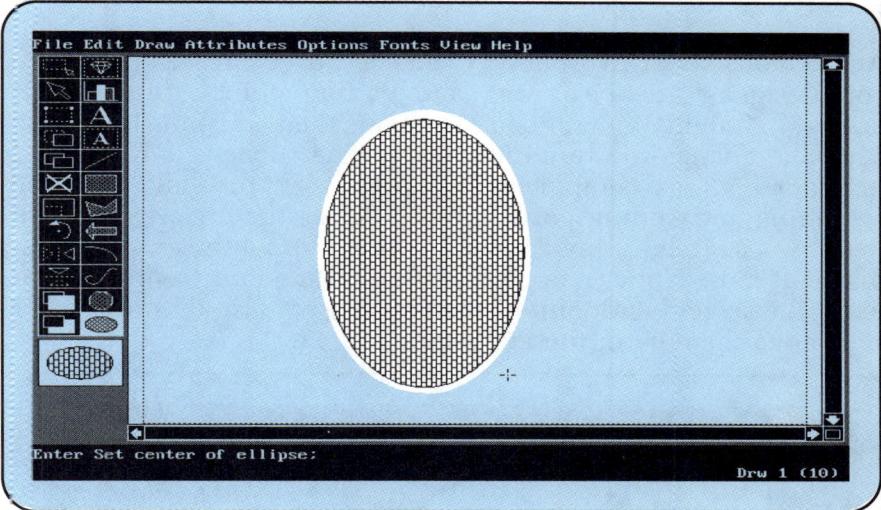

Figure 5.2 Drawing an ellipse

> **Tip:** With the exception of Arrow Width, you can use any of the options in the Attributes menu to modify the ellipse.

 **Drawing an Ellipse**

1. Display the Draw menu and select Ellipse (or select the Ellipse icon).

   A prompt appears telling you to press Enter to set the center of your ellipse.

Chapter 5

2. Move the cursor to the point where you want the center to be and press Enter or the left mouse button.

   The prompt changes and tells you to press Enter to end the ellipse.

3. Move the cursor in any direction to size the ellipse and press Enter or the left mouse button to complete it.

   DrawPerfect completes the drawing and fills in the ellipse with the currently selected fill pattern.

Drawing an Arc

An arc consists of two points connected by a curved line. Once you designate the beginning and ending points, DrawPerfect draws a straight line connecting them, then lets you move the cursor to change the line into an arc. The concept is illustrated in Figure 5.3. A completed arc appears on the left, with the beginning and ending points noted. Before the arc was shaped, there was a straight line connecting the two points, as shown on the right side. Notice the prompt line telling you to press Enter to set the second endpoint of the arc. As soon as you press Enter and move the cursor, the arc begins to take shape.

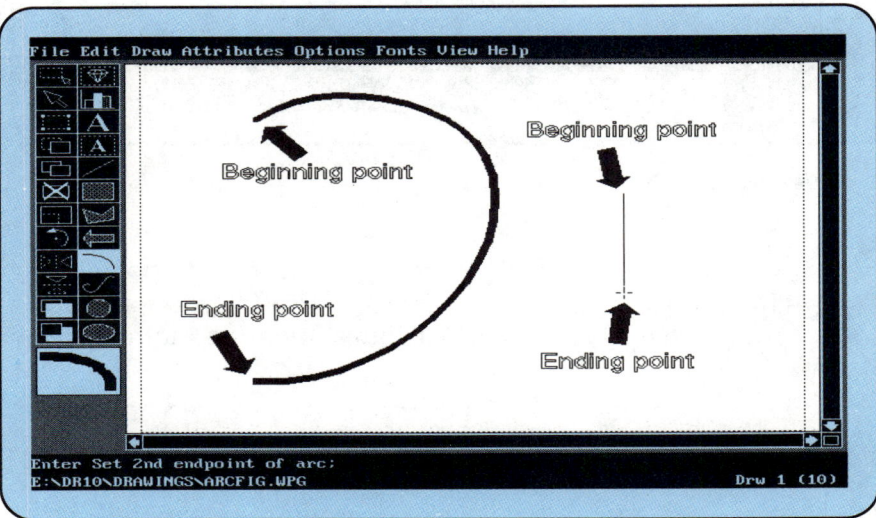

Figure 5.3 An arc with marked beginning and ending points

More About the Drawing Tools and Options

To draw an arc, begin by displaying the **Draw** menu and choosing the **Arc** option or by selecting the Arc icon (the fourth from the bottom in column two). This prompt will appear:

`Enter` Set 1st endpoint of arc;

DrawPerfect is asking you to indicate where you want the arc to start. Position the cursor and press Enter or the left mouse button. The prompt will then change to:

`Enter` Set 2nd endpoint of arc;

This tells you to pick a position for the ending point of the arc. As you move the cursor, you'll see that you are drawing a straight line. Once you have reached your destination, press Enter or the left mouse button once again. This prompt will appear:

`Enter` End arc;

You have just connected the two points and now you can create any type of arc between these two lines. As you move the cursor, the outline of the arc will change accordingly. Keep moving the cursor in any direction until you've completed your arc and then press Enter or the left mouse button to end it.

 Drawing an Arc

1. Display the Draw menu and select the Arc option (or select the Arc icon).

    A prompt will appear telling you to press Enter to set the first endpoint of the arc.

2. Position the cursor where you want the arc to begin and press Enter or the left mouse button.

    The prompt will change and tell you to press Enter to set the second endpoint of your arc.

3. Move the cursor to the end and press Enter or the left mouse button.

    The prompt will change and tell you to press Enter to end the arc.

4. Move the cursor in any direction to shape the arc. When you finish, press Enter or the left mouse button.

Drawing a Curve

The function of the Curve tool is shown by its somewhat distorted S-shaped icon; you use it to draw curved lines. In DrawPerfect, the curve is considered an open figure. To create one, you designate a beginning point, move the cursor to the point where you want the line to curve and press Enter or the left mouse button, then move the cursor to begin shaping the curve and press Enter or the left mouse button. Next, you can either continue moving the cursor to create a second curve (such as an S-shape) or press the Spacebar or right mouse button to end it. That probably sounds more complicated than it really is. Try drawing one and you'll find that it's easy.

To begin drawing a curve, display the **Draw** menu and select the **Curve** option, or select the icon (the third from the bottom). This prompt appears:

`Enter` Start curve

Move the cursor to where you want to start the curve and press Enter or the left mouse button. The prompt changes to:

`Enter` Continue curve; `Space` End curve;

You have just created the starting point for a curved line. Move the cursor and you'll see a straight line forming, not a curved one. This is because you have not designated a point for the first bend in your curve. To do this, press Enter or the left mouse button. Now move the cursor in another direction and watch what happens: The line starts to curve! This is a constant relationship. As you move the cursor, DrawPerfect continually adjusts the first part of the curve with the second part.

Now you have two options. The first is to end the curve by pressing Enter or the left mouse button, then the Spacebar or the right mouse button. The second alternative is to press Enter or the left mouse button and continue to create more curves. When you finish the last one, press Enter or the left mouse button and then press the Spacebar or the right mouse button to complete it. You can draw some fairly complex shapes with this tool, as shown in Figure 5.4.

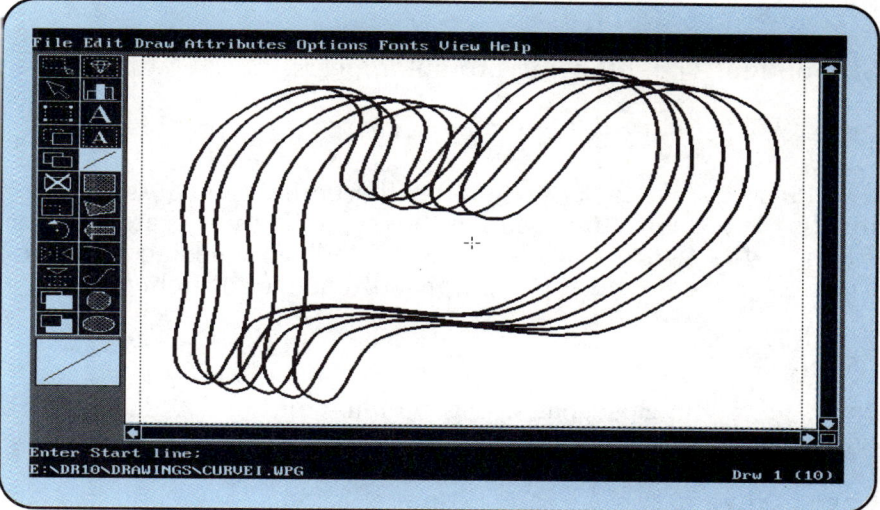

Figure 5.4 Drawing a curve

Using the Size and Stretch Tools

You can use the Size option on the Edit menu to change the size of an object. Note that Size will not change the proportions, just enlarge or reduce the object. To change the proportions you have to use both Size and Stretch, so we'll teach you both in this section.

Using Size

To try the Size tool, you'll need an image or figure on your screen. We used the DOLLAR-3.WPG file from the DrawPerfect Figure Library (under the Business category). If you use this file or one of the other files in the Figure Library, be sure to retrieve it through the Figure option on the Draw menu, and designate a figure box for it that uses no more than half of the screen. (If you forget how to use the Figure option, refer to the last section of Chapter 2, where you used it to retrieve the dog figure.)

Chapter 5

To size the figure, display the **Edit** menu and choose the **Size** option. The following prompt appears:

Enter `Select/Unselect objects`

Place the cursor anywhere on the figure and press Enter or the left mouse button. Marker boxes will appear around the edges of the figure to indicate that it's been selected for modification (sizing), and the prompt will change to include:

Space `Size;`

Next, press the Spacebar or right mouse button. A dashed box will appear around the figure and you will see this prompt:

Arrow Keys `Size object;` **Space** `Drop;`

Use the Arrow keys or the mouse to move the cursor up to enlarge the box or down to reduce it. Once the box has reached the size you want, press the Spacebar or right mouse button. DrawPerfect will then redraw the figure in the new size. If you aren't satisfied with it, just press the Spacebar or right mouse button again and follow the previous procedure. Otherwise, remove the markers by pressing Cancel (F1) or the left and right mouse buttons simultaneously (or the center button if you have one).

> ▶ **Tip:** If you retrieve a figure through the Figure option on the Draw menu, it is considered to be one item when you use an Edit option such as Size. This makes it easier because you can select the entire figure at once by placing the cursor anywhere on it and pressing Enter or the left mouse button. All parts will automatically be included. By contrast, if you use the Retrieve option on the File menu, you have to select each part of the drawing individually and it can be a tedious task.

Q Changing the Size of an Object

1. Display the Edit menu and choose the Size option.

   A prompt appears telling you to press Enter to select or unselect the objects.

2. Place the cursor anywhere on the object you want to size and press Enter or the left mouse button.

   Marker boxes will appear around the edges of the object to show it's been selected, and the prompt will change to include a message telling you to press the Spacebar to size it.

3. Press the Spacebar or right mouse button.

   A dashed box will appear around the figure, and you will see a prompt telling you to press the Arrow keys to size the object or the Spacebar to drop it.

4. Move the cursor up to enlarge the box around the object, or down to reduce it. Once the box has reached the size you want, press the Spacebar or right mouse button.

   DrawPerfect automatically redraws the figure in the new size.

Using Stretch

When you wake up in the morning, do you try to make your arms reach the ceiling and your feet touch the edge of the bed? Imagine what you would look like if your body could really stretch that far (unless you're built for basketball)! Well, that's what the Stretch option will allow you to do with anything you draw. It's like a rubber band and distorts images and text in any direction. You can create some exciting graphics this way and some real disasters. Not only is it an inventive tool, it's a lot of fun and works on anything that DrawPerfect can create.

To try it, retrieve a figure onto the screen. We used the Dollar-3 figure again, retrieving it through the Draw menu's Figure option and embellishing it with some text. Next, display the **Options** menu and select the **Stretch** option. The letters `Str` will appear on the prompt line to remind you that the Stretch option is on. Now display the **Edit** menu and select the **Size** option. This prompt will appear:

`Enter` Select/Unselect objects;

Chapter 5

Place the cursor anywhere on the figure and press Enter or the left mouse button. The prompt will change to include:

`Space` `Size;`

and selection markers will appear around the figure. Your next step is to press the Spacebar or right mouse button. A dashed box appears around the figure and the prompt changes to:

`Arrow Keys` `Size object;` `Space` `Drop;`

Now get ready for some fun! Using the Arrow keys or the mouse, you can stretch your figure in any direction possible, using the dashed box as a guide. Remember how little you were able to change this image in the Size example? Take a look at what we did to it in Figure 5.5!

Figure 5.5   Stretching the dollar

When you're done, press the Spacebar or right mouse button and your new image will appear. You can keep changing the dimensions by pressing the Spacebar or right mouse button, readjusting the dashed lined box, and then pressing the Spacebar or right mouse button for viewing.

To turn off the Stretch option, simply follow the same steps you used to activate it: Display the **Options** menu and select **Stretch** again (or use Clear Options on the Options menu).

> ▶ **Tip:** An asterisk next to one of the options on the Options menu means that it is currently selected. You can select several options for simultaneous use. If more than one option is selected, you can use Clear Options to turn them all off at once.

Constrain

The Constrain option applies to DrawPerfect's Box, Line, and Ellipse tools and restricts how you can use them. For example, if you are using the Box tool, Constrain forces you to draw a square. If you are using Line, it forces you to draw a strictly horizontal or vertical line. If you are using Ellipse, it forces you to draw a circle.

To try the Constrain option, display the **Options** menu and select **Constrain**. The letters Cns will appear in the lower right corner of the screen as a constant reminder that the option is activated. Now you're ready to use Constrain. Begin by drawing a line. Display the **Draw** menu and select the **Line** option. Next, place the cursor on the screen and try drawing a line at a 45 degree angle. Won't work, will it? The Constrain option literally constrains you so that you can only draw a straight vertical or horizontal line. Now try to draw an oval shape with the Ellipse tool or a long rectangle with the Box tool. Get the idea?

You may be wondering when such a tool would be useful. The most common scenario would be when drawing with the mouse. Using the mouse makes it hard to draw strictly horizontal or vertical lines, but Constrain makes it impossible not to! Another situation would be if you wanted to draw a perfectly square box. Whether you are using the Arrow keys or the mouse, Constrain makes it easier because it forces you to draw a square when using the Box tool.

Before continuing, be sure to turn off the Constrain option. To do this, just display the **Options** menu and select **Constrain** or **Clear Options**.

Zoom and Pan

The *Zoom* option on the View menu lets you change the way your drawing is displayed. You can enlarge a section so that only part of the drawing is visible in the drawing window, zoom in and make the entire drawing larger, or zoom out and reduce it. With Zoom on, you can use the *Pan* option to shift your perspective left, right, up, or down, so you can work on other areas of the figure.

When you use Zoom, all the drawing tools and editing tools are available for you to use, even though you have changed your vantage point. Be aware that zooming doesn't change the size of the drawing, just the viewpoint. To change the size, you have to use the Size option on the Edit menu, discussed in an earlier section of this chapter.

Using Zoom

When you select the Zoom option, a menu appears with three more choices: *Area*, *In*, and *Out*. Just like a telephoto lens, the Zoom Area option lets you zoom in on and enlarge a section of your drawing. You can Zoom In to make the whole figure larger or Zoom Out to make it smaller.

To try it, you'll need something in the drawing window. We used the File menu's Retrieve option to retrieve the butterfly drawing from the Figure Library (it's the BUTTERFLY.WPG file, found under the category of Animals). Next, display the **View** menu and choose the **Zoom** option. A submenu appears listing the three Zoom options: Area, In, and Out. Select **Area** and this prompt will appear:

Enter Set corner of zoom area

The zoom feature will enlarge any rectangular area you designate, so the next step is to draw a rectangle around the area you want to enlarge. Move the cursor to the position where you want the upper left corner of the rectangle and press Enter or the left mouse button (we placed ours left of the butterfly's left wing). This prompt appears:

`Enter` Set opposite corner of zoom area;

Start moving the cursor and a dashed line box begins to form around the area, as shown in Figure 5.6.

Figure 5.6   Selecting an area with Zoom

Once you have completely surrounded the area you want to magnify, press Enter or the left mouse button again. DrawPerfect immediately enlarges the area to fill the whole screen. Figure 5.7 shows how our screen looked when we enlarged the butterfly's wing.

You can now use any of DrawPerfect's editing and drawing tools within this area. When you finish and want to change the perspective back to view the whole figure, just use the Reset View option on the View menu or press the Ctrl-Home Home combination.

Remember the other two options, Zoom In and Zoom Out? You can use Zoom In to enlarge the entire figure or Zoom Out to reduce it. You can use them even if you have already enlarged a

Chapter 5

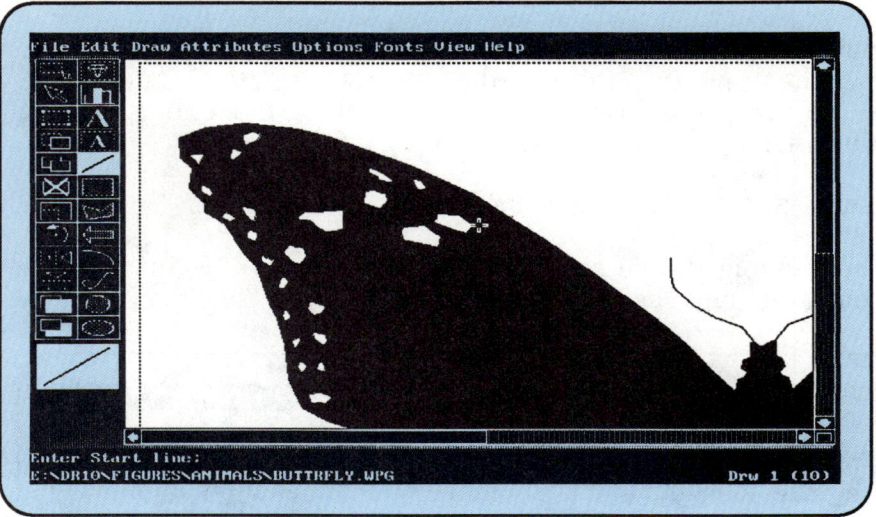

Figure 5.7 Using Zoom Area to enlarge a section of the butterfly drawing

specific area. Zoom In and Zoom Out differ from Zoom Area in that they enlarge or reduce the entire screen, not a specific area. To understand, compare Figure 5.7 to Figure 5.8. In Figure 5.7 we used Zoom Area to zoom in on the left wing, and in Figure 5.8 we used Zoom In, which enlarged the entire butterfly. If we had moved in closer (using Zoom In), we would have focused on the insect's body, because Zoom In moves in towards the center of the drawing. Figure 5.9 shows how the screen looked after we used Zoom Out. Notice the dashed box around the figure; it represents the edge of the drawing, which has been reduced.

To use Zoom In or Out, just select it from the **View** menu. A much quicker method is to press the Page Up key for Zoom In, or the Page Down key for Zoom Out. You can control the degree to which your drawing will be reduced or enlarged by changing the Cursor Step. You may remember from Chapter 1 that the Cursor Step is the number appearing in parenthesis in the lower right-hand corner of the screen. It is usually 10 when you start DrawPerfect, but you can change it to 1 or 25 by pressing the Insert key. Changing it to 25 increases the amount of reduction or enlargement that occurs each time you press Page Up or Page Down (or select Zoom In or Zoom Out from the View menu). Changing the Cursor Step to 1 decreases the amount of reduction or enlargement.

More About the Drawing Tools and Options

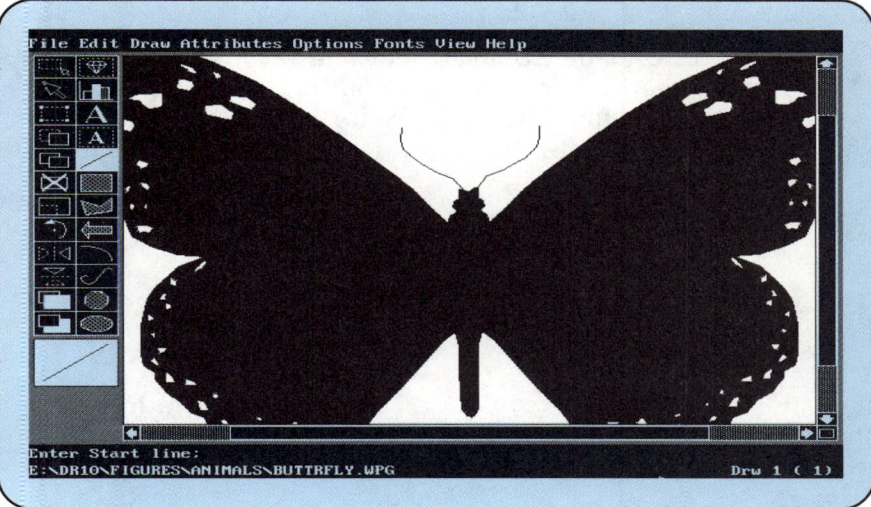

Figure 5.8   Using Zoom In to enlarge the entire butterfly drawing

Figure 5.9   Using Zoom Out to reduce the butterfly drawing

> **Tip:** While using Zoom to focus in on a specific area of your chart or drawing, you can print the area that's visible in the drawing window. To do this, display the File menu (or press Shift-F7), select Print, then select Print Window.

Using Pan

The Pan option only works when Zoom Area or Zoom In is activated. Once you have enlarged an area, you can use Pan to move the drawing up or down, or to the right or left.

To try it, use Zoom Area to enlarge a section of the butterfly figure, then display the **View** menu and select the **Pan** option. A submenu will appear asking you which direction to pan: *Up*, *Down*, *Left*, or *Right*. When you select one, the drawing will shift in the opposite direction. For instance, if you select Left, the figure will move to the right, and if you select Up, it will move down. The degree to which the drawing shifts is regulated by the Cursor Step number.

DrawPerfect has four key combinations that you can use instead of selecting the Pan options from the View menu: Press Ctrl and Right Arrow to pan left, Ctrl and Left Arrow to pan right, Ctrl and Down Arrow to pan up, and Ctrl and Up Arrow to pan down. They are summarized in Table 5.1.

Table 5.1   Key combinations

Key	Effect
Ctrl-Right Arrow	Moves drawing to the left
Ctrl-Left Arrow	Moves drawing to the right
Ctrl-Down Arrow	Moves the drawing up
Ctrl-Up Arrow	Moves the drawing down

Drawing with Freehand

If you use a mouse, you can use the Freehand option to draw lines that loop, zigzag, curve, and go anywhere the mouse goes. You can also use it to draw irregular polygons, as shown in Figure 5.10.

Figure 5.10   A polygon drawn with Freehand

Try using Freehand with the Line tool. Begin by displaying the **Draw** menu and selecting **Line**. Next, select **Freehand** from the Options menu, or press the Freehand key, Shift-F9. Notice that the letters Frh appear on the prompt line to remind you that Freehand is now activated. Normally, you could only draw a straight or angled line. With Freehand, these limits become obsolete. Now you can scribble all over the screen! Press the left button on the mouse and continue to hold it down as you drag the mouse around on the pad. Draw loops, zigzags, or even write your name, then release the left mouse button and end your line by pressing the right mouse button. Once you release the left mouse button, you can draw straight lines again. To reactivate Freehand, just press the left mouse button again and hold it while drawing. That's all there is to it.

The same procedure applies when you use Freehand to draw a polygon. If one or more sides of the polygon are irregular, simply hold down the left mouse button while drawing the irregular side. To draw a straight side, release the left button.

All the options on the Attributes menu are at your disposal when you use Freehand. If you are using the Line tool to draw, you can change the line color, style, and width. If you are using the Polygon tool, you can also change the fill color and fill pattern.

To turn off the Freehand option, use the same steps that you used to turn it on: Either display the **Options** menu and select **Freehand**, or press Shift-F9. The more you experiment with the Freehand option, the more exciting it will become. With repeated attempts, you soon will realize that the possibilities are endless. Have fun!

What You Have Learned

In this chapter, you've learned how to use four drawing tools, Arrow, Ellipse, Arc, and Curve, and several options that are helpful for drawing, Constrain, Stretch, Zoom, and Pan. You should now be familiar with the following:

- ▶ You can draw arrows, ellipses, arcs, and curves by selecting these tools from the Draw menu or icon panel. After you select one of them, prompts appear at the bottom of the screen with specific instructions about how to use it.
- ▶ To draw an arrow, you select the Arrow option from the Draw menu, press Enter or the left mouse button to position the head of the arrow, move the cursor to size the arrow, and press Enter or the left mouse button to complete it.
- ▶ To draw an oval-shaped object, you select the Ellipse option from the Draw menu, press Enter or the left mouse button to define the center, move the arrow to the perimeter, and press Enter or the left mouse button to complete it.
- ▶ An arc consists of two points connected by a curved line. To draw one, select Arc from the Draw menu, designate the beginning and ending points by pressing Enter or the left mouse button, and move the cursor to change the line into an arc. To complete the arc, press Enter or the left mouse button.

- ▶ To draw a curved line, select the Curve tool from the Draw menu. Next, move the cursor onto the beginning point and press Enter or the left mouse button, move the cursor to the point where you want the line to curve and press Enter or the left mouse button, and continue to move the cursor to shape the first curve. End the first curve by pressing Enter or the left mouse button. After that you can continue drawing more curves in your line, or press the Spacebar or right mouse button to complete it.
- ▶ To reduce or enlarge an object, select the Size option from the Edit menu.
- ▶ To change the proportions of an object, use the Size and Stretch options simultaneously.
- ▶ The Constrain option on the Options menu restricts how you can draw with the Box, Line, and Ellipse tools. It forces you to draw a square when using the Box tool, a strictly horizontal or vertical line when using the Line tool, and a circle when using the Ellipse tool.
- ▶ The Zoom option on the View menu lets you magnify a section of your drawing so that only part of it is visible in the drawing window. You can also use it to zoom in and make the entire drawing larger, or zoom out and reduce it. Zoom changes the display, but does not change the actual size of the drawing.
- ▶ When Zoom Area or Zoom In is on, you can use the Pan option on the View menu to shift your perspective left, right, up, or down to view areas of the figure.
- ▶ You can use the Freehand option on the Options menu to draw irregular polygons and lines that loop, zigzag, curve, and follow any path the mouse takes. You can only use Freehand with a mouse.

Chapter 6

More About DrawPerfect's Editing Tools

In This Chapter

▶ *Selecting an item or area to edit*
▶ *How to delete items and restore them again*
▶ *How to move and copy items*
▶ *How to change the size of an object*
▶ *The front and back options on the Edit menu*
▶ *Using the Rotate and Mirror options*
▶ *How to edit text*
▶ *Using Modify to alter a drawing object*

You have already used a few of the options on the Edit menu in previous chapters. For instance, in Chapter 2 you used *Move* to reposition the title and *Modify* to edit the bar graph and change some of its data. After retrieving the dog figure, you used *Back* to change its position so the dog would appear behind the bar chart instead of in front of it. In Chapter 3 you used *Copy* to make several copies of the planet figure and use them as bullets. In this chapter, we will review these options and teach you how to use some of the other important options on the Edit menu.

Selecting an Item or Area

Before you can use Move, Delete, Copy, or any of the other options on the Edit menu, you must designate the item or area to be affected. If you're only editing one object (and have not been using the Select Area option), selecting the object is easy: As soon as you choose an option like Move from the Edit menu, this prompt appears:

`Enter Select/Unselect objects;`

and the Arrow icon that represents Select Item appears in the Status box, as shown in Figure 6.1. At that point, all you have to do is place the cursor anywhere on the item and press Enter or click the left mouse button. Several markers in the form of tiny boxes appear around the item. When two objects are close together, sometimes the markers appear around the wrong item. If so, you can unselect it by pressing Enter again or clicking the left mouse button; then press Enter or click the left mouse button again to select the other item.

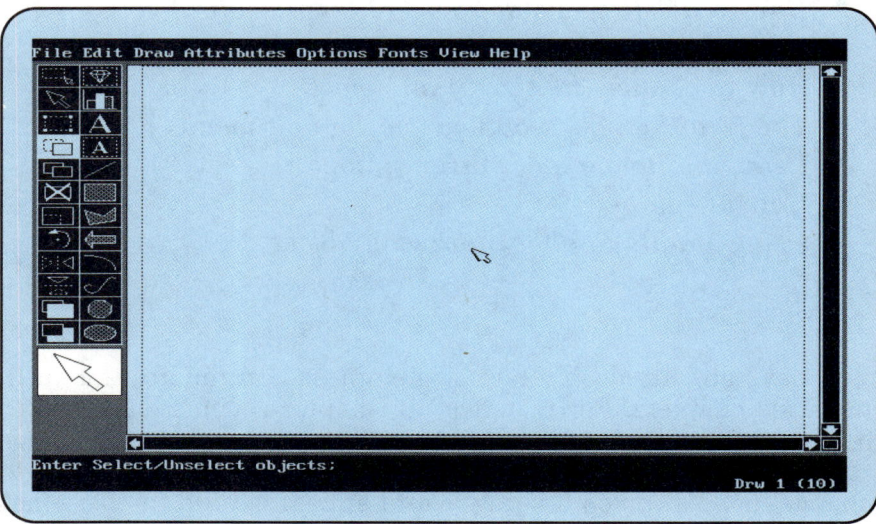

Figure 6.1   The Select Item icon in the Status box

After you select an object, the prompt line changes to include instructions about your next step. For instance, if you choose Move and select an item, the prompt changes to:

`Enter` Select/Unselect objects; `Space` Move;

If you want to select several items to edit, don't press the Spacebar right away (or its mouse equivalent, the right button). Instead, move the cursor onto the next item and press Enter again (or click the left mouse button) and repeat until you've selected all the items you want to include, then proceed with your editing action.

Selecting an Item to Edit

1. Display the Edit menu and select one of the editing tools (Move, Copy, Delete, Size, Rotate, etc.).

    An Arrow icon representing Select Item appears in the Status box, and DrawPerfect prompts you with this message: `Enter` Select/Unselect objects;

2. Move the cursor onto the item you want to edit and press Enter or click the left mouse button.

    Several tiny boxes appear around the item, signifying that it has been selected.

3. Follow the instructions on the prompt line to proceed with the editing action.

A faster way to select a group of objects is to use the Select Area option on the Edit menu. This option lets you draw a box around an area. This selects all objects that are completely inside the box to be included in your next editing action. To use it, begin by displaying the **Edit** menu and choosing **Select Area** (or select the first icon in column one). If you want to select everything in the drawing window, press Enter or click the left mouse button twice. Otherwise, move the cursor to the starting position, usually above and slightly left of the area, and press Enter or click the left mouse button. Next, move the cursor down and to the right until the entire area is surrounded by a dashed box and then press Enter or click the left mouse button. The dashed box disappears, and all the items inside the area are surrounded by markers. If you make a mistake, press Cancel (F1) or both mouse buttons and start again.

Figure 6.2 shows an example. Since we wanted to move the entire legend, we chose Select Area, placed the cursor above the legend title (*Product*) and pressed Enter, then used the cursor keys to draw the dashed box around the area. Next, we pressed the Enter key. At that point the box disappeared and all the items inside the box were surrounded by markers (tiny boxes), as shown in Figure 6.3. If we had selected these items individually, it would have required many more keystrokes, since there are five separate items in the area.

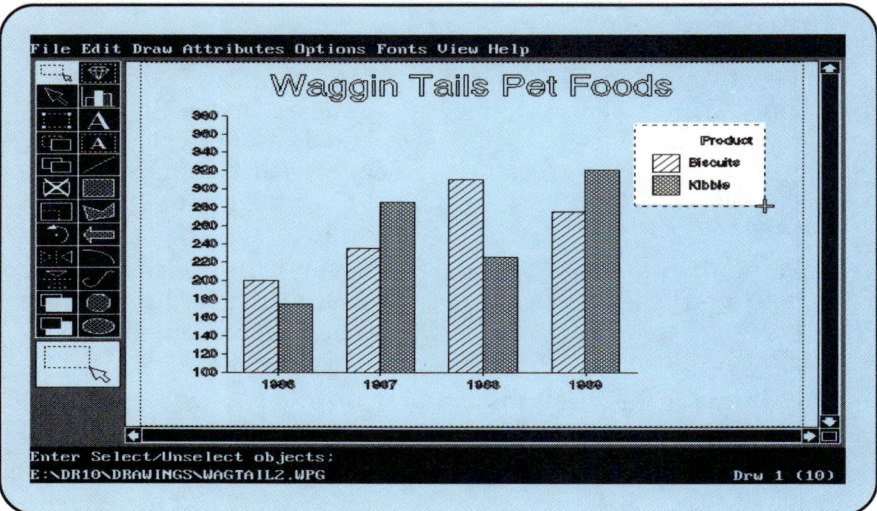

Figure 6.2 Using Select Area to draw a box around an area

Once you have used Select Area for an editing action, the next time you select an Edit option, such as Copy, Move, or Delete, Select Area will still be in effect. Instead of letting you select an individual item, DrawPerfect will wait for you to draw a box around the selected area. If this happens and you want to select an individual item—not an area—press Cancel (F1) or both mouse buttons, choose **Select Item** from the Edit menu, then choose your Edit option and proceed as normal.

More About DrawPerfect's Editing Tools

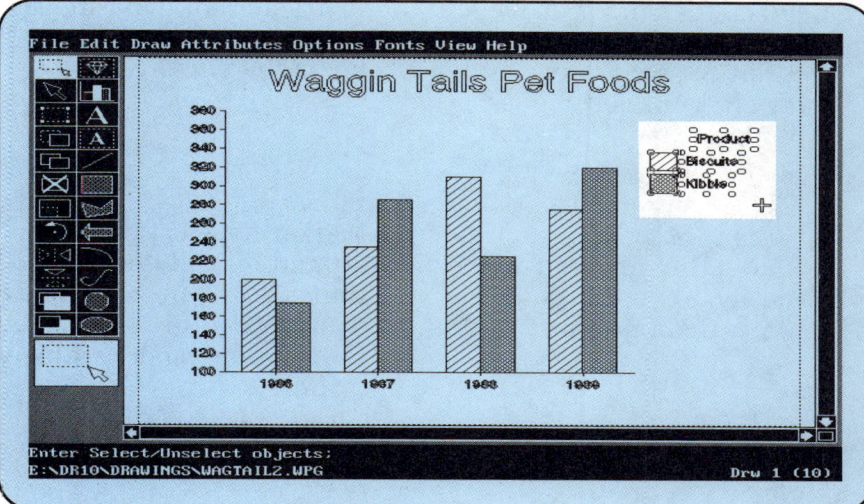

Figure 6.3 *The markers that appear after selecting an area to edit*

In the remaining sections of this chapter when we show you how to use options like Delete, Copy, and Move, we usually assume that Select Item is in effect when you first use the option. In other words, if we ask you to select Delete without telling you to choose Select Item or Select Area first, we are assuming that Select Item will automatically be used. This is always the case when you start DrawPerfect. In fact, Select Item will always be used unless you choose Select Area for an editing action. After that, if you want to select individual objects, you have to choose Select Item from the Edit menu *before* selecting an option like Delete or Copy.

 Selecting an Entire Area to Edit

1. Display the Edit menu and choose Select Area.

   An icon showing a box with an arrow pointing at its lower right corner appears in the Status box, and DrawPerfect prompts you with this message: `Enter Select/Unselect objects;`

2. Place the cursor above and to the left of the area you want to select, press Enter or click the left mouse button, then move the cursor down and to the right.

A dashed box will appear around the area as you move the cursor.

3. When the box surrounds the entire area you wish to designate, press Enter or click the left mouse button.

Marker boxes appear around all the items inside the selected area. Now you can proceed to select an Edit option, such as Move or Delete. ☐

Delete

DrawPerfect includes two methods of deleting an item or area: the Delete option on the Edit menu and the Delete key (or Backspace key). To erase an individual object using the first method, display the **Edit** menu and choose **Delete**, or select the Delete icon from the icon panel (it's the sixth one in the first column, represented by a box with a large X through it). Next, move the cursor onto the item and press Enter or the left mouse button to select it. Markers appear around the item. Press the Spacebar or right mouse button to delete it.

To delete an area, begin by choosing **Select Area** from the Edit menu. Next, form a box around the area by pressing Enter or the left mouse button, moving the cursor, then pressing Enter or the left mouse button again. The last step is to select Delete from the icon panel or Edit menu.

If the Redraw prompt appears in the lower right corner of the screen after you've used Delete, press F9 or select ReDraw from the View menu.

To use the Delete key method, choose either **Select Area** or **Select Item** from the Edit menu, designate the items to be affected, then press the Delete key.

Deleting an Item or Area

1. Use Select Item or Select Area to designate the item or area to be deleted.

   Markers appear around the object or objects.

2. Display the Edit menu and select Delete, or select the Delete icon (the sixth one in the first column), or press the Delete key.

   The selected item or items disappear.

Restoring Deleted Items

If you erase an item or area and then change your mind and decide you want it back, DrawPerfect has the solution. Before you erase anything else, select the **Undelete** option on the Edit menu (there is no corresponding icon). Alternatively, you can press the Cancel key (F1) or the left and right mouse buttons simultaneously (or center button). You will see this prompt:

`Undelete: 1 Restore; 2 Previous Deletion: 0`

and whatever you last erased will reappear in the drawing window, surrounded by marker boxes. For instance, in Figure 6.4 markers appear around the gas pump handle that we just deleted and the Undelete prompt appears. To bring the pump back, we could select the Restore option. If we had deleted an item or area prior to that, we could use the Previous Deletion option to view it and (optionally) restore it. In fact, DrawPerfect retains the last three items that you delete, so you can select Previous Deletion twice to restore the second-to-last and third-to-last deletion.

Copy

Occasionally, you may need to copy an item or area from one section of your drawing to another. To do this, you can use the Copy option on the Edit menu. To copy one item at a time, just select **Copy** from the Edit menu (or select the fifth icon in column one). Next, move the cursor onto the item you wish to copy and press

Figure 6.4 Using the Undelete option to restore a deleted item

Enter or click the left mouse button. Marker boxes surround the item, and this prompt appears:

`Enter` Select/Unselect objects; `Space` Copy;

Press the Spacebar or right mouse button to begin copying. A box appears connecting the markers, and the prompt changes to:

`Arrow Keys` Copy object; `Space` Drop;

Use the mouse or Arrow keys to move the box; then press the Spacebar or right mouse button to copy it.

To copy an area, choose **Select Area** from the Edit menu and draw a box around the area by pressing Enter or the left mouse button, then moving the cursor and pressing Enter or the left mouse button again. After the markers appear, select **Copy** from the Edit menu (or select the icon, the fifth one in column one). A box appears connecting the markers, and the prompt changes to:

`Arrow Keys` Copy object; `Space` Drop;

Use the Arrow keys or mouse to move the box into position and then press the Spacebar or right mouse button to make the copy.

After you've finished copying an area or item, remove the markers by pressing Cancel (F1) or both mouse buttons simultaneously. If you see the `Redraw` prompt in the lower right corner of the screen, press F9 or select **ReDraw** from the View menu.

Move

The procedure for moving items is almost identical to copying, except that the selected item or items are erased from the current position. Figures 6.5 and 6.6 illustrate the difference. In Figure 6.5 we used Move to move the cactuses from the right side of the drawing to the left. In Figure 6.6, we used Copy to make extra copies and place them on the left side.

Figure 6.5 **Moving the cactus**

Chapter 6

Figure 6.6 Copying the cactus

To move an item, display the **Edit** menu and select **Move** (or select the Move icon, the fourth one in column one). Place the cursor on the item and press Enter or the left mouse button. Markers appear, and the prompt changes to include:

`Space` Move;

Press the Spacebar or right mouse button. The new prompt tells you what to do next:

`Arrow Keys` Move object; `Space` Drop;

Use the Arrow keys or mouse to move the box into the new position and then press the Spacebar or right mouse button. As you'll see, this erases the original item, which reappears at the new position.

To move an area, use **Select Area** to designate the section you wish to move. When the markers appear, display the **Edit** menu and select **Move** (or select the fourth icon in column one). Next, move the box into the new position and press the Spacebar or right mouse button again.

After moving an area or item, erase the markers by pressing Cancel (F1) or both mouse buttons simultaneously. If you see the `Redraw` prompt, be sure to select **ReDraw** from the View menu (or press F9).

Size

The Size option on the Edit menu is useful when you want to change the size of an item or area. To use it to enlarge or reduce one item, begin by selecting **Size** from the Edit menu (or select the icon, the seventh in column one). The `Enter Select/Unselect objects;` prompt appears. Next, place the cursor on the item and press Enter or click the left mouse button. The prompt will change to include these instructions:

`Space Size;`

Press the Spacebar or right mouse button, and a dashed box will appear around the object. Use the Up and Down Arrow keys or mouse to change the box's size, as shown in Figure 6.7. When you are satisfied with the size, press the Spacebar or the right mouse button to complete the process and "drop" the item.

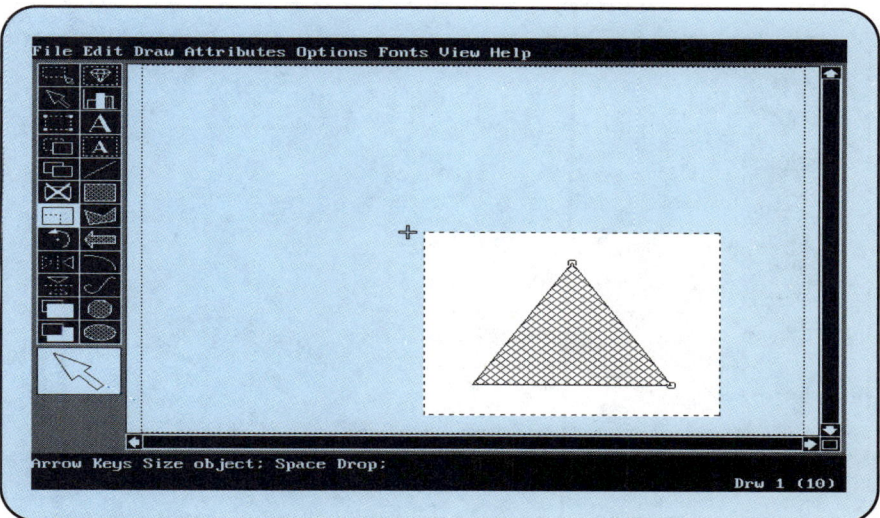

Figure 6.7   Sizing a triangle

Chapter 6

To change the size of an area, begin by using **Select Area** to designate the section. After the markers appear, select **Size** from the Edit menu (or select the icon, the seventh in column one). A dashed box appears around the area, and the prompt changes to:

`Arrow Keys` Size object; `Space` Drop;

Use the Up and Down Arrow keys or mouse to change its size and then press Spacebar or the right mouse button to complete the process.

After sizing an area or item, erase the markers by pressing Cancel (F1) or both mouse buttons simultaneously and then press F9 or select ReDraw from the View menu.

If an item is too close to the border, you may not be able to increase the size as much as you'd like. Look again at Figure 6.7. Notice the triangle's position near the lower right corner of the drawing window and the dashed lines surrounding it, showing how large it will become if we press Enter. In Figure 6.8, we tried to enlarge it even more. Dashed lines appear above and to the left of it, but none appear below and to the right. This indicates that the triangle is too large to fit inside the window. Sure enough, when we pressed the Spacebar, nothing happened. If this happens to you, shrink it back down until dashed lines appear on all four sides.

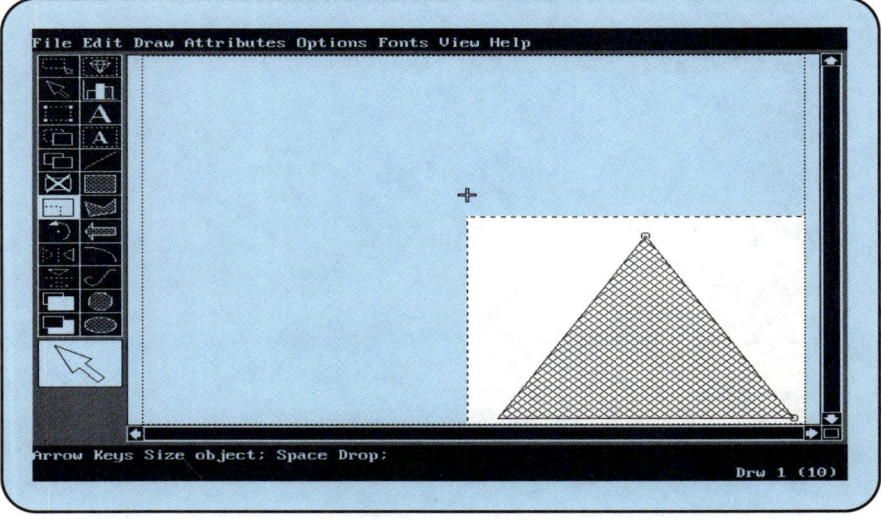

Figure 6.8   Trying to make a box too big for the window

Changing the Size of an Item or Area

1. Use Select Item or Select Area to designate the item or area you want to change.

    Markers appear around the object or objects.

2. Display the Edit menu and select Size (or select the icon, the seventh in column one).

    A dashed box appears around the area, and the prompt changes to `Arrow Keys` Size object; `Space` Drop;

3. Use the Up and Down Arrow keys or mouse to increase or decrease the item or area. When you finish sizing it, press Spacebar or the right mouse button.

    The dashed box disappears but the markers remain.

4. Erase the markers by pressing Cancel (F1) or both mouse buttons simultaneously and then redraw the screen by pressing F9 or selecting ReDraw from the View menu.

The Front and Back Options on the Edit Menu

You can use *Front* and *Back* on the Edit menu to rearrange objects that overlap. Front brings an item forward, in front of the other object, while Back pushes it back, behind the other object. These options can be invaluable when you are trying to draw an object that belongs behind another one. For instance, Figure 6.9 shows a gray oval that we drew to represent the shadow of the 8-ball. You can't tell that it is supposed to be a shadow until we select the Back option and move it behind the grid and 8-ball, as shown in Figure 6.10.

Chapter 6

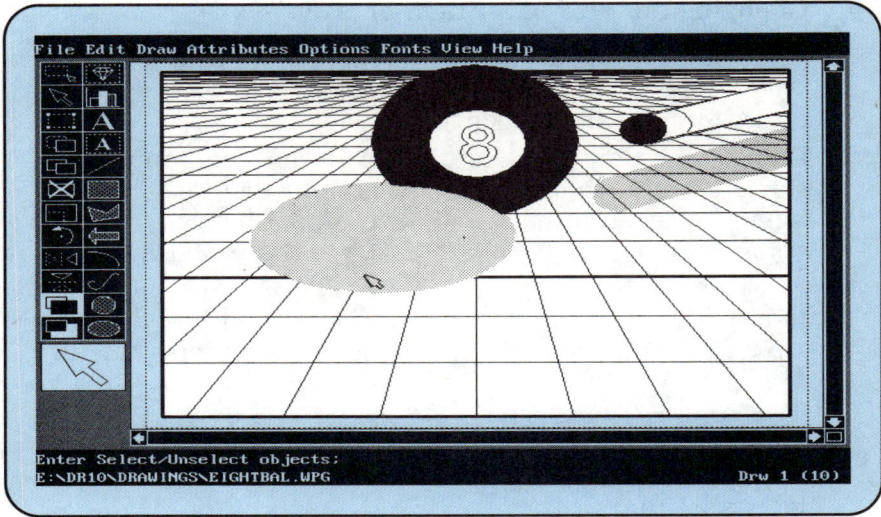

Figure 6.9 *Drawing a shadow*

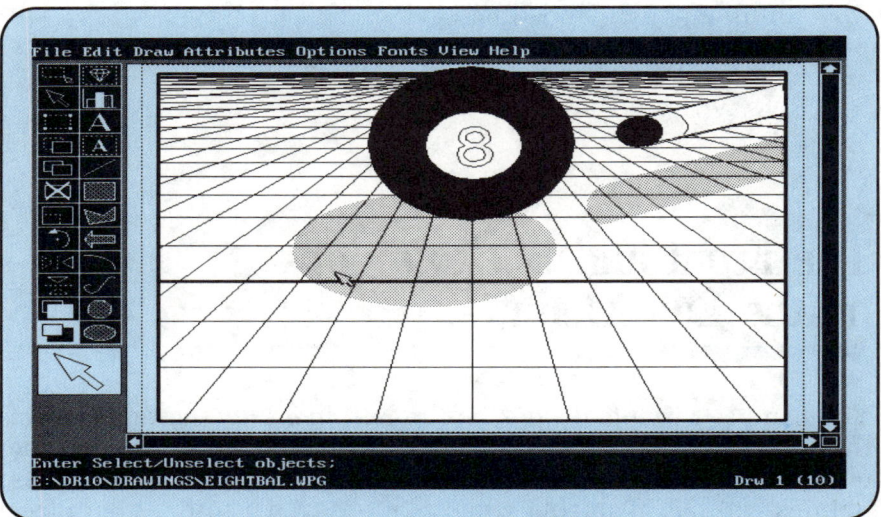

Figure 6.10 *After using Back to move the shadow behind the grid*

To use Front or Back, begin by selecting it from the **Edit** menu or icon panel (Back is the last icon in the first row, and

Front is the second to last). Next, move the cursor onto the object whose position you want to change and press Enter or the left mouse button to select it. Markers appear around the item and the prompt changes to tell you what to do: If you selected Back, you press the Spacebar to push it to the back. If you selected Front, you press the Spacebar to bring it to the front. Once you press the Spacebar or right mouse button, the object moves to the front or back. To remove the markers, press Enter or click the left mouse button.

Rotate and Mirror

The *X Mirror* and *Y Mirror* options are useful when you want to reverse an image on the X- or Y-axis. The *Rotate* option lets you rotate an object in any direction. Figure 6.11 shows three versions of a directional indicator that we drew for a map. The original version shows how it looked after we created the circle and retrieved one of the arrow figures from DrawPerfect's Figure Library. Since the arrow pointed down instead of up, we selected Y Mirror to change it. The results appear in the second version, *Mirror drawing*. Notice how the position of the shadow around the arrow was reversed, since it is a mirror reflection of the arrow in the original drawing. Since north on our hypothetical map was to the left, we then used Rotate to shift the whole figure to the left, as you can see in the third version, *Rotated drawing*.

To use one of the mirror options, just select it from the Edit menu or select the corresponding icon. The X Mirror icon is the ninth in column one, with two triangles and a dashed line between them. The position of the triangles gives you a clue about how the object will be reversed: left and right. The Y Mirror icon is the tenth in the first column. It shows triangles above and below a dashed line, symbolizing that this option will reflect an image up and down. After selecting X Mirror or Y Mirror, place the cursor on the item that you want to mirror, select it by pressing Enter or the left mouse button, and then press the Spacebar or right mouse button.

To use the Rotate option, just select it from the Edit menu or icon panel (it is the eighth icon in column one). Next, move

Chapter 6

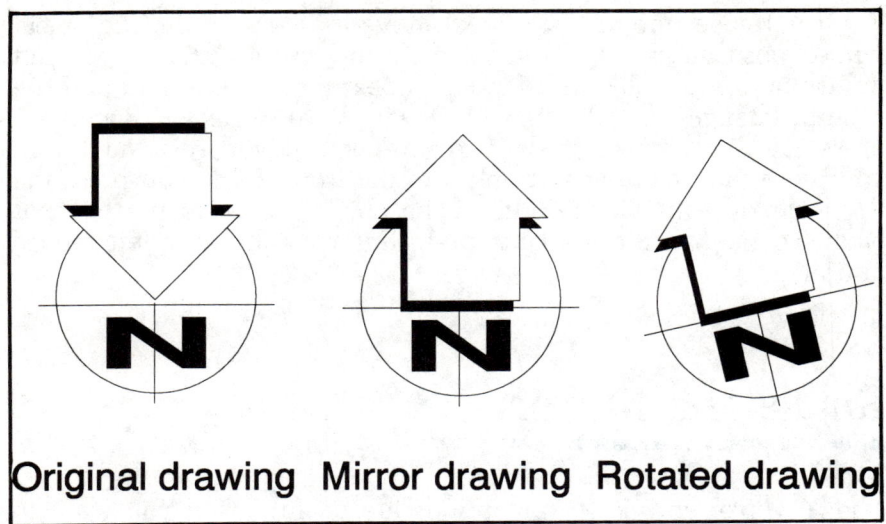

Figure 6.11   Using Y Mirror and Rotate

the cursor onto the item you want to rotate and press Enter or the right mouse button. The prompt changes to include:

`Space` Rotate;

Press the Spacebar or right mouse button, and then use the mouse or Arrow keys to rotate your item. When you're finished and are ready to "drop" it, press the Spacebar or right mouse button.

Modify

In Chapter 2 you learned how to use the Modify option on the Edit menu to change the data in a bar chart. You can also use this option to edit text in a Text Line or Window, or to alter a figure that you've drawn. In the three sections that follow, we'll show you how.

Using Modify to Edit Text

If you've used the Text Line or Window Text option on the Draw menu to type text in a drawing or chart, you can edit it with the Modify option on the Edit menu. To use this option, begin by displaying the **Edit** menu and selecting **Modify** (or select the icon, the third in column one). Next, place the cursor anywhere on the text and press Enter or the left mouse button to select it. Markers appear around the text, and the prompt changes to include:

`Space Modify;`

Press the Spacebar or right mouse button to begin editing. The prompt changes to:

`Input text;`

and the text cursor appears at the beginning of the text. You can then retype, delete, change the font, or otherwise modify your text. When you're finished, press Exit (F7) or use the mouse to drag the cursor onto the **Exit** option at the bottom of the screen and click the left button. To remove the markers, press Cancel (F1) or click both mouse buttons simultaneously. Select **ReDraw** from the View menu if you see the `Redraw` prompt.

Q Editing Text

1. Display the Edit menu and select Modify (or select the icon, the third in column one).	DrawPerfect prompts you to press Enter to select or unselect an object.
2. Place the cursor anywhere on the text and press Enter or the left mouse button to select it.	Markers appear around the text, and the prompt changes to include: `Space Modify;`
3. Press the Spacebar or right mouse button to begin editing.	The text cursor appears at the beginning of the text.
4. Edit the text, then press Exit (F7) or use the mouse to select the Exit option at the bottom of the screen.	The markers remain.

Chapter 6

5. To remove the markers, press Cancel (F1) or click both mouse buttons simultaneously. You may need to select ReDraw from the View menu. ☐

Modify Drawing Objects

When you're working with drawing objects, such as boxes, polygons, arrows, or circles, Modify has another function: to move the points that define an object. For example, in Figure 6.12 we changed the shape of the ice cream cone by choosing Modify, selecting the point at the bottom of the cone, and moving it down with the cursor. You can clearly see the outline of the new cone, which will be larger and narrower than the original one.

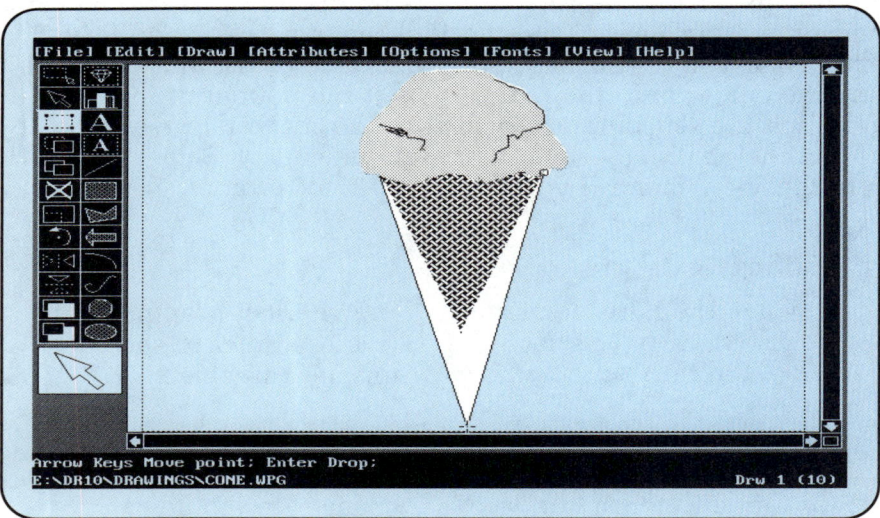

Figure 6.12   Using Modify to alter a point on the ice cream cone

To use Modify, begin by selecting it from the **Edit** menu or by selecting the Modify icon, the third one in the first column. The `Enter Select/Unselect objects;` prompt appears. Move the cursor onto the item you want to change and press

Enter or click the left mouse button. The prompt changes to include:

`Space` Modify;

Press the Spacebar or right mouse button. This prompt appears:

`Arrow Keys` Select point; `Enter` Move point;
`Space` Exit;

Place the cursor on the point you want to change and press Enter or click the left mouse button. The prompt changes to:

`Arrow Keys` Move point; `Enter` Drop;

Next, use the Arrow keys or mouse to move the point, as shown in Figure 6.12. When you reach the position you want, press the Enter key or left mouse button, then the Spacebar or right mouse button. If you want to move another point on the selected object, place the cursor on it, and then press Enter and repeat the process. Otherwise, press the Spacebar or right mouse button and then select ReDraw. Remove the markers by pressing Cancel (F1) or the two mouse buttons simultaneously.

Modify Figure

If you have used the Figure option on the Draw menu to retrieve a DrawPerfect file into one of your charts or drawings, the Modify option works differently. For example, in Figure 6.13 we used the Figure option to retrieve the ice cream cone into our bar chart. When we select the ice cream cone and choose the Modify option from the Edit menu, DrawPerfect zooms in on the ice cream cone, as shown in Figure 6.14.

Notice the prompt lines at the bottom of the screen:

`Enter` Select/Unselect objects;
`Modify Figure Mode; F7` exit modify

To edit the enlarged figure, you place the cursor on the area you want to change and press Enter or the left mouse button. The first line of the prompt then changes to include:

`Space` Modify;

Next, you press the Spacebar or right mouse button and this prompt appears:

`Arrow Keys` Select point; `Enter` Move point;
`Space` Exit;

The rest of the procedure is the same as the one you studied in the previous section. You move the cursor onto a point that you want to edit and press Enter or the left mouse button to select it and then use the Arrow keys to move it. To complete the move, you press Enter or the left mouse button, then the Spacebar or right mouse button.

When you've finished editing the enlarged figure, you can return to the drawing window by pressing F7 or by using the mouse to select the **Exit Modify** option at the bottom of the screen.

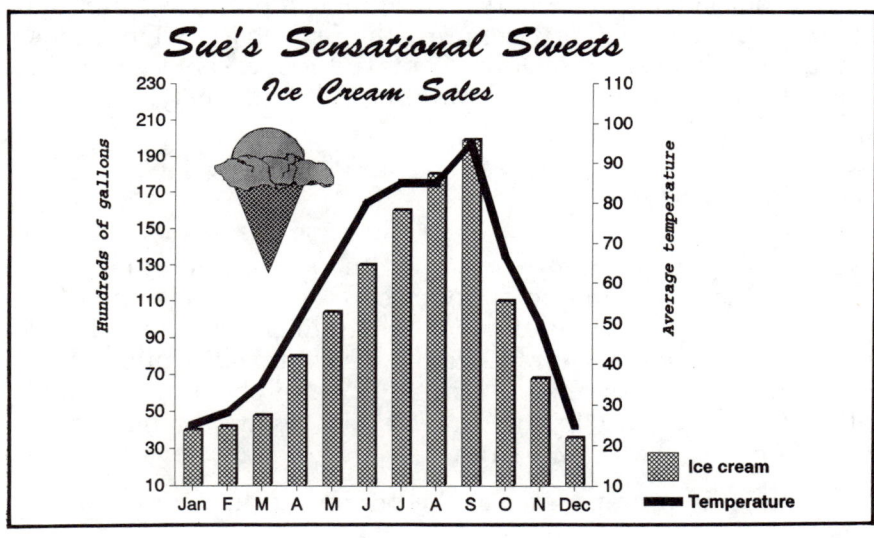

Figure 6.13 *A bar chart with ice cream cone figure*

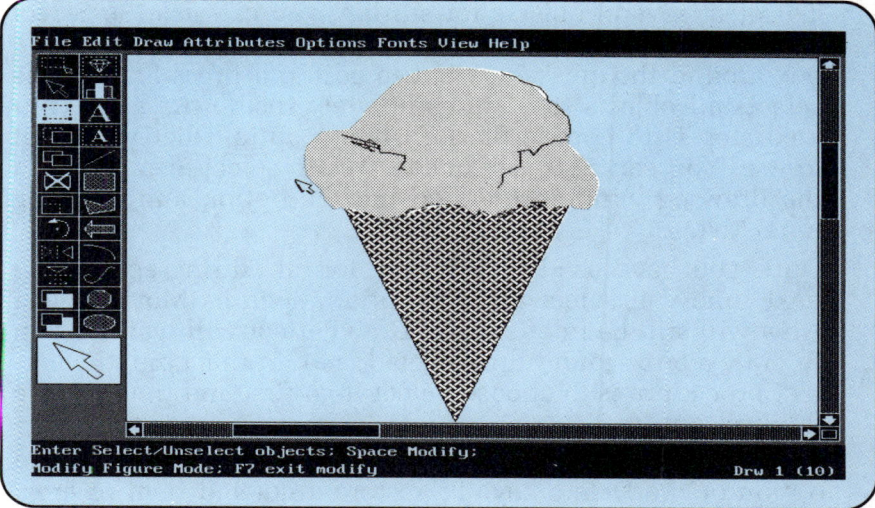

Figure 6.14 Using Modify on the ice cream cone

What You Have Learned

In this chapter, you've learned how to use the Edit menu to modify, move, copy, delete, size, rotate, and mirror items in your drawings and charts. You should now be familiar with the following Edit menu options:

▶ Before you can use Edit menu options, such as Move, Delete, Copy, Size, and Rotate, you must designate the item or area to be affected using Select Item or Select Area on the Edit menu.

▶ Each time you start DrawPerfect, Select Item is automatically in effect. Unless you change it to Select Area, selecting an individual object to edit is easy: First you select an Edit menu option, such as Move, and then you place the cursor on the item and press Enter or click the left mouse button. Several marker boxes appear around the object to signify that it has been selected and you can proceed to edit it.

▶ To select several objects for editing, you can use the Select Area option on the Edit menu. After choosing it, you draw a box around the area you want to edit and press Enter. This selects all objects that are completely inside the box. Your next step is to choose the Edit menu option that you want to use. You can also use Select Area to select everything in the drawing window by choosing the option and pressing Enter twice.

▶ Once you have used Select Area for an editing action, the next time you select an Edit option, such as Move, Select Area will still be in effect and DrawPerfect will wait for you to draw a box around the selected area. In this case, the correct procedure is to choose Select Item first and then choose the Edit option.

▶ To erase an item or area, you can either use the Delete option or the Delete key. To restore a deleted item or area, you can use the Undelete option or the Cancel key (F1).

▶ To copy an item or area from one section of your drawing to another, you can use the Copy option.

▶ To move an item or area from one section of your drawing to another, you can use the Move option.

▶ You can use the Size option to enlarge or reduce an item or an area.

▶ If two objects overlap, you can rearrange them using the Front or Back option. Front brings an item forward, in front of the other object; while Back pushes it back, behind the other object.

▶ To reverse an image on the X- or Y-axis, you can use the X Mirror or Y Mirror option.

▶ You can rotate an object in any direction using the Rotate option.

▶ You can use Modify to edit text in a Text Line or Window, or to alter an object that you've drawn.

Chapter 7
Printer Control

In This Chapter

- How to print your charts and drawings
- Printing an enlarged section of a chart or drawing
- Two methods of printing a file without retrieving it
- Controlling the printer
- Previewing the printed version of a drawing or chart
- Print options

Printing Your Work

DrawPerfect features several methods that you can use to print your charts and drawings. The Print menu includes three: *Print Drawing, Print Window,* and *Drawing on Disk.* The List Files menu also includes a Print option, and you can use it to print one or more DrawPerfect files from the disk without retrieving them into the drawing window. In this section, we'll teach you how to use them all.

Printing the Entire Chart or Drawing in Your Drawing Window

If you read Chapter 2, you have already learned about the Print Drawing option on the Print menu, probably the most commonly used method. Select this option whenever you want to print the chart or drawing currently in your drawing window. To use it, display the **File** menu and select **Print** (or press the Print key, Shift-F7). This brings up the main Print menu shown in Figure 7.1.

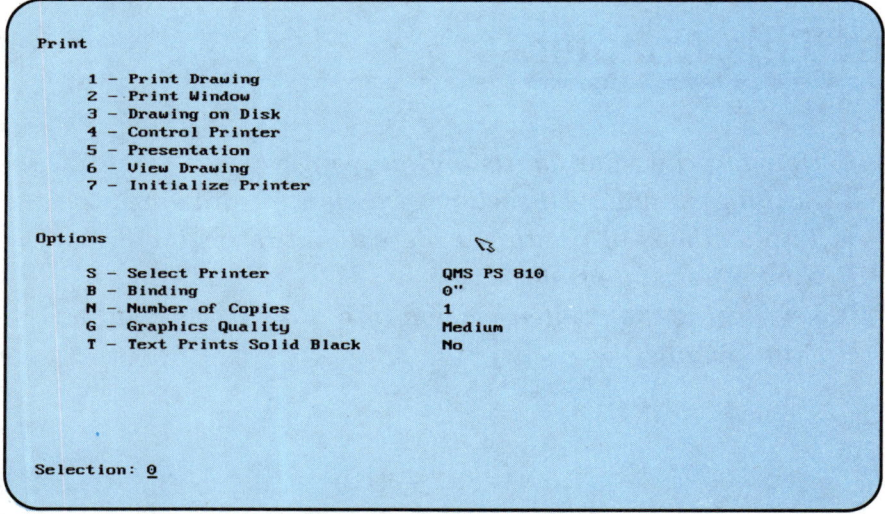

Figure 7.1   The main Print menu

Before printing, always check the Options section of this menu for your printer's name; it should appear next to `Select Printer`. If you don't see it, your printer may not be installed correctly and you may not be able to print at all. If so, choose the Select Printer option and look for your printer's name in the list that appears at the top of the screen. An example of this screen is shown in Figure 7.2. Notice that we have two printers to select from, HP LaserJet Series II and QMS PS 810. An asterisk appears next to QMS PS 810, indicating that it is the currently selected printer. We installed both of these printers when we originally installed DrawPerfect, choosing from among hundreds of printers supported by the program. If your printer does not appear in the list on this screen, you will have to install it before printing (to learn how, see Appendix A). If it is on the screen, select it by typing **1** or S (or highlight the printer's name and choose the Select option with the mouse). After that, your printer should work correctly.

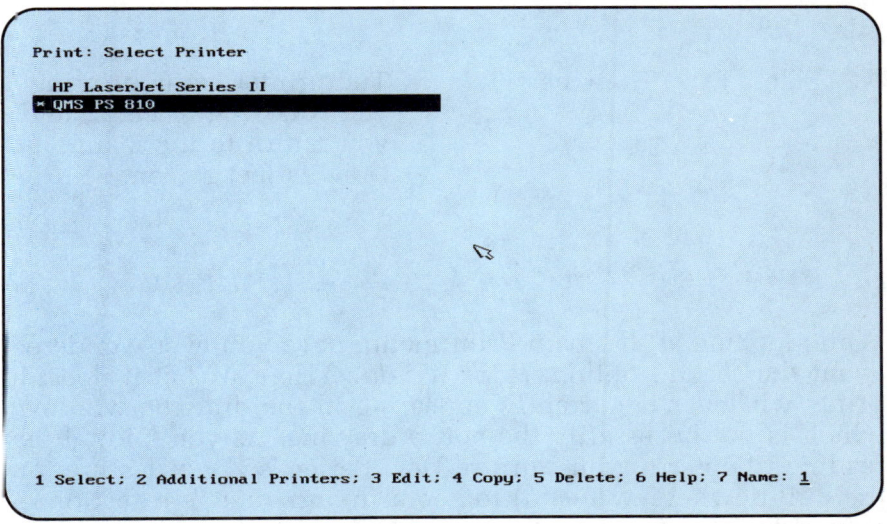

Figure 7.2 *Selecting a printer*

To print the chart or drawing in your drawing window, your next step is to select **Print Drawing**. The printer should start printing almost immediately. If it doesn't, do not select Print Drawing again because it just won't work! When a printer refuses to start after you issue a print command, such as Print Drawing, there is usually a printer connection problem, such as a loose cable, an on-line button that is currently switched off, or an incorrectly installed printer. Furthermore, DrawPerfect remembers everything you ask it to print, regardless of whether or not the printer is actually functioning. Each time you select Print Drawing or one of the other print methods, the program assigns a job number to your request and places it in a job list, where it waits until the printer is ready. Once you do get the printer working, it will print the chart or drawing once for each time you selected Print Drawing (or another print method). In the Control Printer section of this chapter, we will teach you more about the job list.

Q Printing the Drawing or Chart Currently in the Drawing Window

1. Display the File menu and select the Print option (or press the Print key, Shift-F7).

   The Print menu appears.

2. Select Print Drawing.

   The printer starts printing your drawing or chart, and you return to the main DrawPerfect screen. ☐

Printing a Section of a Chart or Drawing

While looking at the main Print menu, have you ever wondered about the second option, *Print Window?* Here's what it does: It prints whatever is currently appearing in the drawing window, which is not necessarily the entire drawing. As you know from reading Chapter 8, you can use DrawPerfect's Zoom feature (on the pull-down View menu) to zoom in and enlarge a section of your drawing so that only part of it is visible in the drawing window. While using Zoom, you can select Print Window to print this enlarged section.

For example, Figure 7.3 shows the drawing window with a picture of an eight ball and a cue stick. We used Zoom to focus in on the eight ball, and our results appear in Figure 7.4. If we had selected Print Window at that point (while viewing just the eight ball), DrawPerfect would have printed only the section shown in Figure 7.4.

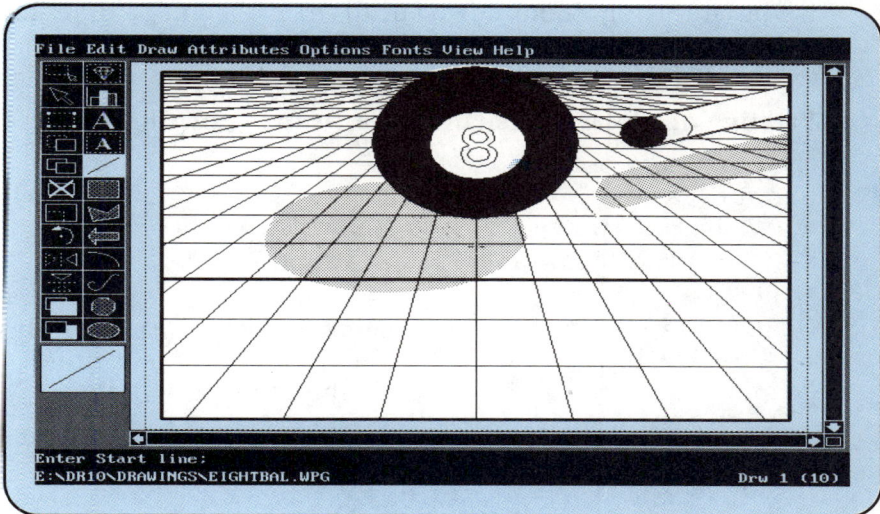

Figure 7.3   The drawing before using Zoom

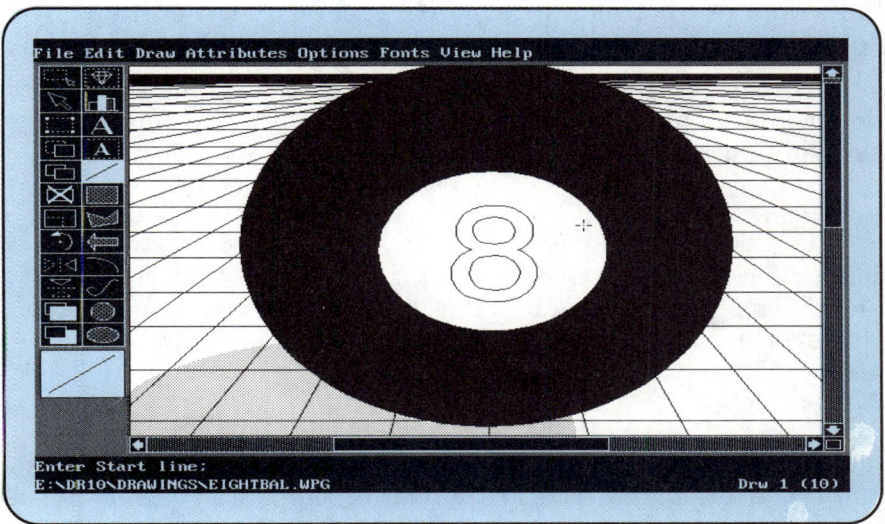

Figure 7.4   The drawing after zooming in on the eight ball

If you are using Zoom but want to print the entire drawing or chart, just select Print Drawing instead of Print Window.

◗ Printing an Enlarged Section of a Drawing or Chart

1. Use the Zoom option (on the pull-down View menu) to enlarge the section of the drawing that you want to print.
2. Display the File menu, select Print, then select Print Window. · DrawPerfect will print only the section that is visible in the drawing window. ☐

Printing Without Retrieving

You do not have to retrieve a DrawPerfect file (WPG file) to print it. Instead, you can use the Drawing on Disk option on the main Print menu, or the List Files menu's Print option. You can use these options to print a file even if a different chart or drawing is currently in the drawing window.

To use the Drawing on Disk option, just display the pull-down **File** menu, select **Print**, and then select the third option, **Drawing on Disk**. This prompt will appear:

```
Drawing name:
```

asking for the file name. Type the file name and then press Enter. The printer should start printing almost immediately. However, if you see this message:

```
ERROR: File not found
```

it means that DrawPerfect cannot find the file, probably because you typed the name incorrectly. If this happens, you may wish to try the List Files method of printing. When you use this method, you don't have to type the file name; instead, you select it from a list.

To use the List Files method of printing without retrieving, display the pull-down **File** menu, select **List Files**, and press Enter. You will see a List Files screen similar to the one shown in Figure 7.5 (except that your file names will be different). Next, move the cursor onto the file that you want to print and select the **Print** option. If you don't see the file, press Page Down a few times — sometimes the list is too large for one screen!

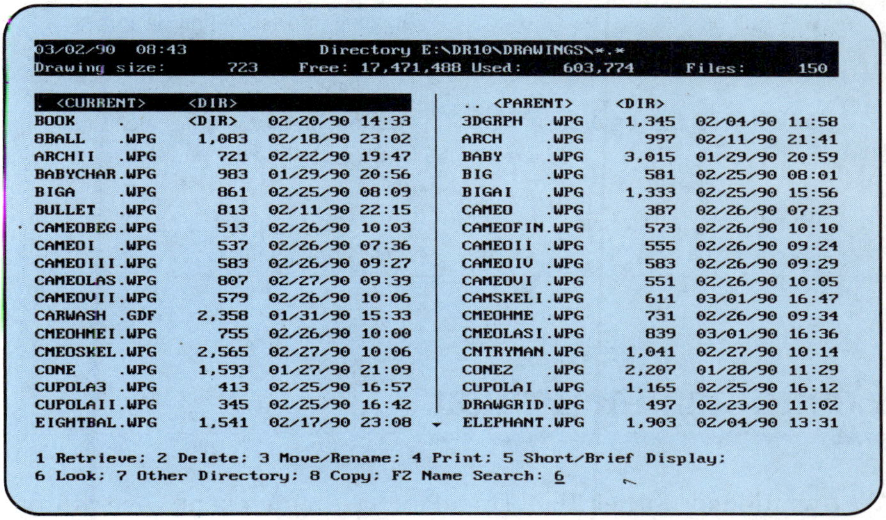

Figure 7.5   The List Files screen

You can also use the List Files method to print a group of files. To do this, place the cursor on the first file that you want to print and mark it by typing an asterisk. Repeat for each file that you want to print. The asterisks will appear after the number in the third column (which represents file size). When you finish marking your files, select the Print option. You will then see this prompt:

`Print marked files? No (Yes)`

Select Yes. We will explore the List Files print method in more detail in Chapter 9, so you may wish to read that section for more information, such as how to use it to print files in a different subdirectory.

A summary of DrawPerfect's printing techniques appears in Table 7.1.

Table 7.1 Printing techniques

To print a	Use
Chart or drawing in the drawing window	Print Drawing option on Print menu
WPG file on disk	Drawing on Disk option on Print menu, or Print option on List Files menu
Several WPG files on disk	Print option on List Files menu (mark each file with an asterisk first)
Partial chart or drawing	Use Zoom to enlarge it; then select Print Window

Controlling the Printer

We mentioned earlier that DrawPerfect "remembers" everything you ask it to print, and places each request into a printer job list. If you ask it to print more than one chart or drawing, the program will assign sequential numbers to your requests and print them in order. To view the list of drawings waiting to be printed, cancel a print job, or stop the printer, you can use the Control Printer option on the main Print menu. When you select this option, the menu shown in Figure 7.6 appears.

The menu line at the bottom of the Control Printer screen includes five options. You can select **Cancel Jobs** to cancel one or more print jobs; **Rush Job** if you've asked DrawPerfect to print several files and want to change the order so that one of them will begin printing immediately; **Display Jobs** to show any jobs that can't fit on this screen; **Stop** to stop the printer temporarily in case it is jammed or out of paper; and **Go** to start it again.

Figure 7.7 shows another Control Printer menu. Notice that three print jobs appear in the Job List section in the middle of the screen. We used Drawing on Disk to select 8BALL.WPG and CONE.WPG for printing, so their file names appear in the middle column under the heading `Drawing`. We selected the third print job when it was in our drawing window, using the Print Drawing option, so the word `(Screen)` appears in the Drawing column instead of a file name. Since Additional Jobs Not Shown is 0, there are no other print jobs in the list. If there were, we would have to select Display Jobs to see them.

```
Print: Control Printer

Current Job

Job Number:   None                    Page Number:   None
Status:       No print jobs           Current Copy:  None
Message:      None
Paper:        None
Location:     None
Action:       None


Job List

Job  Drawing             Destination         Print Options




Additional Jobs Not Shown: 0



1 Cancel Job(s); 2 Rush Job; 3 Display Jobs; 4 Go (start printer); 5 Stop: 0
```

Figure 7.6 *The Control Printer menu*

```
Print: Control Printer

Current Job

Job Number:   1                       Page Number:   None
Status:       Initializing            Current Copy:  None
Message:      Printer not accepting characters
Paper:        None
Location:     None
Action:       Check cable, make sure printer is turned ON


Job List

Job  Drawing             Destination         Print Options
 1   E:\...\BBALL.WPG    LPT 1
 2   E:\...\CONE.WPG     LPT 1
 3   (Screen)            LPT 1

Additional Jobs Not Shown: 0



1 Cancel Job(s); 2 Rush Job; 3 Display Jobs; 4 Go (start printer); 5 Stop: 0
```

Figure 7.7 *A Control Printer menu with three print jobs*

A prompt appears in the Current Job section, next to `Message:`, warning us that something is wrong with the printer:

`Printer not accepting characters`

The Action area suggests what to do:

`Check cable, make sure printer is turned ON`

Here's evidence of what we told you earlier: DrawPerfect remembers all your print requests, and they remain here in the list until you get the printer working. (Incidentally, if you exit DrawPerfect while there are still print jobs in the list, you will see a prompt asking if you want to cancel all print jobs.) To cancel one or more print jobs, you select the Cancel option. This prompt appears:

`Cancel which job? (*=All Jobs) 1`

Note that the number at the end of the prompt will correspond to the first number in your job list, and may not be 1. Numbering begins with the first print request that you issue after starting DrawPerfect. Once you exit, the first job will be number 1 the next time you use DrawPerfect.

In response to the `Cancel which job?` prompt, type the number that appears next to the job you want to cancel and then press Enter. Next, you will see this prompt in the Action area:

`Press "G" to restart, "C" to cancel`

and it means DrawPerfect is waiting for you to start the printer again by typing **G** for Go. It pauses here in case you need to remove the paper or adjust the printer after canceling the last print job. Once you type G, the printer will start again with the next print job.

To cancel all print jobs, type an **asterisk** in response to the `Cancel which job?` prompt. This prompt will appear:

`Cancel all print jobs? No (Yes)`

and the assumption will be no. Type **Y**. Soon all the print jobs will be canceled and the screen will change. The prompt `No Print jobs` will appear next to the status line.

> **Tip:** Most printers have some memory of their own, called a *printer buffer*. DrawPerfect may not be able to stop the printer or cancel a print job if the data has already been sent to your printer's buffer. Even if it does stop it, you may still need to clear this buffer. To do this, you can use the Initialize option on the main Print menu. When you select it, a prompt appears asking if you want to proceed with printer initialization. Select Yes.

To stop the printer temporarily, just select the **Stop** option from the Control Printer screen. After you fix the printer, type **G** to restart it.

Canceling Print Requests

1. Display the File menu and select Print.

   The main Print screen appears.

2. Select Control Printer.

   The Control Printer screen appears.

3. To cancel a print request, select Cancel and type the job number of the job you want to cancel (it appears under the heading `Job` in the Job List section of the screen). When you have reset the printer and are ready to print again, type G. To cancel all print jobs, type an asterisk and then type Y in response to the `Cancel all print jobs?` prompt.

Previewing the Printed Drawing

The screen version of a chart or drawing is not always an exact representation of the printed version. For example, text appears in outline on screen, but is solid black when printed (unless you have changed the default setting for Text Quality While Editing). DrawPerfect's View Drawing option lets you preview the printed version, an invaluable feature that can help you save paper if you find that your work isn't exactly what you expected. Also, it lets you view your work in a larger format, without all the menus, icons, and prompts that you see in the main DrawPerfect screen. We discussed View Drawing in Chapter 3, so we'll just review it briefly in this section.

The View Drawing option is on the main Print menu. To use it, display the **File** menu, select **Print**, and then select **View Drawing** from the main Print menu. Note that you cannot edit while in this screen. In fact, pressing almost any key returns you to the main Print menu! When you finish looking at the preview, press Enter (or almost any other key) to return to the Print menu or press Exit (F7) to bypass the Print screen and return to the main DrawPerfect screen.

If you have a color monitor, View Drawing displays your charts and drawings in color. Unless you are using a color printer, this is not really the way they will look when printed! Fortunately, DrawPerfect's Setup menu includes an option that you can use to change the display to black and white. When you do, colors will appear as patterns in the View Drawing screen, just as they do when printed. To use this option, display the **File** menu, select **Setup**, then select **Display**. Next, select **View Drawing in Black and White** and type **Y** and then press Exit (F7) to return to the drawing window.

Print Options

The Options section of the main Print menu includes several useful features. We discussed the Select Printer option earlier in this chapter, so we'll cover the others in this section.

You can use the Binding option to add extra blank space on the left side of the printed page if you plan to bind your material. To use it, select **Binding**, type the number in inches or decimals, and then press Enter.

You can use Number of Copies to print multiple copies of a chart or drawing. To use it, just select the option, type the number, and press Enter.

By default, the Graphics Quality option is set to *Medium*. You can change it to *High* to increase the printed quality of your graphics or to *Draft* to obtain a rough draft at a lower print quality. Increasing the graphics quality decreases printer speed.

Unless you have a color printer, when you print a chart or drawing whose screen version includes colors, they will be represented by patterns in the printed version. If you have used colors for text, sometimes the text pattern doesn't show up well, especially if you've used one of the lighter colors. To solve this problem, change the Text Prints Solid Black option to Yes and all text will be printed in black, even though it appears in color on your screen.

Once you have changed a print option, the change remains in effect until you either change it again or exit DrawPerfect. To change an option permanently, display the **File** menu, select **Setup**, then **Initial Settings**, then **Print Options**. Changes you make in this screen will remain in effect even after you exit DrawPerfect.

What You Have Learned

In this chapter, you've studied several methods that you can use to print your charts and drawings, and you learned how to control the printer and use several print options. You should now be familiar with the following:

- ▶ The File menu includes a Print option that brings up a full-screen Print menu.
- ▶ To print the chart or drawing currently in your drawing window, use the Print Drawing option on the Print menu.
- ▶ The Print Window option on the Print menu prints whatever is currently appearing in the drawing window. If you have used DrawPerfect's Zoom feature to enlarge a section of your drawing, Print Window prints this enlarged section.

▶ You can use the Drawing on Disk option on the main Print menu to print a DrawPerfect file, even if a different chart or drawing is currently in the drawing window.

▶ You can use the Print option on the List Files menu to print one or more DrawPerfect files from the disk without retrieving them into the drawing window.

▶ Each time you select Print Drawing or one of the other print methods, DrawPerfect assigns a job number to your request and places it in a job list where it waits its turn to be printed. To view the list of drawings waiting to be printed, cancel a print job, or stop the printer, you can use the Control Printer option on the main Print menu.

▶ When a printer refuses to start after you issue a print command, such as Print Drawing, don't ask it to print again. Instead, check for a loose cable, an on-line button that is currently switched off, or an incorrectly installed printer. DrawPerfect remembers all your print requests, and they remain in the job list until you get the printer working.

▶ The main Print menu includes options that you can use to change the binding width and add extra blank space on the left side of the printed page; to print multiple copies; to change the Graphics Quality option from Medium to High or Draft; and to print text that appears in color on screen (if you have a color monitor) in black instead of using a pattern.

Chapter 8

More About Business Graphs

In This Chapter

▶ *Pie charts*
▶ *Line charts*
▶ *Area charts*
▶ *Stacked bar charts*
▶ *Graph options: grid lines, 3-D, format, X-pie, data values, markers, fill styles*
▶ *Creating a chart using data in a spreadsheet*

In Chapter 2 you learned how to create, save, and print your first business graph, a bar chart. You also learned how to make some modifications to it, such as changing it to a line graph, moving the title, changing some of the data, rotating the Y-label, and enhancing it with the dog drawing from DrawPerfect's Figure Library. In this chapter we'll teach you how to create several other types of business graphs, including pie charts, line charts, area charts, and stacked bar charts. You'll also learn how to enhance your graphs with grid lines, a 3-dimensional effect, different formats for the numeric values on the Y-axis, different fill styles, and more. We'll finish by showing you how easy it is to create graphs using data from a spreadsheet such as PlanPerfect, Excel, or Lotus 1-2-3.

Pie Charts

Pie charts differ from all the other types of charts you can create in DrawPerfect because they represent only one set of data, such as total annual sales, and are designed to show what percent of the total each item in the set represents. Figure 8.1 shows an example. The set of data is 1989 sales for the bakery, broken down by product. You can tell with one glance which products were the most popular that year: cookies and cakes. Another example would be annual births in the United States, broken down by month. Each slice of the pie would represent total births in one month. Contrast these examples to the bar chart you created in Chapter 2, which represented four sets of data: 1986, 1987, 1988 and 1989 sales data for two pet products, biscuits and kibble. A pie chart would be totally inappropriate for that application because it could only display biscuits and kibble sales for one year.

Figure 8.1 **A pie chart showing annual sales data by product**

Creating a pie chart is just like creating a bar chart, except that you only enter one set of data in the Graph Data screen, and it all belongs in the first column. In the rest of this section, we'll teach you how to create the pie chart shown in Figure 8.1.

Begin with a clear drawing window. Display the **Draw** menu, select the **Chart** option, and then select **Pie** from the submenu that appears. You should see the Pie Chart icon in the Status box, and this prompt:

`Enter Set corner of chart area (twice for full page);`

If you want the pie chart to fill the entire page, just press Enter or the left mouse button twice. Otherwise, move the cursor to the position where you want the upper left corner of the pie chart and press Enter or the left mouse button. Then move the cursor to the lower right corner and press Enter or the left mouse button again.

Depending on how your version of DrawPerfect is set up, you will either be in DrawPerfect's Graph Edit screen looking at a sample pie chart, or in the Graph Data screen. If you're in the Graph Edit screen, you'll see the title *Sample Chart* and a pie chart with sample data for apples, oranges, peaches, and pears. You may remember from Chapter 2 that DrawPerfect provides this data to help you learn how to create a chart. If you see the Graph Data screen instead of the sample graph, it means you've used the Setup menu to prevent DrawPerfect from displaying this information (Appendix B includes a section about how to change this option).

Your next step is to enter the new data, titles, and legends. If you are in the Graph Edit menu, select the **Define** option to go to the Graph Data menu. Delete the sample data by pressing F1 or using the mouse to select the Clear option. Select **Yes** in response to the prompt that asks if you want to clear all current data. The next step (for everyone) is to type the titles, legend titles (Bread, Cake, etc.), and data shown in Figure 8.2. When you finish, your screen should be identical to Figure 8.2.

As we mentioned earlier, you can only type one set of data in a pie chart, and it all belongs in the first column. If you're still unclear about this, you may want to compare Figure 8.2 to Figure 2.6 in Chapter 2, where you entered four sets of data for a bar chart.

Chapter 8

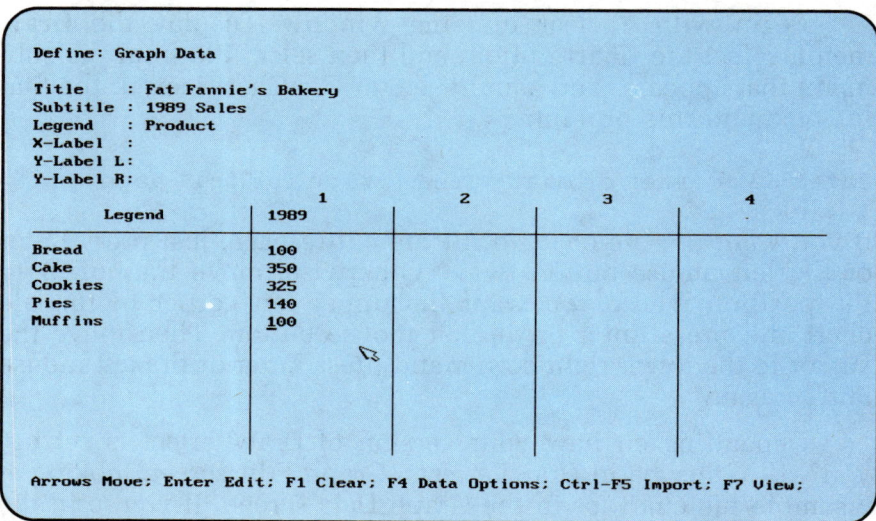

Figure 8.2 The Graph Data screen for the pie chart shown in Figure 8.1

> **Tip:** You can create two pie charts that will appear next to each other on the screen. To do this, type the first pie's data in column one, and type the second pie's data in column two.

Once you've entered the titles and data, select the **View** option to return to the Graph Edit screen and have a look at your pie chart. Wasn't that easy?

Creating a Pie Chart

1. Display the Draw menu, select the Chart option, then select Pie from the submenu that appears.

The Pie Chart icon appears in the Status box, and a prompt appears telling you to press Enter to set the corner of the chart area.

2. To designate the size of the chart, either press Enter or the left mouse button twice to fill the entire page, or move the cursor to the upper left corner and press Enter or the left mouse button. Next, move the cursor to the lower right corner and press Enter or the left mouse button.

    The Graph Edit screen and sample pie graph or the Graph Data screen appears (depending on how your version of DrawPerfect is set up).

3. If you are in the Graph Edit menu, select the Define option and then delete the sample data by pressing F1 and typing Y, or by using the mouse to select the Clear option and then Yes.

    You should be in the Graph Data menu and the sample data should be erased.

4. Type the data, titles, and legends for your pie chart. Be sure to type the data in the first column only. When you finish, select the View option to see the pie chart.

Using the Options Menu to Add a 3-Dimensional Effect and Data Values

Now let's have some fun with the pie, using the Options menu to make a few improvements. The first improvement will display a number next to each slice telling what percent of the whole pie that slice represents. The second will give the pie a 3-dimensional effect. You should be in the Graph Edit screen, where your new pie chart appears. Begin by selecting **Options**, which takes you to the Graph Options screen shown in Figure 8.3.

```
Graph Options:

 1 - Display Values                              No

 2 - Graph Orientation/3D                        Vertical, Normal

 3 - Fill Style                                  Both

 4 - Proportional Pies                           No

 5 - Bar Configuration                           Normal

 6 - Representation Line                         Lines Only
                   Scatter                       Markers Only

 7 - Display the Y Axes Separately               No

 8 - Alternate X Names                           No

 9 - Axes            Type      Scaling    Stack  Gridlines  From zero  Format
     Y Axis Left     Linear    Automatic  No     No         No         General
     Y Axis Right    Linear    Automatic  No     No         No         General
     X Axis          Linear    Automatic  N/A    No         No         General

Selection: 0
```

Figure 8.3 The Graph Options screen

Select the first option, **Display Values**, and change it to **Yes**. Next, select **Graph Orientation/3D**. You'll see this prompt:

`1 Vertical; 2 Horizontal: 0`

Select **Vertical**, which is the current orientation. The prompt changes to:

`1 Normal; 2 3-Dimensional: 0`

Select the second option, **3-Dimensional**. Now press Enter or the right mouse button to return to the Graph Edit screen and see the results. Ours appear in Figure 8.4.

Notice that some of the values in parentheses are too far away from the pie slices they represent, and some are actually on the pie. You may remember using the Move option in Chapter 2 to move the Y-axis label, which had disappeared off the top of the screen. Here you can use Move to reposition these errant values. Select **Move** and you'll see a letter next to each item in the pie chart. Select the letter of the item you want to move, use the mouse or Arrow keys to reposition the item, then press the Spacebar or right mouse button to drop it. Repeat for each item that you want to move, and then press Enter or the right mouse button to redraw the screen.

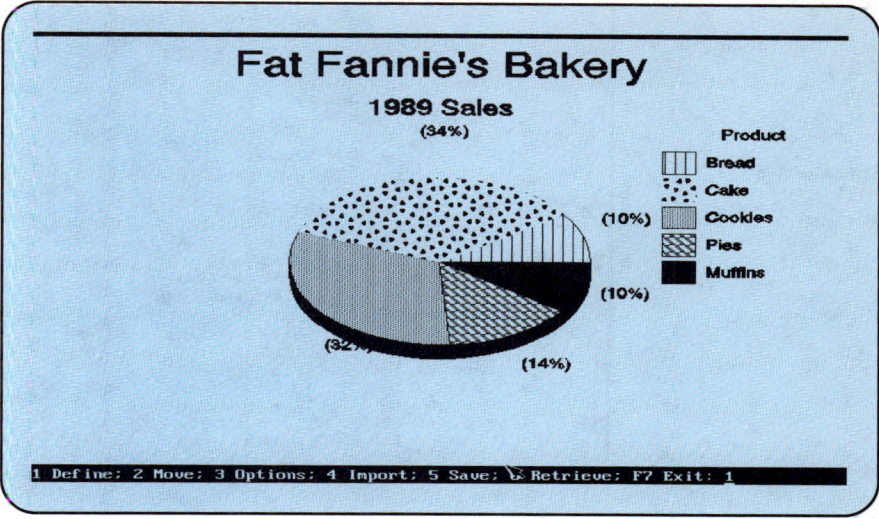

Figure 8.4 A 3-dimensional pie with data values displayed for each slice

Exploding a Slice of the Pie

Another fun effect is to blow out the largest slice of the pie so it moves away from the rest of the pie and really stands out. You can't explode a slice unless you change the Graph Orientation back to Normal, so that will be your first step. Select **Options**, then **Graph Orientation**, then **Vertical** and **Normal**. Press Enter or the right mouse button to see the pie again.

To explode a pie slice, select **Define** and then select **Data Options** from the menu line (or press F4). This takes you to the Graph Data Options screen shown in Figure 8.5, which should be familiar from Chapter 2. Move the cursor into the Cookies row and place it in the Type column, as shown by the pointing arrow in Figure 8.5. Your cursor should be on the word *Pie*. Press Enter or the left mouse button and you'll see this menu at the bottom of the screen:

```
1 Pie; 2 XPie; 3 Bar; 4 Area; 5 Line; 6 Scatter; 7 Hi-Lo;
8 None: 3
```

Select **XPie**. Now return to the Graph Edit screen to see your pie by pressing F7 or selecting the View option with the mouse.

Chapter 8

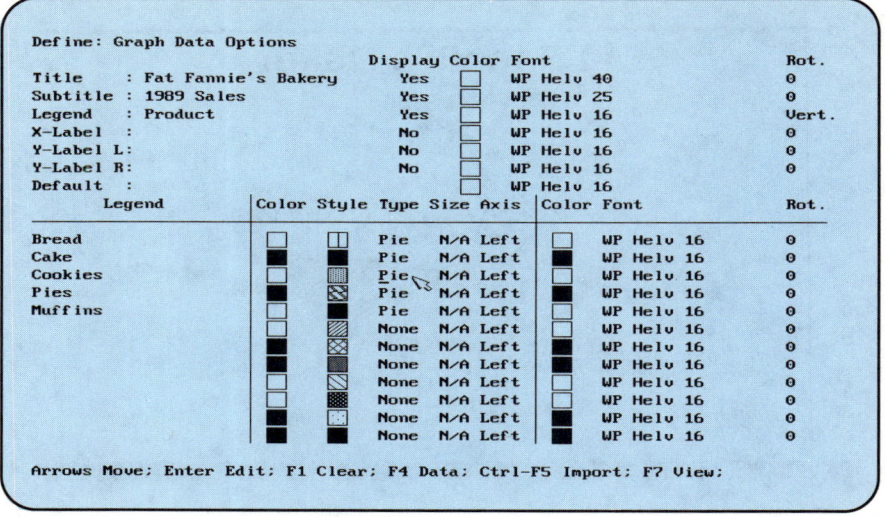

Figure 8.5 Using the Graph Data Options screen to explode a slice of the pie

Line Charts

Line charts are often used to represent data that changes over a period of time, such as monthly, quarterly, or annually. The lines connect each numeric value in a data set, and reveal the general trend of change. They also imply a carryover of the data through the time period. When there is more than one set of data, a separate line is used for each one. For example, Figure 8.6 shows a line chart that graphs two sets of data for a tire company: monthly inventory for the first three months of 1988 and for 1989. Compare the two lines and you can easily see that there was more inventory in 1989 than in 1988. The chart also suggests a trend: Inventory is high in January and decreases gradually throughout the quarter.

To create the line chart shown in Figure 8.6, follow the same initial steps that you used to create a pie chart in the previous section. Begin by displaying the **Draw** menu and selecting **Chart** and then select **Line** from the chart submenu. You should see the Line Chart icon in the Status box, and the prompt that

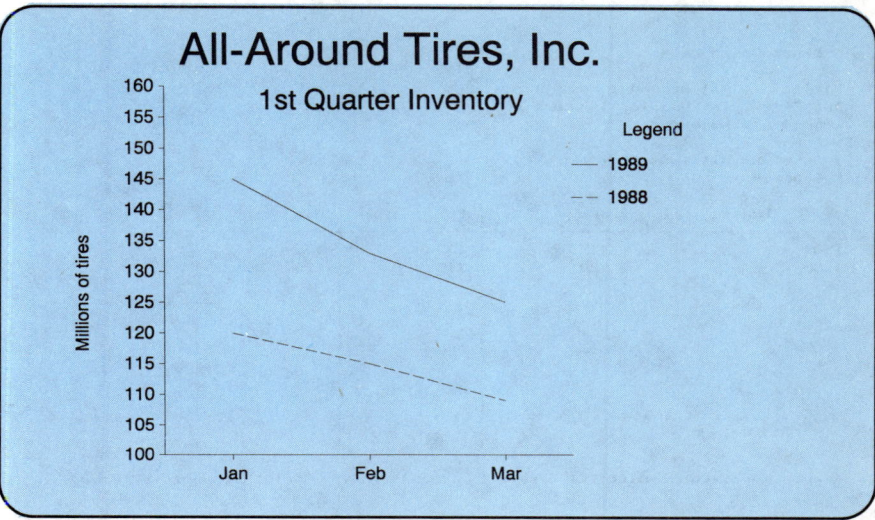

Figure 8.6   The All-Around Tires line chart

tells you to press Enter to set the corner of the chart area. Use the Enter key or mouse (as described in the previous section) to designate the size of the chart. After you do that, either the Graph Edit screen or the Graph Data screen will appear. If you are in the Graph Edit screen with a sample chart, your next step is to select the **Define** option, then press F1 and type **Y** to erase the sample data. Now type the data, titles, and legends shown in Figure 8.7. When you finish typing them, select the **View** option to see your new line chart.

> **Tip:** Once you've drawn a line chart, you can easily change it to an Area, Pie, Bar, XPie, Scatter, or HiLo chart by selecting the Type option on the Graph Data Options menu and choosing one of the other types from the menu that appears. Incidentally, if you select Pie and have two sets of data, you'll see two pie charts side-by-side.

Chapter 8

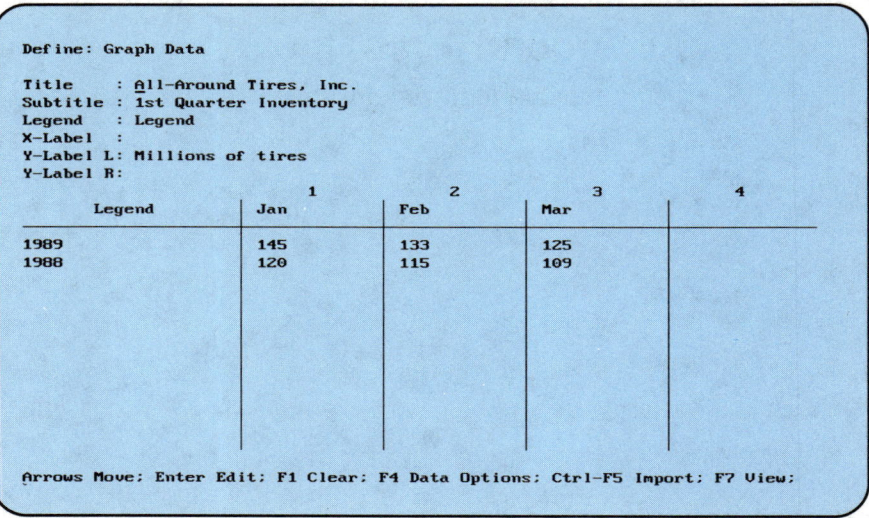

Figure 8.7 *The Graph Data screen for the All-Around Tires line chart*

Creating a Line Chart

1. Display the Draw menu, select the Chart option, then select Line from the submenu that appears.

    The Line Chart icon appears in the Status box, and a prompt appears telling you to press Enter to set the corner of the chart area.

2. To designate the size of the chart, either press Enter or the left mouse button twice to fill the entire page, or move the cursor to the upper left corner and press Enter or the left mouse button. Next, move the cursor to the lower right corner and press Enter or the left mouse button.

    The Graph Edit screen and sample line graph or the Graph Data screen appears (depending on how your version of DrawPerfect is set up).

3. If you are in the Graph Edit menu, select the Define option and then delete the sample data by pressing F1 and typing Y, or by using the mouse to select the Clear option and Yes.

   You should be in the Graph Data menu and the sample data should be erased.

4. Type the data, titles, and legends for your line chart. When you finish, select the View option to see the chart.

Grid Lines

Sometimes it's helpful to include grid lines in a chart. For example, in Figure 8.8 we used the Type option on the Graph Data Options menu to change the All-Around Tires line graph to a bar graph and then added grid lines. Notice the grid lines are aligned with the tick marks on each axis, such as the numbers 120, 125, 130, and 135 on the Y-axis. You can display horizontal or vertical grid lines, or use both simultaneously. For horizontal lines, you select grid lines for the Y-axis. For vertical ones, you select grid lines for the X-axis. For both horizontal and vertical lines, select grid lines for both axes.

To draw grid lines, select **Options** (assuming you are still in the Graph Edit screen looking at your line chart). The Graph Options menu shown in Figure 8.3 appears. Select the last option, **Axes**, and you'll see this menu at the bottom of the screen:

`1 Y Axis Left; 2 Y Axis Right; 3 X Axis: 0`

Although you can have three axes in a graph, yours only has two, an X Axis and Y Axis Left. (See Figure 2.13 in Chapter 2 for an example of why you would want to include a second Y-axis.) Now look in the Gridlines column and notice that all three entries are set to No. To change them, select the first option, **Y Axis Left**, and then the **Grid Lines** option. As soon as

Chapter 8

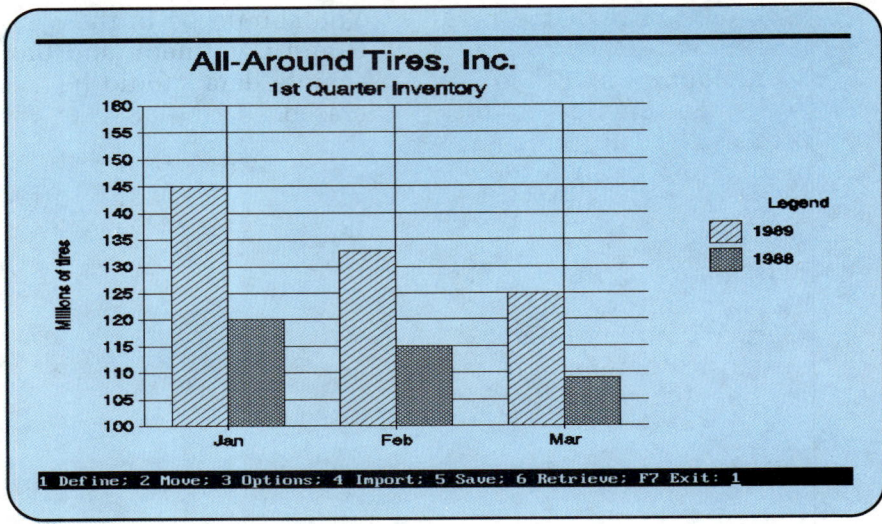

Figure 8.8   The All-Around Tires bar chart with grid lines

you select the Grid Lines option, the Gridlines entry for that row changes from No to Yes. Press Enter or click the right mouse button, and then select **X Axis** and change Gridlines to **Yes**. Press Enter or the right mouse button three times to return to the Graph Edit menu. Note that we used the Move option to move the subtitle up and away from the grids.

Formatting the Numbers on the Y-Axis

When you were using the Graph Options menu to include grid lines in your chart, you may have noticed another of the selections under the Axes option: *Format*. You can use Format to change the appearance of the numbers on the Y-axis (but you can only use it to format the X-axis if you are creating a scatter chart). For example, if you change the format to *Currency*, instead of displaying numbers like 10, 20, and 30, DrawPerfect displays $10.00, $20.00, and $30.00. The other choices are *General, Integer, Fixed, Percent, Scientific, Comma,* and *Other*.

To use the Format option, select **Options** from the Graph Edit screen where your chart appears. Next, select **Axes** and then **Y Axis Left**. This menu line appears:

```
1 Type; 2 Scaling; 3 Stack; 4 Grid Lines; 5 Graph From
Zero; 6 Format: 0
```

Select the last option, **Format**. The menu line changes to display these options:

```
1 General; 2 Currency; 3 Integer; 4 Fixed; 5 Percent;
6 Scientific; 7 Comma; 0 Other: 0
```

If you select General, Currency, or Integer, this prompt will appear:

```
Divisor Value:
```

followed by a number like 1 or 100. For display purposes, the numbers on your Y-axis will be divided by the number you type in response to this prompt. For example, if the numbers on your Y-axis are 100, 200, and 300 and you type 100 here, they will be displayed as 1, 2, and 3 when you use the General format.

If you select Fixed, Percent, Scientific, or Comma, you will see this prompt:

```
Enter number of digits: (0-15)
```

followed by a number like 0 or 2. After you type a number between 0 and 15 (and press Enter), the Divisor Value prompt will appear. After you type a divisor value, press Enter or the right mouse button three times to see the chart in the Graph Edit screen.

The last Format option, Other, is more complex than the other seven because it leads to several more menus. You use the first one to select a method for decimal placement: *Floating*, *Fixed*, or *Scientific*. If you select Fixed or Scientific, a prompt appears requesting the number of digits. Type a number and press Enter. The next menu asks how you want to display negative numbers: with minus signs, parentheses, or CR/DR symbols. Select one of these and another menu appears providing two formatting options, *Currency* and *Percent*. After you select Currency or Percent, a prompt appears asking if you want to include commas. After you select Yes or No, a prompt appears asking for the Divisor Value. After you type a divisor value, press Enter or the right mouse button three times to see the chart in the Graph Edit screen.

Chapter 8

Adding Markers for the Data Points

As you can see from Figure 8.6, DrawPerfect's line charts consist of lines that connect invisible numeric values (from the Graph Data screen), but the numeric values themselves aren't represented. Occasionally, you may want to include markers showing exactly where each data point is located on the Y-axis, as shown in Figure 8.9 (we thickened the lines so you could see them and the markers more easily). To do this, you can use the *Representation* option on the Graph Options menu. You can also use this option to exclude the lines altogether, so that only the markers appear in the chart.

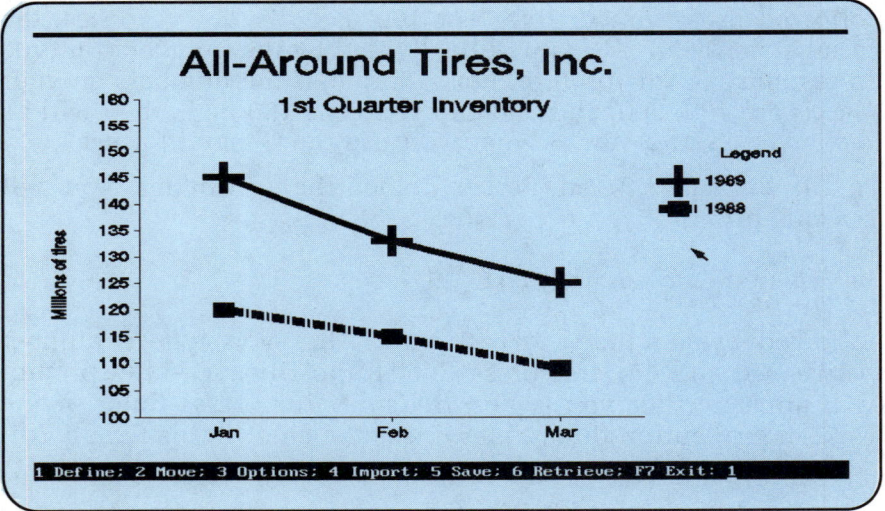

Figure 8.9 The All-Around Tires line chart with markers

To add markers to a line chart, select **Options** from the Graph Edit menu. The Graph Options menu shown in Figure 8.3 appears. Select the sixth option, **Representation**. This prompt appears:

`1 Lines; 2 Scatter: 0`

Since you are using a line chart (not a scatter chart), select **Lines**. The prompt changes to:

```
1 Lines Only; 2 Lines And Markers; 3 Markers Only: 0
```

Select **Lines and Markers** and press Enter or the right mouse button to return to the Graph Edit screen and see your line chart with markers. It should resemble Figure 8.9. Notice that DrawPerfect uses a different style of markers for each line, such as boxes, asterisks, dots, and plus signs.

Stacked Bar Charts

A stacked bar chart is useful when you want to show cumulative totals for two or more sets of data. The data sets are stacked on top of each other so you can tell at a glance the combined total. For example, the chart in Figure 8.10 shows the change in duck populations for the years 1961 through 1985. The chart shows how much both types of ducks have been declining since the peak year of 1971. It also shows that the mallard population has been consistently higher than the pintail population.

To create a stacked bar chart, follow the same steps you use to create a line chart, except select **Stacked Bar** instead of Line from the menu that appears after you display the **Draw** menu and select **Chart**.

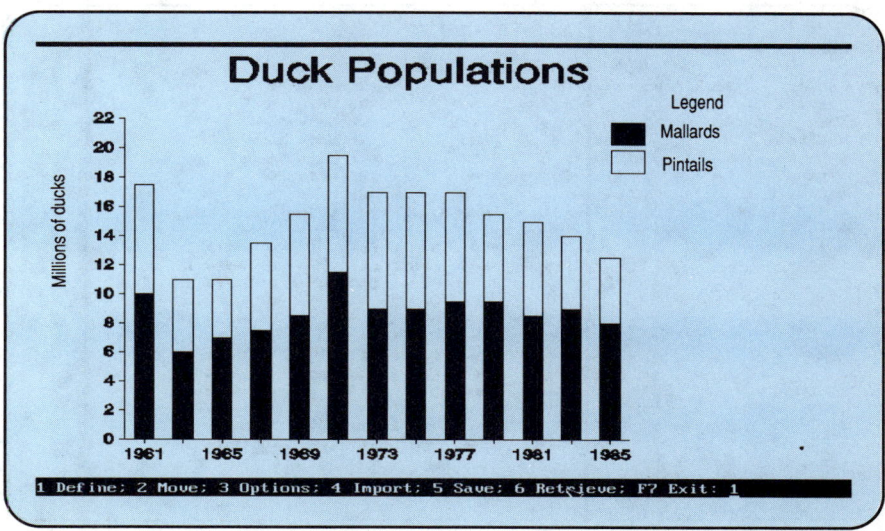

Figure 8.10 *A stacked bar chart*

Changing the Fill Style and Colors for the Bars

In the stacked bar chart displayed in Figure 8.10, we changed the fill patterns and colors so the two data sets would be very distinct. DrawPerfect provides 64 patterns and 256 colors that you can use to change the appearance of your bar charts, stacked bar charts, area charts, or pie charts.

To change the color or pattern, you use the Graph Data Options menu. If you are in the Graph Edit screen, you can get there by selecting the **Define** option. Next, you'll either see the Graph Data screen or the Graph Data Options screen, depending on which one you were last using. If you see the Graph Data screen, either press F4 or select **Data Options** from the menu that appears at the bottom of the screen. Now move the cursor into the Color or Style column for the first data item you want to change, and then press Enter or the left mouse button. A list of colors or patterns (style) appears at the bottom of the screen. For instance, Figure 8.11 shows the fill patterns that appeared when we selected Style. Notice that there is only room for 16 of them on the screen. To see more, select **Next** (or type N). When you find the one you want to use, type the number next to it and press Enter, or select it with the mouse. To return to the Graph Edit screen and view the changes to your graph, select **View** or press F7.

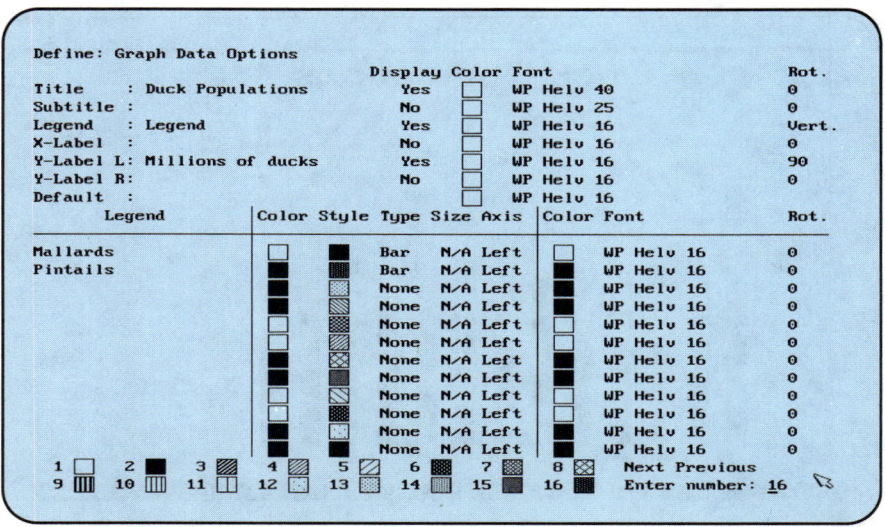

Figure 8.11   Using the Style option to select a fill pattern

Area Charts

Area charts are similar to line charts in that a line is drawn for each set of data. However, the area under each line is filled in with a different pattern or color (or both) and the chart represents total volume, not trends. Area charts display cumulative values, like stacked bar charts. Each data set is stacked on top of the other, and the top line shows the total of all the values. For example, the chart in Figure 8.12 shows total emissions of hydrocarbons (which create smog), broken down to compare the difference between cars built before 1980 and those built after 1980. As you can see, cars built before 1980 produce much higher levels of hydrocarbons. The chart suggests that smog levels will decrease significantly by 2000, as these cars wear out and are taken off the road.

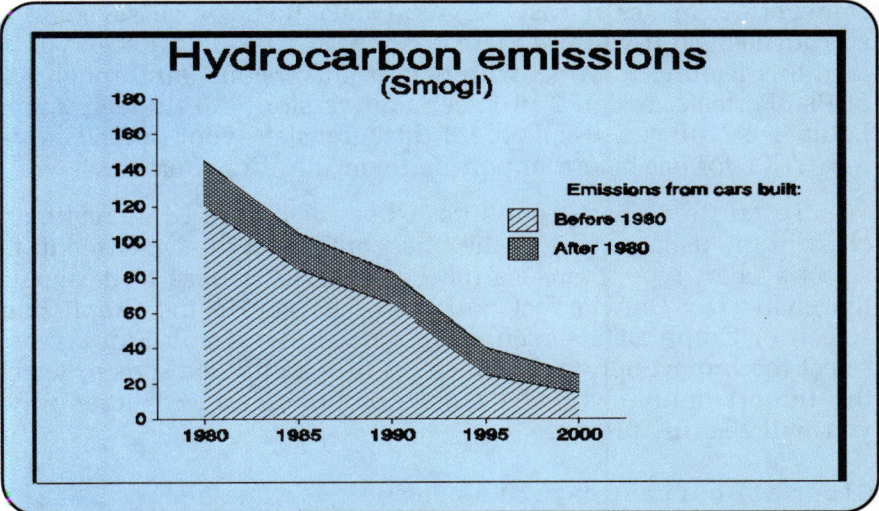

Figure 8.12   An area chart showing hydrocarbon emissions

The data that we used for the area chart in Figure 8.12 appears in the following chart. Notice that the 1980 value for pre-1980 cars is 120, and it is 25 for cars built after 1980. Together they total 145, which is the value corresponding to the top line of the area chart for 1980.

	1980	1985	1990	1995
Before 1980	120	85	65	25
After 1980	25	20	18	15

The steps that you use to create an area chart are identical to the ones you use to create a line chart, except that you select Area instead of Line from the menu that appears after you display the Draw menu and select Chart.

Creating a Chart Using Data in a Spreadsheet

DrawPerfect makes it easy to graph data that you've saved in a spreadsheet, so if you use PlanPerfect, Lotus 1-2-3, or Excel, you'll love this feature! It works with data from versions 3.0 through 5.0 of PlanPerfect, version 2 of Excel, and versions 1.0 through 2.2 of Lotus 1-2-3. If you use Lotus 3, just translate your spreadsheets into WK1 format before importing them into DrawPerfect.

To create a chart from spreadsheet data, begin by creating a chart in the usual way: Use the Chart option on the Draw menu to select a chart type, then use the Enter key or mouse to designate the chart size. DrawPerfect will then take you to the Graph Edit screen or Graph Data screen. If you are in the Graph Edit screen, select the **Import** option. If you are in the Graph Data screen, select the **Import** option with the mouse or press Ctrl-F5. Either way, you will see this prompt:

```
Clear all current data? No (Yes)
```

Select **Yes**. The screen changes and displays the Import Data menu shown in Figure 8.13. Your next step is to select **Filename**. This prompt appears:

```
File to be Imported:
```

Type the full name (including the three-character extension, such as .WK1) of the PlanPerfect, Lotus, or Excel file that you want to use and press Enter. If the file is not in the current directory, you'll also have to type the path so DrawPerfect will know where to find it. For instance, to import a Lotus 1-2-3 file named *SALES89.WK1* that is in a subdirectory named *LOTUS,* you would type this name:

C:\LOTUS\SALES89.WK1

If you don't understand how to use path names and directions, see Chapter 9 for more information.

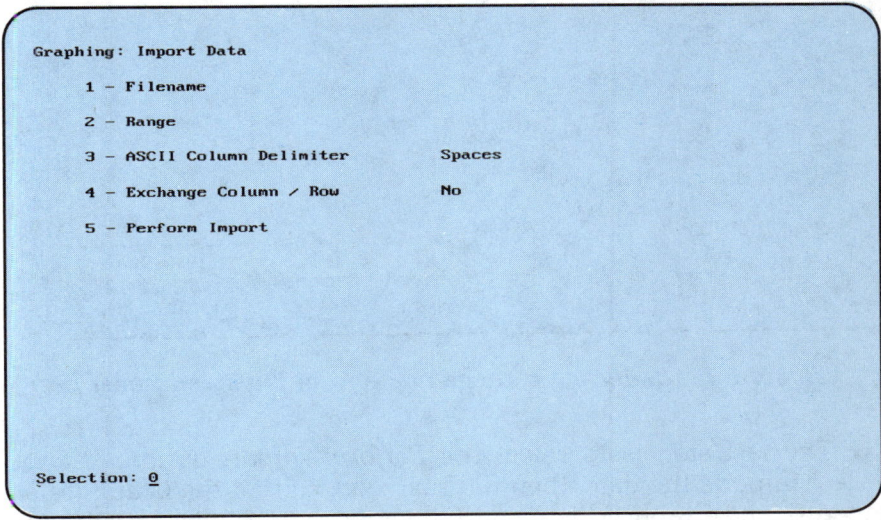

Figure 8.13   The Import Data menu

DrawPerfect assumes that you want to use all the data in the spreadsheet. If not, you can use the *Range* option to restrict it to a rectangular block of cells. When you select Range, this prompt appears:

Enter Range:

followed by the cell numbers DrawPerfect assumes you want to use, such as A1.. E8. At this point you can type a different range, separating the first and last cell numbers by one or two periods or a colon, such as A1.G45, B2..S30, or C5:M25. Alternatively, if you used your particular spreadsheet's special command to assign a range name for the cells, you can type the range name. If you aren't sure of the range names, press the List Files key (F5). A box appears showing the ranges in your spreadsheet. It should resemble Figure 8.14. To select one of the range names, just move the cursor bar onto it and press Enter or select it with the mouse.

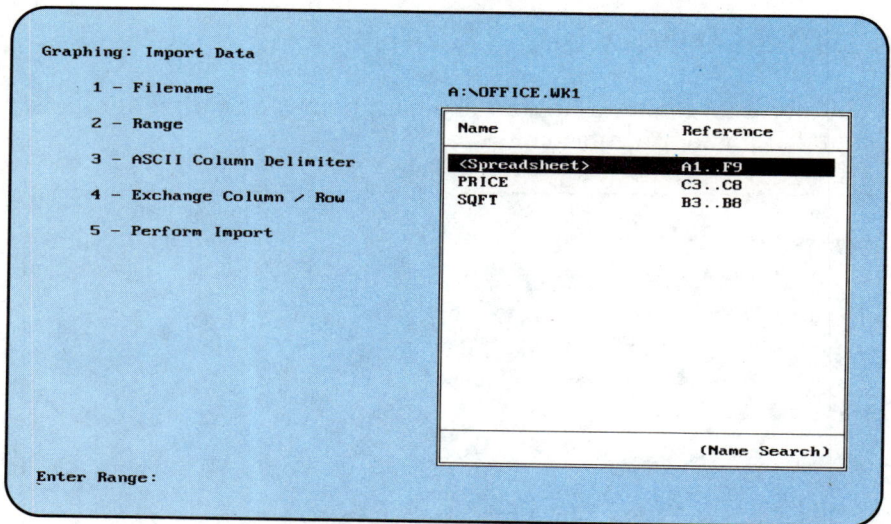

Figure 8.14 Selecting a range name from the spreadsheet

The last step is to select the *Perform Import* option. DrawPerfect imports the data, then returns you to either the Graph Data screen or the Graph Edit screen (depending on which screen you were using when you selected Import). If you are in the Graph Data screen, select the View option to see the resulting chart. In either case, after viewing it you'll want to select Define to return to the Graph Data screen and change or add an appropriate title, legend, and legend titles. When you finish, you can save it like any other DrawPerfect chart.

Creating a Chart from Spreadsheet Data

1. Use the Chart option on the Draw menu to select a chart type and then use the Enter key or mouse to designate the chart size.

    DrawPerfect will then take you to the Graph Edit screen or Graph Data screen.

2. If you are in the Graph Edit screen, select the Import option. If you are in the Graph Data screen, select the Import option with the mouse or press Ctrl-F5.

   A prompt will appear asking if you want to clear all the current data.

3. Select Yes.

   The screen changes and the Import Data menu appears.

4. Select Filename.

   A prompt appears asking for the name of the file to be imported.

5. Type the full name and extension (and path if it is not in the current directory) of the spreadsheet file and press Enter.

6. If you want to restrict the data to a specific range, select the Range option. If not, go to the last step.

   A prompt appears asking you to enter the range.

7. Type the range or range name, or press F5 and select a range name from the list that appears.

8. Select the Perform Import option.

   DrawPerfect imports the data, and you return to either the Graph Data screen or the Graph Edit screen (depending on whether you had Sample Data when you began). If you are in the Graph Data screen, select the View option to see the chart. You may wish to select Define to change or add an appropriate title, legend, and legend titles. ☐

Chapter 8

What You Have Learned

In this chapter, you've learned how to create pie charts, line charts, area charts, and stacked bar charts; how to enhance them using options such as grid lines, 3-D, format, markers, and fill styles; and how to graph data from a spreadsheet. You should now be familiar with the following:

▶ Pie charts can only include one set of data, such as total annual sales broken down by product. Creating a pie chart is almost identical to creating a bar chart, except that you select Pie from the Chart submenu and type all the data in the first column.

▶ You can use DrawPerfect's Options menu to enhance a pie chart with a 3-dimensional effect, or to add values showing what percent of the whole pie each slice represents.

▶ You can use the Graph Data Options menu to explode one slice of a pie chart, so that it stands out from the rest of the pie.

▶ Line charts represent data that changes over a time period, such as quarterly or annually, and reveal general trends. Creating a line chart is almost identical to creating a bar chart, except that you select Line from the Chart submenu.

▶ Once you have created a chart, you can use the Type option on the Graph Data Options menu to experiment with it, changing it to any of the following types: Pie, Bar, Area, Scatter, Line, or HiLo.

▶ You can use the Graph Options menu to add grid lines to your horizontal or vertical axis, or to both axes.

▶ You can change the appearance of the numbers on the Y-axis using the Axes Format option on the Graph Options menu. You can change the format to General, Currency, Integer, Fixed, Percent, Scientific, Comma, or Other.

▶ To include markers that show each data point in a line chart, you can use the Representation option on the Graph Options menu.

- ▶ Use a stacked bar chart when you want to display cumulative totals for two or more sets of data. Creating a stacked bar chart is identical to creating a bar or line chart, except that after selecting Chart from the Draw menu, you select Stacked Bar.

- ▶ You can use the Graph Data Options menu to change the fill style and colors for your bar, pie, or area charts. You can select from among 64 patterns and 256 colors.

- ▶ In an area chart, each data set is represented by an area filled in with a different pattern or color. Area charts show cumulative values, and each data set is stacked on top of the other. The steps that you use to create an area chart are nearly identical to the ones you use to create a line or bar chart, except that after selecting Chart from the Draw menu, you select Area.

- ▶ You can create a graph from data saved in a spreadsheet such as PlanPerfect, Excel, or Lotus using the Import option on the Graph Edit screen or Graph Data screen. You can import all of the data in the spreadsheet, or a named range.

Chapter 9
File Management

In This Chapter

- ▶ The List Files screen
- ▶ Viewing a file without retrieving it from the disk
- ▶ How to retrieve a file if you don't know the exact name
- ▶ Making backup copies of your drawings and charts
- ▶ How to delete, move, and rename files
- ▶ Printing several files in one command
- ▶ How to create and use directories

All DrawPerfect files have to be stored on a disk, and whether you use a hard disk or floppy disk for this purpose, you will soon need help managing them. For instance, if you use a hard disk, there is usually enough space for you to accumulate thousands of files on it. However, unless you divide it into separate areas called *directories*, you can only store 512 files. Even if you do subdivide it, at some point you may find that your hard disk is full. If this happens, you will want to delete old files that you never use or archive files to a floppy disk that you aren't currently using but may need in the future. Also, since hard disks often fail and all files are destroyed, it is imperative that you make backup copies of all important files. DrawPerfect can help you with all of these tasks, and much more, through the List Files menu.

List Files is a remarkable collection of tools that you can use to perform important file management tasks such as creating directories, changing the default directory, moving a group of files to another directory, and copying several files from a hard disk to a floppy disk. You can also use it to retrieve, print, copy, rename, or delete files. Many of these tools can be used in place of the equivalent DOS commands (Disk Operating System), which are much harder to use. Also, tools such as copy, move, and delete are not restricted to DrawPerfect files, so you can use them to manage files from your other programs. As you find yourself creating more and more files on your disk, we think you will come to agree that List Files is indispensable.

If you use WordPerfect, you may already be familiar with the List Files tools. If you're not, you'll benefit doubly from reading this chapter because the same tools are available in WordPerfect, and you should be taking advantage of them!

The List Files Screen

To display the List Files screen, you can either use the List Files key (F5) or display the File menu and select the List Files option. Here's how:

 Press List Files (F5) or type **F L**.

 Drag the cursor onto **File**, click the left button, and hold it. Drag the cursor onto **List Files** and release the button.

A Dir prompt appears in the lower left corner of the screen. It may be similar to this one:

`Dir C:\DR10\DRAWINGS\*.*`

Let's analyze the prompt. *Dir* is a command that comes from DOS, the disk operating system, and it stands for *Directory*. When you use it, Dir displays a list of all files in the default directory. Whenever you save or retrieve a file, DrawPerfect uses the default directory unless you specify another one when typing the file name. Since the subject of directories and subdirectories is often confusing to beginners, let's explore it.

A directory is a subdivision of the disk. All disks, whether hard or floppy, have a root directory. DOS automatically creates the root directory when you format the disk, and you can divide it into one or more divisions called *directories,* where you store a group of related files. You can further subdivide each directory into one or more divisions called subdirectories. The whole structure resembles an upside-down tree, and each directory is like a branch of the tree. Figure 9.1 illustrates this concept.

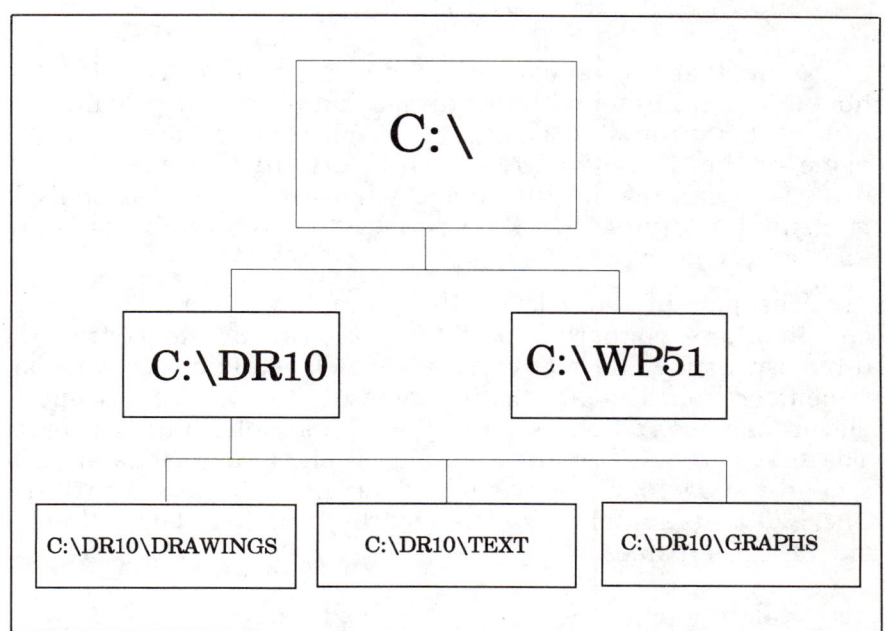

Figure 9.1 A disk divided into directories and subdirectories

The root directory is the top level and is always represented by the backslash symbol (\). In Figure 9.1 there are two directories below the root directory: *DR10* and *WP51.* The DR10 directory has three subdirectories of its own, *Drawings, Text,* and *Graphs.* The diagram also shows each subdirectory's *path,* the route from the root directory to the subdirectory. For instance, the path to DRAWINGS is C:\DR10\DRAWINGS. The drive and

Chapter 9

directory names in a path are always separated by backslashes. You must specify the path when performing operations such as copy and move.

> **Tip:** Before you can use a new disk, you must format it using the DOS Format command. This is a one-time process that prepares the new disk to accept the files you save. Formatting completely erases any files that may exist on a disk, so be very careful when you format. If you turn on your computer and see a C prompt or if a menu appears, the disk has already been formatted, so don't do it again!

Now that we've clarified the subject of directories (we hope), let's continue with our discussion of the Dir prompt. The rest of the prompt, C:\DR10\DRAWINGS*.*, tells you the name of the default drive and directory. In this example, the drive is C: and the default directory is DRAWINGS. DRAWINGS is a subdirectory of DR10, which is a directory one level below the root directory, C:\.

The pair of asterisks in the prompt represent file names, and they are wonderful tools that you can use to restrict the directory listing. Bear with us and we'll explain. As you may remember from Chapter 2, file names can contain from one to eleven characters (letters and/or numbers) split into two parts. The first part can contain from one to eight characters, and the second part, which is optional, can contain from one to three. The two parts are always separated by a period. The following are valid file names:

    cookies.wpg   barchar1.wpg
    films   films.wpg
    orbital.gdf   orbital.wpg

File names cannot include a blank space or any of the following symbols:

    * ? < > : ; = [ ] / \ " + = ,

For instance, this name would not be valid: films 1.wpg.

Back to the asterisks: The first asterisk represents the first one to eight characters in a file name, such as *cookies* and *barchar1* in the examples. The second asterisk represents the last one to three characters, such as *wpg* and *gdf*. Therefore, when you use the Dir command with the two asterisks, it will list all file names in the subdirectory. You can restrict the listing in a variety of ways. For example, to display only files that end in wpg you could change the prompt to:

`Dir C:\DR10\DRAWINGS\*.wpg`

or you could restrict it to files names that begin with the letter F by typing it this way:

Dir C:\DR10\DRAWINGS\f*.*

So now that you know all about the Dir command, go ahead and use it to display all files in your default directory.

 Press Enter.

 Click the right button.

You should see a screen that resembles Figure 9.2. However, since you have different files on your disk, your screen won't look exactly the same as ours.

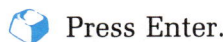

Figure 9.2 The List Files screen

The screen is divided into a header area, a file list, and a menu line at the bottom. The *header area* is the first two lines at the top of the screen. The first line tells you the current date and time (if your computer keeps track of it correctly!) and the current disk drive and directory. The second line tells you the file size of the drawing on the main DrawPerfect screen, if there is one; the amount of free space available on your disk; the total number of files in the directory, and the amount of disk space they use. Let's study this header:

```
02/20/90 14:33        Directory E:\DR10\DRAWINGS\*.*
Drawing size:      20 Free: 18,806,784 Used: 634,743
                      Files: 130
```

The first line tells you:

▶ The date is 02/20/90.
▶ The time is 14:33 (or 2:33 p.m.).
▶ The current directory is DRAWINGS, it is on drive E, and it is a subdirectory of DR10.

The second line tells you:

▶ The drawing window in the main DrawPerfect screen is blank (the *Drawing size* is 20 because of the file header information that DrawPerfect will add to any new file you create).
▶ 18,806,784 bytes of free space remain on drive E.
▶ The files in this directory (DRAWINGS) use 634,743 bytes on drive E.
▶ There are 130 files in the DRAWINGS directory.

The *file list* includes all file names, directories. and subdirectories, including two directory names that we will explain in the next paragraph: <CURRENT> <DIR> and <PARENT> <DIR>. Directory and subdirectory names always come first in the list, such as <CURRENT> <DIR>, <PARENT> <DIR>, and <BOOK> <DIR> in Figure 9.2. The file names follow. File names that begin with numbers come first, and the others are in alphabetical order from left to right, separated by a line. For instance, in the List Files screen shown in Figure 9.2, there are three directories at the top of the list: CURRENT, PARENT, and BOOK. The file names are next. Notice that the first two begin with numbers, 3DGRAPH.WPG and 8BALL.WPG. The others are in alphabetical order: ARCH.WPG on the right, then AUSBULLE.WPG on the left, BABY.WPG on the right, BABYCHAR.WPG on the left, BEN.WPG on the right, etc.

In addition to the file names and extensions (the last three characters following the period in the file name), the display includes each file's size and the date and time it was last saved. For instance, the GAZEBO.WPG file in our list is 773 bytes in size, and was created on 2/16/90 at 18:19 (6:19 p.m.).

Notice the small triangle at the bottom of the screen, under the line that separates the two sides. This tells us there are too many files to display on one screen. To view the others, we could press Page Down a few times or click the left mouse button and hold it while dragging the mouse down to the end.

> **Tip:** In the List Files screen, pressing the Home key twice and then the Down Arrow key moves the cursor to the last file in the list. Pressing the Home key twice followed by the Up Arrow key moves the cursor to the top, onto <PARENT> <DIR>. Pressing the Home key, then the Down Arrow key or Up Arrow key moves the cursor to the top or bottom of the screen.

Let's digress for a minute to clear up a common misunderstanding about the <CURRENT> <DIR> and <PARENT> <DIR> notation. <CURRENT> <DIR> means current directory and <PARENT> <DIR> means parent directory. The current directory is the directory whose file list you are now viewing. The parent directory is the directory one level above the current directory, if there is one. In Figure 9.2 the current directory is DRAWINGS and the parent directory is DR10. If the current directory were DR10, the parent would be E:\. If the current directory were E:\, the parent directory and current directory would be the same (since E:\ is the top level).

Here's where the confusion arises: Many users think that all files on the right side of the screen are in the parent directory, and all the ones on the left side are in the current directory, but it just isn't so! All displayed files are in the current directory. To list the files in the parent directory, you can place the cursor onto the name <PARENT> <DIR> and select the Look option. In the next section, we'll show you how.

Chapter 9

Q Displaying a List of All Files in the Default Directory

1. Press List Files (F5) or type F L. Mouse users can drag the cursor onto File, click the left button and hold it, then highlight List Files and release the button.

   A Dir prompt appears in the lower left corner of the screen.

2. Press Enter. Mouse users can click the right button.

   A directory listing appears. To exit List Files, you can press the Spacebar or click the right mouse button. □

Using Look to View the Contents of a Directory

When the cursor is highlighting a directory name, the Look option allows you to look at the List Files screen for that directory. When the cursor is highlighting a file name, you can look at the file without retrieving it. Let's use it to view the contents of your parent directory. Assuming that you are still in the List Files screen, with the cursor highlighting <CURRENT> <DIR>:

Press the Right Arrow key once and type **L** or 6 (or press Enter, since 6 is the default option that will be used when you press Enter).

Drag the cursor onto <**PARENT**> <**DIR**>, click the left button to highlight it, then drag the cursor onto **Look** in the menu line and click the left button again.

A Dir prompt appears. Ours was:

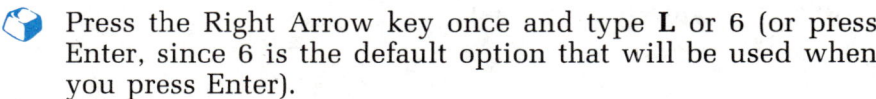

since our parent directory is DR10. A warning: If your prompt shows only the root directory, such as Dir C:*.*, your current and parent directories are the same, so your file list won't change when you perform this exercise. If your prompt includes a directory, such as Dir C:\DR10*.*, then you will see a different set of files in your parent directory. If so, go ahead and try it.

 Press Enter.

 Click the right button.

File Management

There you are! A copy of our screen appears in Figure 9.3. Notice the directory prompt in the header, indicating that this is E:\DR10.

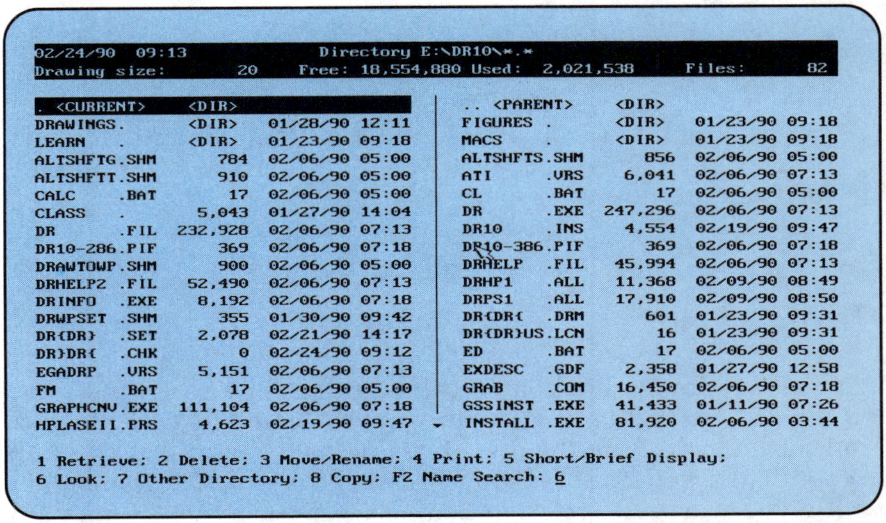

```
02/24/90  09:13              Directory E:\DR10\*.*
Drawing size:      20   Free: 18,554,880 Used:  2,021,538    Files:       82

.    <CURRENT>   <DIR>                  ..   <PARENT>   <DIR>
DRAWINGS.        <DIR>     01/28/90 12:11    FIGURES .      <DIR>     01/23/90 09:18
LEARN    .       <DIR>     01/23/90 09:18    MACS    .      <DIR>     01/23/90 09:18
ALTSHFTG.SHM         784   02/06/90 05:00    ALTSHFTS.SHM        856   02/06/90 05:00
ALTSHFTT.SHM         910   02/06/90 05:00    ATI     .URS      6,041   02/06/90 07:13
CALC    .BAT          17   02/06/90 05:00    CL      .BAT         17   02/06/90 05:00
CLASS   .          5,043   01/27/90 14:04    DR      .EXE    247,296   02/06/90 07:13
DR      .FIL     232,928   02/06/90 07:13    DR10    .INS      4,554   02/19/90 09:47
DR10-286.PIF         369   02/06/90 07:18    DR10-386.PIF        369   02/06/90 07:18
DRAWTOWP.SHM         900   02/06/90 05:00    DRHELP  .FIL     45,994   02/06/90 07:13
DRHELPZ .FIL      52,490   02/06/90 07:13    DRHP1   .ALL     11,368   02/09/90 08:49
DRINFO  .EXE       8,192   02/06/90 07:18    DRPS1   .ALL     17,910   02/09/90 08:50
DRWPSET .SHM         355   01/30/90 09:42    DR{DR{  .DRM        601   01/23/90 09:31
DR{DR}  .SET       2,078   02/21/90 14:17    DR{DR}US.LCN         16   01/23/90 09:31
DR}DR{  .CHK           0   02/24/90 09:12    ED      .BAT         17   02/06/90 05:00
EGADRP  .VRS       5,151   02/06/90 07:13    EXDESC  .GDF      2,358   01/27/90 12:58
FM      .BAT          17   02/06/90 05:00    GRAB    .COM     16,450   02/06/90 07:18
GRAPHCMU.EXE     111,104   02/06/90 07:18    GSSINST .EXE     41,433   01/11/90 07:26
HPLASEII.PRS       4,623   02/19/90 09:47 ▼  INSTALL .EXE     81,920   02/06/90 03:44

1 Retrieve; 2 Delete; 3 Move/Rename; 4 Print; 5 Short/Brief Display;
6 Look; 7 Other Directory; 8 Copy; F2 Name Search: 6
```

Figure 9.3 Using Look to view the parent directory

Although you are now looking at a different current directory, and you can use menu options like Retrieve or Delete on any of the displayed files, you have not changed the default directory. Let's prove it by leaving the List Files menu and then returning to it. To exit List Files:

🖑 Press the Spacebar.

🖱 Click the right button.

Now you should be back in the main DrawPerfect screen. Next, use the List Files option again to display the default directory listing.

🖑 Press List Files (F5) and then Enter, or type **F L** and press Enter.

🖱 Drag the cursor onto **File**, click the left button and hold it while highlighting **List Files**, then release the button. Click the right button.

Chapter 9

As you can see, this returns you to the original directory. In our example, the directory is DRAWINGS, but yours is probably different.

> **Tip:** Pressing the Enter key selects the Look option, since 6 is the default selection in the List Files menu line. If the cursor is highlighting <CURRENT> <DIR>, you can get stuck in an endless loop by pressing Enter over and over again! Remember, <CURRENT> <DIR> is the directory you are now viewing.

Using Look to View the Contents of a File

As we mentioned, Look has a different function when the cursor is highlighting a file: It lets you view the contents of a file without retrieving it from the disk. Imagine how useful this would be if you had saved hundreds of files and had forgotten the name of a file you wanted to retrieve. Rather than retrieving them one by one, and clearing the screen after each one, you could use Look to view them in succession until you found the one you wanted and then retrieve it. Let's find out how.

Since you are back in the default directory, you should be able to find a file that ends in WPG. Place the cursor on it, then select Look.

Type **L** (or type 6 or press Enter).

Drag the cursor onto **Look** and click the left mouse button.

You should see a DrawPerfect file (drawing or chart). For example, we selected HOUSE.WPG and our screen appears in Figure 9.4. Notice the prompt at the bottom of the screen showing the file name on the right side, and this menu on the left:

`1 Next; 2 Previous; 3 Retrieve:`

You can probably guess what these options will do. If you want to view the next file in the list, select **Next**. To view the previous file, select **Previous**. Once you see the file that you want to retrieve, select **Retrieve**. If you want to return to the List Files screen, press the Spacebar or click the right mouse button.

Figure 9.4   Using Look to view a file without retrieving it

If you try to look at a file that is not in WPG format, you will see this error message:

ERROR: Incorrect format

If you do this while in the Look screen (by selecting Next or Previous), the screen will be blank except for the prompt line at the bottom. If this happens, you can continue selecting Next or Previous until you see a WPG file. Once you reach the end of the file list, you'll keep seeing the same file over and over as you continue selecting Next.

Let's exit back to List Files to learn about the Name Search option. Assuming you are still using Look to view a drawing:

🗔 Press the Spacebar or Cancel (F1).

🖱 Click the right button.

Chapter 9

Name Search: Navigating Through the List Files Screen

Name Search is a handy little tool that will help you move the cursor onto any file in the list. If you use the keyboard, it's the fastest way to highlight a file. Even with a mouse, if your directory contains a large number of files and fills up more than one screen, it is still the fastest. Here's how it works: Just select Name Search, then type the first letter of the file name. For instance, if you wanted to move the cursor onto DOG.WPG you would:

 Type **N** (or press F2) and then type **D**.

 Drag the cursor onto **Name Search**, click the left mouse button, then type **D**.

The cursor moves to the first file name that begins with D, in alphabetical order. If there is another file in the list that starts with D, such as *DATES.WPG,* the cursor will highlight that one first. If so, just type the second letter in the file name you are searching for, such as O for the DOG.WPG file. If necessary, continue typing the third and fourth letters until the cursor is highlighting the file you want.

The prompt in the lower right corner of the screen tells you what to do once you've highlighted the file you want to use.

(Name Search; Enter or arrows to Exit)

Pressing Enter or clicking the right mouse button brings back the List Files menu. Pressing an Arrow key brings back the List Files menu, but it also moves the cursor. For example, if the cursor is in the first column and you press the Right Arrow, the cursor will move to the file name on the same line in column two.

Before continuing, exit from Name Search and from the List Files menu.

Using List Files to Retrieve a File

If you read Chapter 2, you learned how to retrieve a document using the pull-down File menu's Retrieve option. There is one major disadvantage to that method: If you don't know exactly how to spell the name, you won't be able to retrieve it. Instead, you will see an error message saying the file was not found. In contrast, when you retrieve through the List Files menu, you don't have to know the exact spelling because it shows you the full names of all files in your default directory. All you have left to do is look for the one you want to retrieve, then move the cursor onto it and select the Retrieve option. Let's try it.

To practice retrieving, find a DrawPerfect file whose name ends in the extension WPG. The easiest way to do this is to narrow the displayed list so that it includes only files ending in WPG. Here's how:

 Type **F L**.

 Drag the cursor onto **File**, click the left button and hold it. Drag the cursor onto **List Files** and release the button.

The familiar Dir prompt appears, followed by the directory name and the two asterisks that indicate all files will be displayed. To restrict the list, change the prompt to Dir *.wpg by typing:

*.wpg

then press Enter or click the right mouse button. Figure 9.5 shows our results. If your default directory does not contain any files with the wpg extension, your file list will be empty.

Now move the cursor onto one of the files so that you can retrieve it.

 Use the Arrow keys to highlight the file that you want to retrieve. Notice that the cursor appears as a highlighted bar in this screen. Type **R** (or 1) to retrieve it.

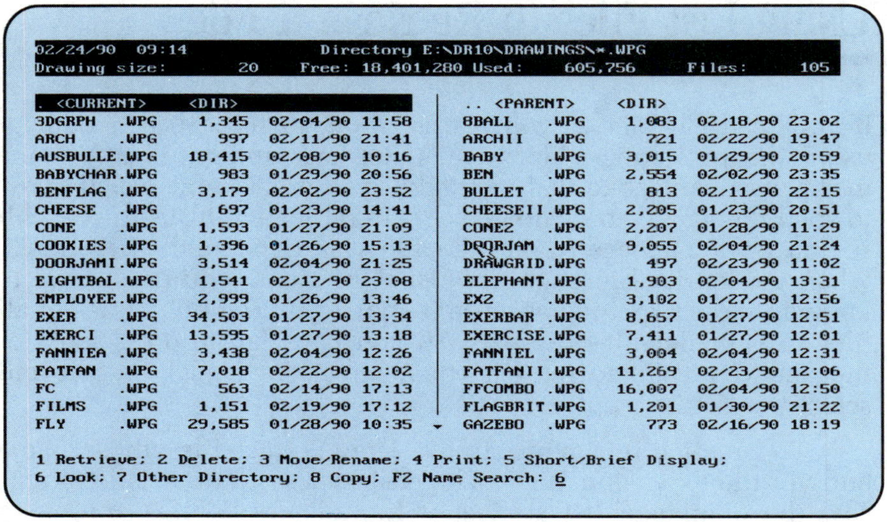

Figure 9.5 *Restricting the list of displayed files*

> ▶ **Tip:** If you press Enter instead of typing R or 1 while trying to retrieve a file, you will see this prompt at the bottom of the screen: `1 Next; 2 Previous; 3 Retrieve:0`. This happens because pressing Enter selects the Look option, not the Retrieve option. If you see this prompt, you can still retrieve the file by typing R (or 3).

 Drag the cursor (arrow) onto the file that you want to retrieve and click the left button. Drag the cursor onto the **Retrieve** option in the menu line at the bottom of the screen and click the left button.

> ▶ **Tip:** When you retrieve, you are actually only retrieving a *copy* of the file into the drawing window, and any changes that you make to it are not made to the disk version. When you save the file on screen, you erase the disk version and replace it with the screen version.

File Management

You should now be back in the main DrawPerfect screen, and the file you just retrieved should appear in the drawing window. Let's take another look at the List Files menu.

 Type **F L** and then press Enter.

 Drag the cursor onto **File**, click the left button, and hold it. Highlight **List Files** and release the button. Click the left button.

We want you to be aware of one statistic in the header area that has changed: *Drawing size* on the second line. Before you retrieved your file, that number was 20, indicating there was no drawing or chart in the drawing window. Now it should be approximately the same as the file size statistic for the file you retrieved. This serves as a warning: That file is still in your drawing window, and if you were to retrieve another file now, you would be adding it to the drawing that is already there. Exit from List Files so you'll believe us.

 Press the Spacebar.

 Click the right button.

Do you see your drawing? The lesson we are trying to get across is that when you display the List Files screen, it does not automatically clear your drawing window. Retrieving another file and adding it to the one already there is a common mistake, so don't feel silly if you make it (but do use Exit without saving to clear the screen so you don't accidentally save the two files together!).

 Retrieving a File Using the List Files Screen

1. Type F L and then press Enter. Mouse users can display the File menu, highlight List Files, click the left button and then the right one.

   The List Files screen appears showing names of all files in your default directory.

2. Use the Arrow keys to move the cursor onto the file that you want to retrieve and then type R or 1. Mouse users can move the cursor (arrow) onto the file, click the left button, then move the cursor onto the Retrieve option and click the left button.

> **Tip:** Whenever you are in the main DrawPerfect screen, you can redisplay the last List Files screen that you were using by pressing F5 twice. For instance, you might select List Files, use the asterisks to display only those files ending in WPG, retrieve a file, and then return to the main DrawPerfect screen. The next time you press F5 twice, you will see the same screen, showing only the files ending in WPG. Likewise, if you had been looking at the parent directory when you last used List Files, pressing F5 twice would display the list of files for that directory. However, if you last used List Files to view the files on a different disk drive, pressing F5 twice does not work (instead, it shows the default directory).

Making Backup Copies

One of the most important options on the List Files menu is the Copy option, which you can use to copy one or more files to another directory or disk drive. Since hard disks and floppy diskettes can and often do fail, you should get into the habit of using this option to back up your charts and drawings.

Copying One File to Another Drive or Directory

To copy one file to another directory, display the List Files menu and highlight the file that you want to copy. Select the Copy option, and you will see this prompt:

`Copy this file to:`

If you want to copy the file to another disk drive, just type the name of the drive and press Enter. For instance, if the file is on drive C and you want to copy it to drive A, type

A:

then press Enter.

If you want to copy it to a subdirectory, you have to type the whole path. For instance, if you want to copy a file from C:\DR10 to C:\DR10\DRAWINGS, type

\DR10\DRAWINGS

then press Enter. If the file is in the DRAWINGS subdirectory and you want to copy it into the DR10 directory one level above, type

\DR10

then press Enter.

Each of these examples assumes that you want to use the same name when you copy the file. If not, you just type a different name after the drive or path name. For instance, if you want to copy a file named ORBITAL.WPG from drive C to a file named SPACE.WPG on drive A, type

A:SPACE.WPG

in response to the `Copy this file to:` prompt.

You can also copy a file to the same directory by assigning a different name to it. To do this, just type the new name (without a directory name) in response to the `Copy this file to:` prompt. Note that you will not see the new file name in the List Files screen until you exit from it and return again. The quickest

Chapter 9

way to do this is to highlight <CURRENT> <DIR> and press Enter twice (to select Look).

> 🚫 **Caution:** If you see a Replace prompt when you try to copy a file, be careful! It means there is another file with the same name on the drive or directory you are trying to copy to, and if you select Yes you will erase that file. To be on the safe side, you can always type N, then select Copy again and type a different file name.

Copying a File

1. Display the List Files menu, highlight the file that you want to copy, then select Copy.

    This prompt appears: `Copy this file to:`

2. To copy the file to another disk drive, type the name of the drive and press Enter. To copy it to another subdirectory, type the path and press Enter. If you want to assign a new name to the copy, type the name of the drive or directory followed by the new file name, and then press Enter.

    The file is copied.

Selecting a Group of Files to Copy Simultaneously

To copy a group of files, you have to mark each one with an asterisk. This is easier than it sounds: Just place the cursor on the first file name and type an asterisk; then repeat for each file you want to copy. The asterisks will appear next to the file size statistic for each file, as shown in Figure 9.6. If you want to copy all files in the current directory, mark them all at once by pressing Home and then typing an asterisk (but if one or more files is already marked, pressing Home asterisk unmarks them all so you have to press Home asterisk a second time). After you've marked the files, select **Copy** from the menu. You will then see a prompt asking if you want to copy the marked files, as in Figure 9.6.

```
02/24/90  09:14           Directory E:\DR10\DRAWINGS\*.WPG
Drawing size:       20   Free: 18,401,280 Used:     46,277    Marked:      13

    . <CURRENT>   <DIR>                  .. <PARENT>    <DIR>
  3DGRPH  .WPG    1,345* 02/04/90 11:58   8BALL   .WPG   1,083* 02/18/90 23:02
  ARCH    .WPG      997  02/11/90 21:41   ARCHII  .WPG     721  02/22/90 19:47
  AUSBULLE.WPG   18,415  02/08/90 10:16   BABY    .WPG   3,015  01/29/90 20:59
  BABYCHAR.WPG      983  01/29/90 20:56   BEN     .WPG   2,554  02/02/90 23:35
  BENFLAG .WPG    3,179* 02/02/90 23:52   BULLET  .WPG     813* 02/11/90 22:15
  CHEESE  .WPG      697  01/23/90 14:41   CHEESEII.WPG   2,205  01/23/90 20:51
  CONE    .WPG    1,593  01/27/90 21:09   CONE2   .WPG   2,207* 01/28/90 11:29
  COOKIES .WPG    1,396  01/26/90 15:13   DOORJAM .WPG   9,055  02/04/90 21:24
  DOORJAMI.WPG    3,514  02/04/90 21:25   DRAWGRID.WPG     497* 02/23/90 11:02
  EIGHTBAL.WPG    1,541* 02/17/90 23:08   ELEPHANT.WPG   1,903  02/04/90 13:31
  EMPLOYEE.WPG    2,999* 01/26/90 13:46   EX2     .WPG   3,102  01/27/90 12:56
  EXER    .WPG   34,503  01/27/90 13:34   EXERBAR .WPG   8,657  01/27/90 12:51
  EXERCI  .WPG   13,595* 01/27/90 13:18   EXERCISE.WPG   7,411* 01/27/90 12:01
  FANNIEA .WPG    3,438* 02/04/90 12:26   FANNIEL .WPG   3,004  02/04/90 12:31
  FATFAN  .WPG    7,018* 02/22/90 12:02   FATFANII.WPG  11,269  02/23/90 12:06
  FC      .WPG      563  02/14/90 17:13   FFCOMBO .WPG  16,007  02/04/90 12:50
  FILMS   .WPG    1,151* 02/19/90 17:12   FLAGBRIT.WPG   1,201  01/30/90 21:22
  FLY     .WPG   29,585  01/28/90 10:35   GAZEBO  .WPG     773  02/16/90 18:19

Copy marked files? No (Yes)
```

Figure 9.6   *Marking several files for copying*

Select **Yes** to copy them, and this prompt will appear:

`Copy all marked files to:`

You can follow the same rules outlined in the previous section to copy the files. For instance, to copy them from drive C to drive A, just type

`A:`

and press Enter. Incidentally, if there is not enough room on the disk for all the files you are copying, when enough files have been copied so the disk is full, DrawPerfect will prompt you to replace it with another one. To copy all marked files to another directory, type the directory name and path, such as \DR10\DRAWINGS, and press Enter.

The other operations you can perform with a group of marked files are deleting, printing, and moving.

Selecting a Group of Files to Copy, Delete, Move, or Print

1. Move the cursor onto the first file that you want to select and then type an asterisk. Repeat for each file that you want to include. To select all files simultaneously, press Home and then type an asterisk (if one or more files is already marked, pressing Home asterisk unmarks them all, so you'll have to press Home asterisk again).

   Asterisks appear next to the file size statistic for each file that you have selected (in the third column).

2. Select the Copy, Delete, Move/Rename, or Print option from the menu and follow the prompts.

Deleting Files

After using DrawPerfect for a while, you may find that you've amassed a large collection of practice files that you never use. All they are doing is wasting precious disk space. If so, you can use the List File menu's Delete option to erase them. Be careful with it though, because once you delete a file you can't get it back. If you think there is even a remote possibility that you'll want to use a file again, consider using the Move option instead of Delete. That way, you can move it onto a floppy disk, file it away in a safe place, and erase it from your hard disk—all in one command! We will discuss Move in the next section; for now, let's study Delete.

Deleting One File

To erase a file, display the List Files menu, move the cursor onto the file name, then select Delete.

 Type **D** (or 2).

 Drag the cursor onto **Delete** and click the left button.

Since this is a drastic action, DrawPerfect gives you a chance to change your mind, displaying a prompt that asks if you want to delete it. For instance, if you try to delete a file named *SALES.WPG* in the DR10 directory, you'll see this prompt:

`Delete C:\DR10\SALES.WPG? No (Yes)`

Notice that the assumption is No. If you really do want to delete it, select Yes.

Type **Y**.

Drag the cursor onto **Yes** and click the left button.

The screen will be updated and the file name will disappear from your list.

Deleting a Group of Files

To erase a group of files, your first step is to mark each one with an asterisk. You can mark a file by highlighting it and typing an asterisk. To mark all files in the list, press Home and then type an asterisk. The asterisks appear after the file size statistic in the third column.

After highlighting all the files you want to erase, select Delete. You should see this prompt:

`Delete marked files? No (Yes)`

Notice that the assumption is No. Select Yes, and you will see this prompt:

`Marked files will be deleted. Continue? No (Yes)`

As you can see, when you delete a group of files, DrawPerfect gives you two chances to change your mind! Select Yes if you want to delete them. You will see a * Please wait * prompt; soon the screen will be updated and the file names will be gone.

Moving Files

The Move/Rename command is one of the most useful tools on the List Files menu. You can use it to move one or more files to another disk drive, to rename a file, or to simultaneously rename a file and move it to another directory or disk drive. In this section, we'll teach you how to move files. Remember, this is a great way to clean up your hard disk. If you have hundreds of files you never use, just move them to a floppy disk and store it away in a safe place in case you ever need your files again.

Moving One File

To move a file to another directory or disk drive, display the List Files menu, move the cursor onto the file name, then select Move/Rename.

Type **M** (or 3).

Drag the cursor onto **Move/Rename** and click the left button.

You should see a prompt asking for the new file name. For instance, if you are in the DR10 directory of drive C and ask to move a file named PROFIT.WPG, you will see:

`New name: C:\DR10\PROFIT.WPG`

To move it onto another disk (simultaneously erasing it from this disk), type the disk name and press Enter. For instance, to move it from C to the disk in drive A, just type

A:

and press Enter. If you want to move it to a subdirectory, edit the prompt to include the subdirectory name. For instance, to move the PROFIT.WPG file to the DRAWINGS subdirectory of DR10, press the Right Arrow key until the cursor is on the letter P in PROFIT, then type

DRAWINGS

and press Enter. If the file is in the DRAWINGS subdirectory and you want to move it up one level to the DR10 directory, just erase DRAWINGS\ from the prompt that appears:

`New name: C:\DR10\DRAWINGS\PROFIT.WPG`

so it looks like this:

`New name: C:\DR10\PROFIT.WPG`

After DrawPerfect has moved the file, the screen will be updated and the old name will be gone from your file list.

Moving a Group of Files

To move a group of files, mark each one with an asterisk (if you've forgotten how, see the section entitled *Selecting a Group of Files to Copy Simultaneously*). After highlighting all the files you want to move, select the **Move/Rename** option. You should see this prompt:

`Move marked files? No (Yes)`

Select **Yes**. Next, this prompt will appear asking where you want to move them:

`Move marked files to:`

To move the files to another disk, type the drive name and press Enter. To move them to another subdirectory, type the full path to the subdirectory, such as \DR10\DRAWINGS, and press Enter. After DrawPerfect has moved the files, their names will disappear from your screen.

Renaming a File

The Move/Rename option is useful when you want to assign a new name to a file. All you have to do is highlight the file that you want to rename, select Move/Rename, and type a new name. For instance, say you wanted to rename the POSTER.WPG file. You would highlight the file and then select the option. This prompt would appear, showing the current name and directory that the file is in:

`New name: C:\DR10\POSTER.WPG`

To rename the file but leave it in the same directory, just type the new name and press Enter. You will see the effect almost immediately, as the screen is updated to place the file in the correct alphabetical order. To rename the file and simultaneously move it to another directory or disk drive, type the drive name or directory name followed by the new file name and press Enter. For example, to rename it BANNER.WPG and move it to the DRAWINGS subdirectory of DR10, type

\DR10\DRAWINGS\BANNER.WPG

then press Enter.

> **Caution:** Whenever you ask to rename a file, DrawPerfect searches the current directory to see if there is another file with the same name. Since two files in a directory cannot have the same name, if DrawPerfect finds one with the same name, you will see a prompt asking if you want to replace the other file. Replace means erase, so if you select Yes you will erase that file. To be safe, select No, select the option again, and think of another name!

Printing Disk Files

You don't have to retrieve a DrawPerfect file to print it. Instead, you can use the Print option on the List Files menu to print one or more WPG files. It's easy. To print one file, just highlight the file with the cursor and then select the Print option. You will see this prompt in the lower left corner (it disappears quickly so look carefully!):

`Please wait---loading WP Graphics file....`

and soon you should see the chart or drawing emerge from your printer. To print a group of files, just mark them with asterisks and select Print. You will see this prompt:

`Print marked files? No (Yes)`

Select **Yes**. The `Please wait` prompt will appear several times (once for each file you selected) and the files will be printed.

> **Tip:** Each time you ask DrawPerfect to print a file, your request is added to a list of print jobs. Chapter 7 teaches you more about this job list, including how to cancel print jobs or stop the printer.

Printing a File Without Retrieving It

1. Display the List Files screen and place the cursor on the file that you want to print. To print several files, mark them with asterisks.

2. Select the Print option.

   If you selected only one file, you will see this prompt: `Please wait---loading WP Graphics file....`; then the file will be printed.

3. If you marked several files to be printed, select Yes when asked if you want to print the marked files.

   You will see a `Please wait` prompt several times (once for each file you selected) and the files will be printed.

Creating and Changing Directories

In this section, we will teach you how to use the List Files menu's Other Directory option to create a new directory and change the default directory. By dividing your hard disk into directories and subdirectories, you can organize your files more logically and make it easier to locate them. Think of the disk as a file cabinet, and each directory or subdirectory as a file folder where you place related information, your files.

Creating a New Directory

To create a new directory or subdirectory (we use the terms interchangeably here since the program does), you display the List Files screen and select Other Directory. The cursor can be anywhere when you do this (either on a file name or on a directory name). If it is on a file name, you will see this prompt:

`New directory =`

followed by the current directory's name and path. If the cursor is on a directory name, the prompt will also include that directory's name. This happens because DrawPerfect assumes that when you highlight a directory name and select the Other Directory option, your intention is to make that directory the default directory, not to create a new directory.

Either way, your next step is to type the new directory name and press Enter. If you want the directory to be a subdirectory of the current directory (one level below it), you don't need to type a path. For instance, if your current directory is DR10 and you want to create DRAWINGS one level below DR10, you would just type

DRAWINGS

However, if you want the directory to be on the same level, you would have to type the path. For instance, if your current directory is C:\DR10\DRAWINGS and you want to create C:\DR10\CHARTS, you would type

\DR10\CHARTS

After you type the new directory name and press Enter, you will see a prompt asking if you want to create it. For instance, if your current directory is DR10 and you are creating DRAWINGS, this prompt will appear:

`Create drawings? No (Yes)`

(However, if the directory already exists, you won't see the prompt asking if you want to create it. Instead, the command just makes it the new default directory. We will cover this in the next section.)

Select **Yes**. DrawPerfect will then create the directory and update the screen. If your new subdirectory is one level below the current one, its name will appear at the top with the other directory names. Note that creating a new directory does not mean it has become the default directory or the current directory. One more step is required, which we'll explain in the next section.

Changing the Default Directory

You can change the default directory to any subdirectory in the list, or to the parent directory one level above, by highlighting the directory name and selecting the *Other Directory* option. Next you will see a prompt indicating that the highlighted directory will become the new directory. For example, if the default directory is DR10 and you want to change it to DRAWINGS, this prompt will appear:

`New directory = C:\DR10\DRAWINGS`

Press Enter to accept this prompt and implement the option. You will then see a Dir prompt:

`Dir C:\DR10\DRAWINGS`

and can press Enter to view the list of files in the new default directory. Be aware that this is not a permanent change, so the next time you use DrawPerfect (after exiting and restarting it) the default directory will revert to the original one (the one you were in before you used Other Directory to change it). You can permanently change the default directory for your drawings using the Location of Files option on the Setup menu. To use it, display the **File** menu, select **Setup**, then select **Location of Files**. From the Location of Files menu that appears, select the fifth option, **Drawing Files**. Type the directory name and path, then press Enter three times to return to the drawing window.

> **Tip:** Any new file you create will automatically be saved in the default directory. Also, when you select List Files and press Enter, DrawPerfect will always display the files in the default directory, unless you type a different directory name before pressing Enter.

Deleting a Directory

You cannot delete a directory unless it is empty, so the first step is to erase or move all files out of it. After that's done, you can delete the directory by highlighting it with the cursor and selecting the **Delete** option from the List Files menu. You will then see a prompt asking if you want to delete it. For instance, if you are deleting the CHARTS subdirectory one level below DR10, it will appear as follows:

`Delete C:\DR10\CHARTS? No (Yes)`

Select **Yes** to delete it. The screen will be updated and the directory name will be erased.

If the directory you were trying to delete was not empty, you will see a different prompt:

`ERROR: Directory not empty`

and the menu will reappear. If this happens, you can use Look to view the file or files in that directory and erase or move them.

What You Have Learned

In this chapter, you've learned how to manage your files using DrawPerfect's List Files screen. You should now be familiar with the following:

▶ The List Files option on the File menu brings up a full-screen menu that you can use to retrieve, print, copy, rename, or delete files. It also includes file management tools for tasks such as creating directories, changing the default directory, moving a group of files to another directory, and copying files from a hard disk to a floppy disk.

▶ A directory is a subdivision of the disk. DOS automatically creates the main directory (called the root directory) when you format the disk, and you can divide it into one or more directories to store related files.

▶ The first two lines of the List Files screen include information about the current date and time (as stored in your computer); the current disk drive and directory; the file size of the drawing on the main DrawPerfect screen; the amount of free space available on your disk; the total number of files in the directory and the amount of disk space they use. The rest of the screen shows the file list.

▶ The file list on the List Files screen includes all file names and directory names. Directory names always come first in the list, such as <CURRENT> <DIR> and <PARENT> <DIR>, and file names follow. File names that begin with numbers come first, and the others are in alphabetical order from left to right, separated by a line.

▶ When the cursor is highlighting a directory name in the List Files screen, you can use the Look option to look at the List Files screen for that directory. When the cursor is highlighting a file, you can use the Look option to view the contents of a file without retrieving it from the disk.

▶ You can use the Name Search option on the List Files screen to quickly move the cursor onto any file in the list by typing the first one or two letters of the file name.

▶ The Retrieve option on the List Files menu brings a copy of the file into the drawing window. If you edit it, you must save it again because it no longer matches the disk version.

► You can use the Delete option on the List Files menu to erase one or more files from the disk. Once you delete a file you can't get it back.
► You can use the Copy option on the List Files menu to copy one or more files to another directory or disk drive.
► You can use the Move/Rename option on the List Files menu to rename a file, to move one or more files to another disk drive or directory, or to simultaneously rename a file and move it to another directory or disk drive.
► You can use the Other Directory option on the List Files menu to create a new directory or change the default directory to any subdirectory in the list, or to the parent directory one level above.

Chapter 10

Using the Shell to Integrate DrawPerfect and WordPerfect

In This Chapter

- ▶ An explanation of the Shell
- ▶ Running DrawPerfect and WordPerfect simultaneously and switching between them
- ▶ Using the Shell to transfer files between DrawPerfect and WordPerfect
- ▶ Retrieving WordPerfect text into DrawPerfect
- ▶ An easy way to spell check DrawPerfect text
- ▶ Creating a bar graph from a WordPerfect table

The Shell is a utility program that is included with DrawPerfect. Overall, it serves as a program integrator. You can use it to set up a menu listing all of your software programs, and then start any of them by typing a single letter such as **W** for WordPerfect or **D** for DrawPerfect. If you are a WordPerfect 5.1 user, you can use the Shell to run DrawPerfect and WordPerfect simultaneously, and switch back and forth between them. You can even exchange files between the two programs. You can also use the Shell to run DOS commands, such as Format, through the menu; to determine how your computer's memory is being used;

to keep track of the time and/or keystrokes you have spent on a project; and much more. It is beyond the scope of this book to explore all the features the Shell has to offer. Instead, we'll cover those that will be helpful if you're using both WordPerfect and DrawPerfect.

This chapter assumes that you have already installed the Shell. If not, turn to Appendix A and do so before continuing.

Starting the Shell

If you want to use the Shell to integrate DrawPerfect and WordPerfect, you must start DrawPerfect through the Shell menu. You may recall from Chapter 1 that there are two ways to start DrawPerfect: by typing the letter D from the Shell menu or by typing several DOS commands to change the directory and start DrawPerfect. You can force yourself to use the Shell by setting up your computer so that the Shell menu automatically appears whenever you turn on your computer. This process involves modifying your Autoexec.bat file, and is explained in Appendix A.

To start the Shell, your first step is to switch to the subdirectory containing the Shell files. Usually the subdirectory will be on drive C and its name will be DR10. If so, type

CD\DR10

(otherwise type **CD** followed by your subdirectory name) and press the Enter key. Next, start the Shell program by typing **Shell** and pressing Enter. The main Shell menu should appear, as shown in Figure 10.1.

DrawPerfect and WordPerfect should appear as options on the left side of the menu. Notice the highlighted letter that appears next to the menu options, such as **D** for DrawPerfect and **W** for WordPerfect. To start a program, just type the letter appearing next to it.

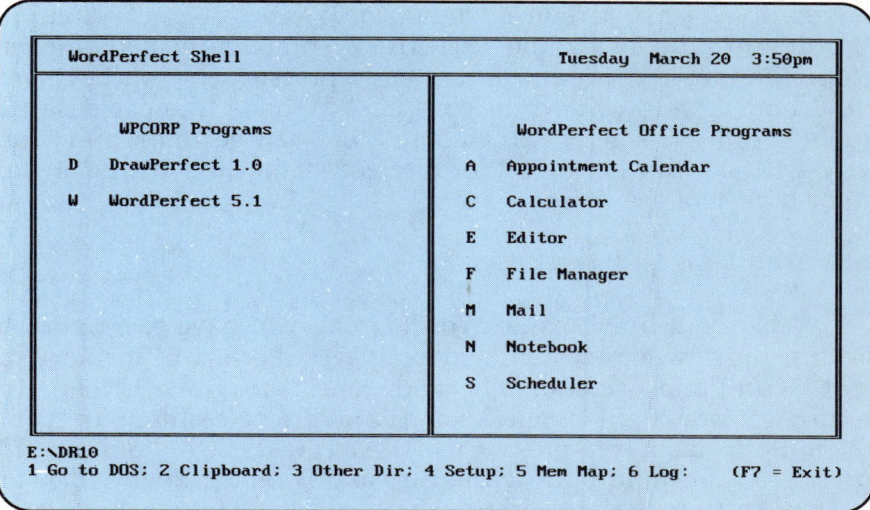

Figure 10.1 The Shell menu

Switching Between WordPerfect 5.1 and DrawPerfect

One of the main advantages of starting WordPerfect or DrawPerfect through the Shell is that you can run both programs simultaneously and switch between them using just three keystrokes. For example, if you are using DrawPerfect and your boss comes in and asks you to print a letter in WordPerfect, you don't have to stop everything and exit DrawPerfect. Instead, you can press Ctrl-Alt-W and you'll find yourself in WordPerfect almost immediately. After you finish printing the letter, you can return to DrawPerfect and the chart or drawing you were creating by pressing Ctrl-Alt-D. Interested? Read on and we'll show you how it works.

Start DrawPerfect through the Shell. You may want to retrieve one of your charts or drawings to verify that it will still

Chapter 10

be there after you return from WordPerfect. Now switch to WordPerfect by using the Ctrl-Alt-W combination as follows: Press the Ctrl key, hold it down while pressing the Alt key, and hold both keys down while you press W once (then release all three keys). The screen will go blank for a few seconds, and soon you will see the familiar WordPerfect status line in the lower right corner of the screen:

`Doc 1 Pg 1 Ln 1" Pos 1"`

When you finish using WordPerfect, you have two options: Return to DrawPerfect while keeping WordPerfect in memory or exit WordPerfect completely and return to DrawPerfect. To return to DrawPerfect but keep WordPerfect resident in your computer's memory, press Ctrl-Alt-D (press Ctrl, hold it and press Alt, and hold both while pressing D once). Soon you will be back in DrawPerfect and the chart or drawing you were working on will be in the drawing window. You can continue using Ctrl-Alt-D and Ctrl-Alt-W to switch between the programs. Later, when you finish using DrawPerfect and select Exit to leave it, you'll return to the Shell menu. An asterisk will appear next to the WordPerfect option, as shown in Figure 10.2, signifying that WordPerfect is still in memory. To return to WordPerfect, press Enter (assuming the cursor is on the WordPerfect option).

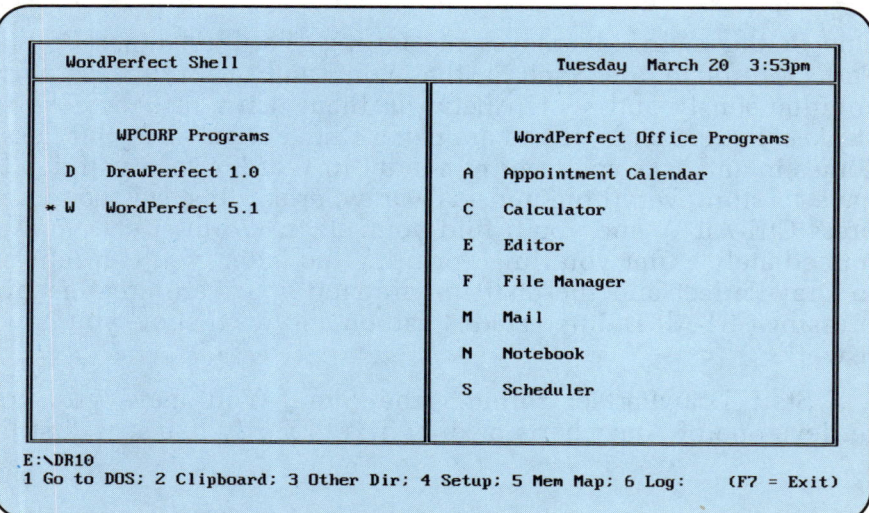

Figure 10.2 *The Shell menu with WordPerfect in memory*

> **Caution:** If you try to exit from the Shell while WordPerfect is in memory (by pressing F7), you'll see this prompt:
>
> `Save information in all programs? (Y/N) Y`
>
> If this happens, press the Cancel key (F1) and return to WordPerfect by typing **W**. Next, use the Exit key (F7) to end your WordPerfect session, saving your WordPerfect document if necessary.

If you've switched from Drawperfect to WordPerfect and wish to exit WordPerfect completely and return to DrawPerfect, press the Exit key (F7). You'll see a prompt asking if you want to save your document. After answering it, you'll see this prompt asking if you want to exit WordPerfect:

`Exit WP? No (Yes)`

Type **Y**. This places you back in the Shell menu, where you'll see an asterisk next to the DrawPerfect option, as shown in Figure 10.3. The asterisk is a reminder that DrawPerfect is already in your computer's memory. To start it again, all you have to do is press Enter.

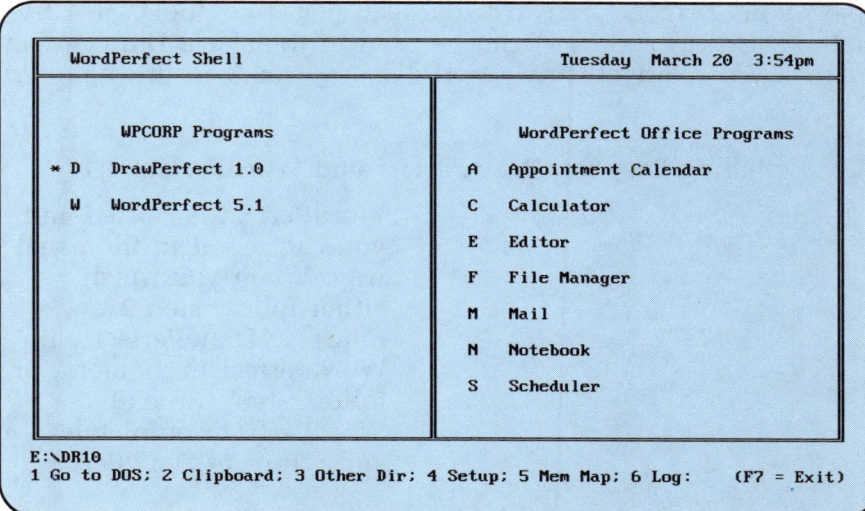

Figure 10.3 *The Shell menu with DrawPerfect in memory*

> **Tip:** You can use the Ctrl-Alt method to switch to any other WordPerfect Corporation product listed on your Shell menu. For example, if you use PlanPerfect, you can switch from DrawPerfect to PlanPerfect by pressing Ctrl-Alt-P.

Another method of switching from DrawPerfect to WordPerfect or another program on your Shell menu is to return directly to the Shell menu. To do this, display DrawPerfect's File menu and select **Go to Shell** (or press the Shell key, Ctrl-F1). This menu appears at the bottom of your screen:

`1 Go to Shell; Clipboard: 2 Save; 3 Retrieve: 0`

Select **Go to Shell**. You will return to the Shell menu, and an asterisk will appear next to the DrawPerfect option to show it is still in memory (as shown in Figure 10.3). Select WordPerfect or any other program or Shell option you want to use by typing the letter next to it or by placing the cursor on it and pressing Enter. When you finish using the other program, exit in the usual way and you'll return to the Shell. Start DrawPerfect again by highlighting it and pressing Enter.

Another method you can use to switch to WordPerfect is to display the File menu and select the WordPerfect option. This takes you directly into WordPerfect just like the Ctrl-Alt-W method. However, it also can be used to transfer a DrawPerfect chart to WordPerfect, so we will discuss it later in this chapter.

Switching Between DrawPerfect and WordPerfect 5.1

1. Start DrawPerfect through the Shell. When you are ready to switch to WordPerfect, press Ctrl-Alt-W.

    WordPerfect is started and you can use it in the usual way. When you finish, either follow step 2 to return to DrawPerfect with WordPerfect in memory, or follow step 3 to exit WordPerfect completely and return to DrawPerfect.

2. To return to DrawPerfect and keep WordPerfect running, press Ctrl-Alt-D.

   The DrawPerfect screen appears, along with the chart or drawing you were working on when you switched to WordPerfect.

3. To exit WordPerfect and return to DrawPerfect, press the Exit key (F7), then type Y to save the file or N to discard it. When you see the `Exit WP?` prompt, type Y. The Shell menu reappears and you can press Enter to return to DrawPerfect.

Using the Shell to Transfer Files Between DrawPerfect and WordPerfect 5.1

There are many reasons to exchange data between DrawPerfect and WordPerfect 5.1. For instance, you may want to transfer a completed chart or drawing from DrawPerfect into a WordPerfect graphics box and use it in a newsletter or some other desktop publishing application. If you are in WordPerfect and want to edit a graphic you've retrieved, you can transfer it into DrawPerfect, edit it, then transfer the edited version back into WordPerfect. If you've entered data into a WordPerfect table or tabular columns, you can transfer it into DrawPerfect and create an attractive business chart (bar, line, pie, etc.). Rather than retyping text that you've already typed in WordPerfect, you can transfer it from WordPerfect into a DrawPerfect text window. In this section, we'll teach you how to do all these wonderful things.

However, before we plunge in and teach you about these features, let's be sure that your system is set up correctly to use them. To begin with, you must be using WordPerfect 5.1; earlier versions of WordPerfect won't work. Since all data is transferred between DrawPerfect and WordPerfect through a Shell feature called the *Clipboard*, another requirement is that both WordPerfect 5.1 and DrawPerfect must appear as options on your Shell menu. Also, when you use DrawPerfect or WordPerfect, you must start them through the Shell. Finally, you must have the following files in the directory that contains your Shell files: ALTSHFTG.SHM, ALTSHFTT.SHM, ALTSHFTS.SHM, WPTODRAW.SHM, and DRAWTOWP.SHM. These are macros that have been included with the Shell. A macro is a special type of file that includes all the keystrokes required to perform a certain task so that you can have the program run these keystrokes automatically. Although we won't be teaching you any more about Shell macros, we have dedicated an entire chapter (Chapter 12) to DrawPerfect macros, and the concepts are similar.

If you used DrawPerfect's automatic installation program to install the Shell, the five Shell macro files should have been copied for you automatically. To check, you can use the List Files option. To do this (from DrawPerfect or WordPerfect) display the **File** menu and select **List Files**. In response to the Dir prompt that appears in the lower left corner of the screen, type the name of the subdirectory that contains your Shell program files and press Enter. For instance, if your Shell files are in the DR10 subdirectory, type

C:\DR10

then press Enter (if the correct subdirectory name already appears next to the Dir prompt, just press Enter). Next, look for the files (ALTSHFTG.SHM, etc.). Since three of them begin with A you should see them near the top of the list, as shown in Figure 10.4. To search for the last one, type **N** to select Name Search, then type **WPT** and press Enter. If you don't see the files, you'll have to copy them from the Shell disk (it's labelled *WordPerfect Shell 3.0, DrawPerfect Shell Macros*). If you forget how to copy files, refer to the previous chapter, *File Management*.

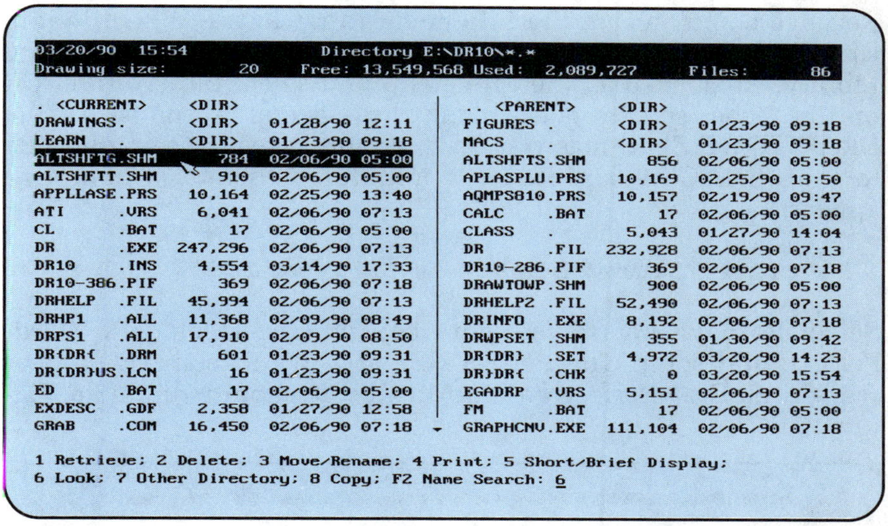

Figure 10.4   Using List Files to verify that the Shell macro files are in the Shell subdirectory

Transferring a DrawPerfect Chart into WordPerfect

When you are in DrawPerfect, transferring a chart or drawing into WordPerfect is easy. You simply retrieve a graphic file into DrawPerfect, then select the WordPerfect option on the File menu. This option copies the image into WordPerfect via the Shell Clipboard. In the process, it automatically creates a WordPerfect figure box to place the graphic in, since you cannot retrieve a graphic file directly into WordPerfect. If you did not start DrawPerfect through the Shell menu, exit and do so before trying this procedure.

The image you are transferring must be in the drawing window, so you'll begin by retrieving a practice file. Use the

Retrieve command on the File menu to retrieve a WPG file into DrawPerfect. We retrieved the LAPTOP.WPG file from the Figure Library. Next, display the File menu and select the WordPerfect option. The screen goes blank for several seconds as the DRAWTOWP Shell macro takes over and saves your graphic file to the Shell Clipboard. After a minute or so this prompt will appear:

1 Retrieve Figure; 2 Leave in Clipboard: 2

Select Retrieve Figure. A figure box will be created in WordPerfect, and soon WordPerfect's Figure Edit screen will appear with your DrawPerfect graphic inside. It should resemble Figure 10.5.

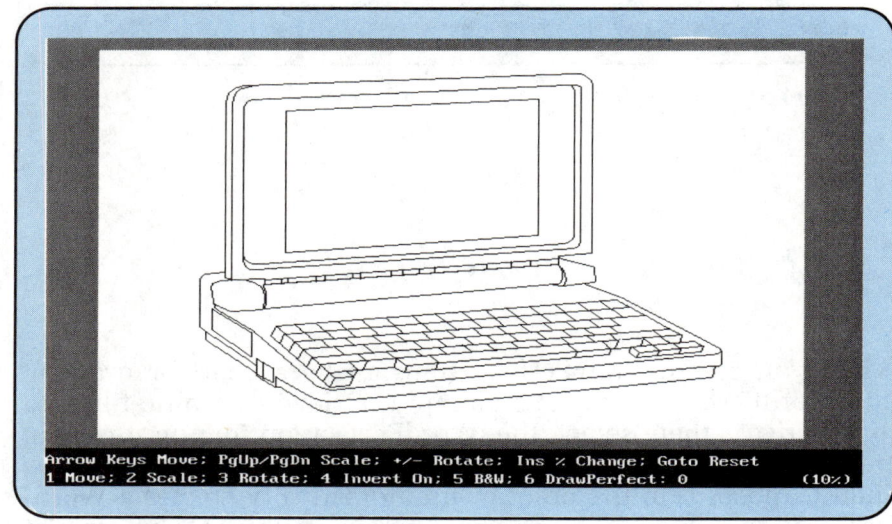

Figure 10.5 *WordPerfect's Figure Edit screen with transferred DrawPerfect graphic*

You can use this menu to move, scale, and rotate the figure (but we won't go into detail since this book is not about WordPerfect!). When you finish using the Edit menu, press Exit (F7) once. This places you in the Definition Figure menu shown in Figure 10.6. You can use this menu to edit the figure box containing your graphic, changing its size, position, caption, and more (also beyond the scope of this book). When you finish, press Exit (F7) once. You will then be in the main WordPerfect screen, where an outline of the figure box will appear at the top of the screen. If you press Enter several times, it will take on the shape of a box, as shown in Figure 10.7. As you can see, the graphic image is not visible in WordPerfect's edit screen (but you can see it using the View Document option on the Print menu).

```
Definition: Figure

    1 - Filename
    2 - Contents            Graphic
    3 - Caption
    4 - Anchor Type         Paragraph
    5 - Vertical Position   0"
    6 - Horizontal Position Right
    7 - Size                3.25" wide x 2.44" (high)
    8 - Wrap Text Around Box Yes
    9 - Edit




Selection: 0
```

Figure 10.6 *WordPerfect's Definition Figure menu*

Figure 10.7 *The figure box in the WordPerfect edit screen*

You can then use the graphic figure in a newsletter, flyer, or other WordPerfect document. After you finish using WordPerfect and exit from it, you will be back in the Shell menu. An asterisk will appear next to the DrawPerfect option to indicate that Draw-Perfect is still in memory. Press Enter to return to DrawPerfect, where you'll find that the graph you transferred into Word-Perfect is still in the drawing window. DrawPerfect transferred a copy of the file to WordPerfect, and the original remained here.

If you are in WordPerfect and want to retrieve a Draw-Perfect file, you don't have to switch to DrawPerfect at all. Instead, just create a graphic box, then retrieve the file. Here's how. Press Graphics (Alt-F9), select **Figure**, then **Create**. The Definition Figure menu appears, as shown in Figure 10.6, and you select the **Filename** option. Type the name (and path, if necessary) of the WPG file you want to retrieve, then press Enter. A prompt appears telling you that WordPerfect is loading a WP Graphics file, and then the file name appears next to the Filename option.

Transferring a DrawPerfect File into WordPerfect

1. If the drawing or chart that you want to transfer is not in the drawing window, use the Retrieve command on the file menu to retrieve it.

2. Display the File menu and select the WordPerfect option.

    The screen goes blank, and after several seconds a prompt will appear asking if you want to retrieve the figure or leave it in the Clipboard.

3. Select Retrieve Figure.

    A Figure box will be created in WordPerfect, and soon WordPerfect's Figure Edit screen will appear with your DrawPerfect graphic inside.

Transferring a Graphic Image from WordPerfect to DrawPerfect

There may be times when you want to edit a figure that's already in a WordPerfect graphic box. For instance, say you had transferred several bar charts and pie charts from DrawPerfect into WordPerfect to use in an important sales report. Before the final printing, you realize that some of the data has changed. Rather than erasing all the charts from WordPerfect and starting over after you modify them in DrawPerfect, you can transfer them into DrawPerfect (one at a time), edit them, then transfer the revised charts back into WordPerfect. Here's how.

Start WordPerfect from the Shell menu. Next, create a graphic box and retrieve a chart or drawing into it. To do this, press Graphics (Alt-F9), select **Figure**, then **Create**. The Definition Figure menu appears, and should be similar to Figure 10.6. Select the **Filename** option. Type the name of the graphic file you want to edit, then press Enter. For instance, we wanted to retrieve the *Wagtail3* file (created in the Chapter 2 exercises), so we typed

\DR10\WAGTAIL3

and pressed Enter. A prompt appears briefly telling you that WordPerfect is loading a WP Graphics file, then the file name appears next to the Filename option at the top of the screen. Your next step is to select the *Edit* option, which places you inside the Figure Edit screen shown in Figure 10.5 (your graphic will be different). Notice the sixth option, *DrawPerfect*. Once you select it, the WPTODRAW Shell macro will take over and transfer the image into DrawPerfect where you can edit it. Go ahead and select **DrawPerfect**.

After a minute or so, you will be in DrawPerfect with the graphic you transferred in the drawing window. Now you can use DrawPerfect's editing tools to make your changes. When you finish, display the File menu and select the *WordPerfect* option. After a few minutes, you will be back in DrawPerfect's Figure edit screen, where your newly modified graphic will appear. Wasn't that easy?

> **Tip:** If this procedure doesn't work and you end up in the Shell menu instead of DrawPerfect, try this: Go back to WordPerfect and press Exit (F7) twice to return to the WordPerfect edit screen. Next, use the Other Directory option on the List Files menu to change the default directory to the one containing the WPTODRAW.SHM file. (If you don't remember how to change the default directory, see the previous chapter, *File Management*.)

Retrieving WordPerfect Text into DrawPerfect

Practically speaking, you can only retrieve short amounts of text from WordPerfect into DrawPerfect but you may still find this feature helpful. Here's how to do it. Be sure to start WordPerfect through the Shell. Type or retrieve the text (in WordPerfect) and then place the cursor at the beginning of the section you want to transfer. Turn on block mode by pressing the Block key, Alt-F4. Next, move the cursor to highlight all the text you want to transfer. To transfer it, press Alt-Shift-T (press Alt, then Shift, and hold both while pressing T). This starts the Shell macro that switches you into DrawPerfect. Your screen should now resemble Figure 10.8. Notice this prompt at the bottom of the drawing window:

```
Position Cursor to Upper Left Corner of Text Window
(Press ENTER):
```

It means that DrawPerfect is waiting for you to designate the size and position for the new text window. This process is exactly like creating a figure box, which you did in Chapter 2 (*Your First Business Chart*). Place the cursor wherever you want to place the upper left corner of the text window, and then press Enter. As soon as you press Enter, DrawPerfect automatically creates the text window and retrieves your WordPerfect text, as shown in Figure 10.9. The cursor will remain inside the text window, where you can edit or format it as you wish. When you finish, press F7 or use the mouse to select **Exit** from the menu at the bottom of the screen. To complete the process, select **ReDraw** from the View menu (or press F9). After you finish using DrawPerfect, be sure to return to WordPerfect and clear the text from your edit screen. When you transferred the text from WordPerfect into DrawPerfect, you transferred a copy, so the original text remains in WordPerfect.

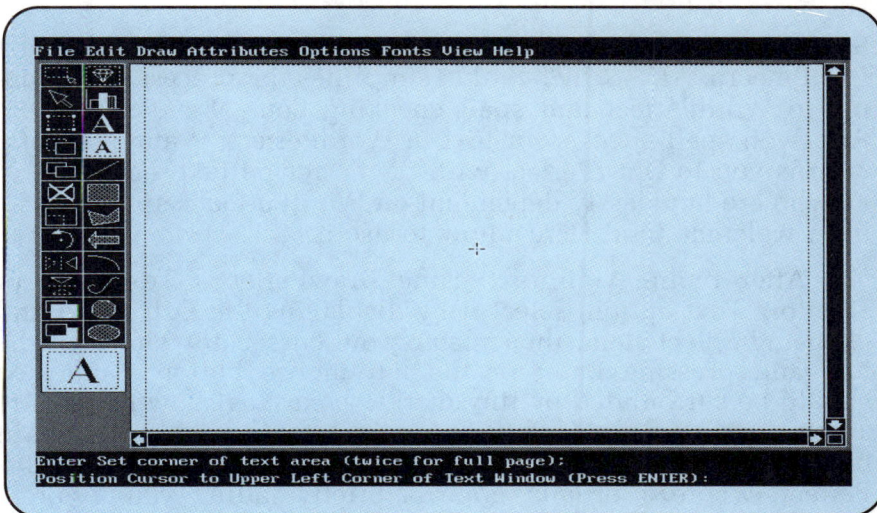

Figure 10.8 *Transferring Text from WordPerfect into DrawPerfect*

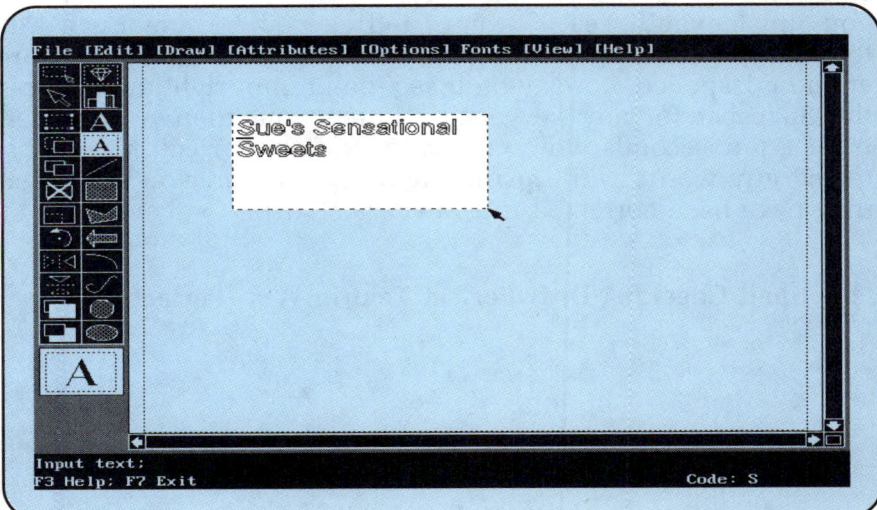

Figure 10.9 *After the text has been transferred*

Spell Checking DrawPerfect Text in WordPerfect

Since DrawPerfect does not have a spell checker, it includes a Shell macro, ALT-SHIFT-S, that simplifies the process of switching to WordPerfect and spell checking your DrawPerfect text. After you spell check your text in WordPerfect, it automatically returns you to DrawPerfect with the corrected text. For those of us who are hopelessly dependent on WordPerfect's speller, it's a most welcome tool! Here's how to use it.

After typing your text using DrawPerfect's Text Line or Window Text option, select it by displaying the **Edit** menu and choosing **Select Item**, then placing the cursor anywhere on the text and pressing Enter or the left mouse button. Your text should be surrounded by tiny marker boxes, as shown in Figure 10.10. Next, press Alt-Shift-S (press Alt, then Shift and hold both while pressing S once). This switches you into WordPerfect, where a prompt appears briefly telling you to press Enter when you finish spell checking, to return to DrawPerfect. The WordPerfect speller starts automatically and stops on the first misspelled word it finds (if there is one). Use the WordPerfect spell menu in the usual way to correct your words. When you finish, you'll see a prompt telling you how many words there are and asking you to press any key to continue. If there are no misspelled words, you'll see the prompt right away. Press the Spacebar (or any key except Enter), and then press Enter. After a few seconds, you will return to DrawPerfect. If you corrected any words while using the spell checker, you'll see that they have been corrected in DrawPerfect also.

 Spell Checking DrawPerfect Text in WordPerfect

1. Type your text using DrawPerfect's Text Line or Window Text option.

2. Display the Edit menu and choose Select Item; then place the cursor anywhere on the text and select it by pressing Enter or the left mouse button.

    Your text should be surrounded by tiny marker boxes.

Using the Shell to Integrate DrawPerfect and WordPerfect

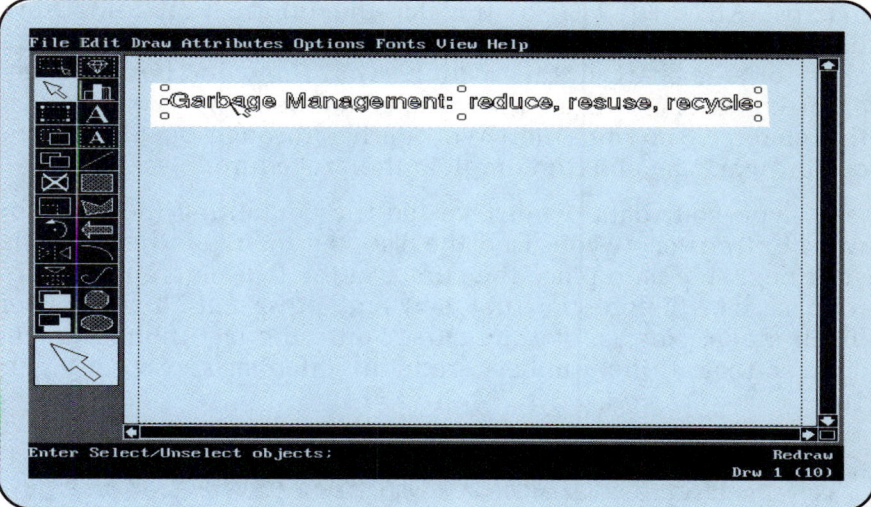

Figure 10.10   Selecting text to spell check in WordPerfect

3. Press Alt-Shift-S.   This switches you into WordPerfect, and the spell checker starts automatically and stops on the first misspelled word, if there is one.

4. Use the WordPerfect spell menu to correct your words.   When you finish, a prompt appears telling you how many words there are and asking you to press any key to continue.

5. Press the Spacebar, and then press Enter.   You return to DrawPerfect with the corrected words in your text line or window.

Creating a Bar Chart from a WordPerfect Table

If you've used WordPerfect's tabular columns or Table feature to type data into rows and columns, you can use one of the Shell

Chapter 10

macros, ALT-SHIFT-G, to transfer the information into Draw-Perfect and create an attractive chart, such as a bar graph, line chart, or area chart. In this section, we'll show you how to create a bar chart. As with all the transfer methods we've covered in this chapter, you must start WordPerfect through the Shell menu or you won't be able to complete the procedure.

Type your data or retrieve the file containing the data you want to transfer. If you used the Tab key to create the columns, your next step is to place the cursor at the left margin of the first row of data (before the first tab) and press Alt-F4 to turn on block mode. Next, move the cursor onto the last number in the table so that all the numbers are highlighted, as shown in Figure 10.11.

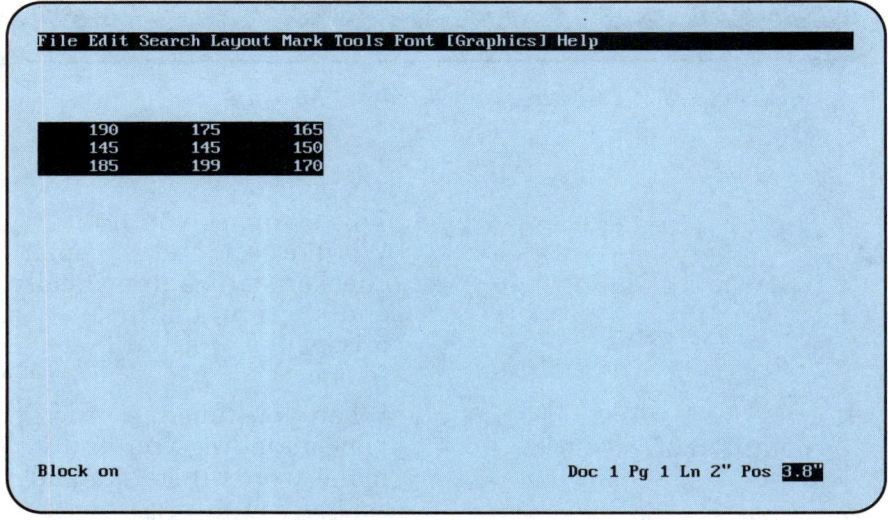

Figure 10.11 *Blocking data in a tabular column*

If you typed data in a WordPerfect Table, start with the cursor on the first number and then press Alt-F4 to turn on block mode. Next, move the cursor onto the last number in the table, highlighting all numbers in the process. In the example shown in Figure 10.12, we started with the cursor on the first number (*125*), then turned on block mode, and moved the cursor to the last one, *400*.

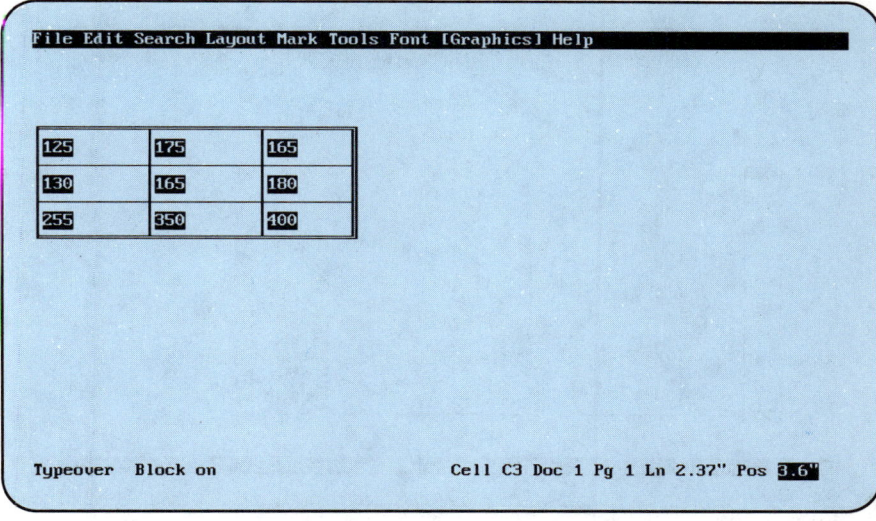

Figure 10.12 Blocking data in a table

Your next step is to press Alt-Shift-G. After a few minutes you will be in DrawPerfect's Graph Edit screen, where your data will have been converted into a bar chart. Also, you'll probably see the title *Sample Chart* that DrawPerfect provides by default. For example, the bar chart that DrawPerfect created using the data in Figure 10.11 is shown in Figure 10.13. From there you can edit your chart and save it using the techniques that you studied in Chapter 2 (*Your First Business Chart*). When you finish using DrawPerfect and select Exit from the main menu, you'll be back in the Shell. An asterisk will appear next to the WordPerfect option to remind you that it is still in memory. To switch back to WordPerfect, just press Enter.

What You Have Learned

In this chapter, you've learned how to use the Shell to integrate DrawPerfect and WordPerfect and exchange files between them. You should now be familiar with the following:

Chapter 10

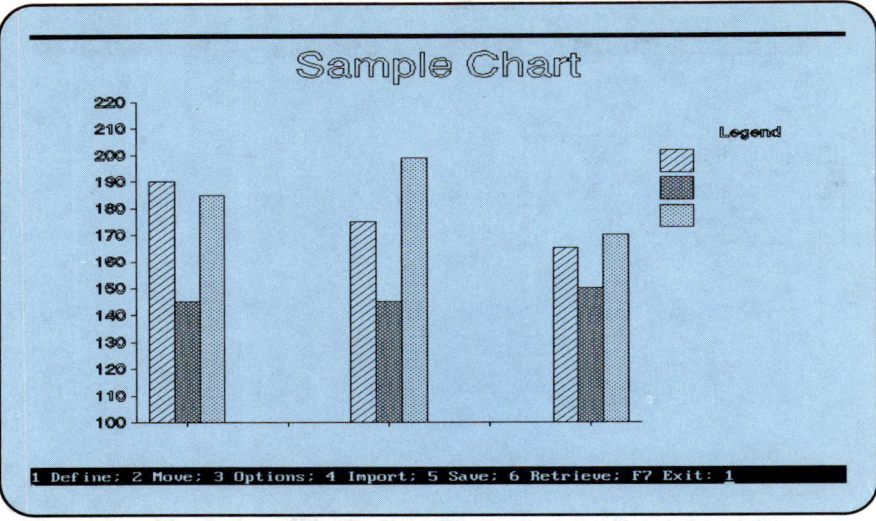

Figure 10.13 *The bar chart created from the data shown in Figure 10.11*

▶ To integrate DrawPerfect and WordPerfect 5.1, you must install the Shell utility program that has been included with DrawPerfect and set it up so that both DrawPerfect and WordPerfect are listed as options on your Shell menu. Also, whenever you use DrawPerfect or WordPerfect, you must start them through the Shell menu.

▶ You can run DrawPerfect and WordPerfect simultaneously, and switch between them using just three keystrokes: Ctrl-Alt-W to switch from DrawPerfect to WordPerfect and Ctrl-Alt-D to switch from WordPerfect to DrawPerfect.

- ▶ Another way to switch between DrawPerfect and WordPerfect is to use the Shell key (Ctrl-F1) or the Go to Shell option on the File menu (for both programs) and then select the DrawPerfect or WordPerfect option from the Shell menu.
- ▶ All data is transferred between DrawPerfect and WordPerfect through the Shell Clipboard and five Shell macros: ALTSHFTG.SHM, ALTSHFTT.SHM, ALTSHFTS.SHM, WPTODRAW.SHM, and DRAWTOWP.SHM. You should have copied these files from the Shell disk when you installed the Shell.
- ▶ To transfer a chart or drawing from DrawPerfect into WordPerfect, you retrieve it into DrawPerfect and then select the WordPerfect option on the File menu. This uses the DRAWTOWP Shell macro to copy the chart or drawing to the Shell Clipboard, start WordPerfect, create a figure box, and place the graphic inside it.
- ▶ To edit a chart or drawing that's already in a WordPerfect graphic box, you can transfer it through the shell Clipboard into DrawPerfect, edit it, then transfer the revised version back into WordPerfect. To do this, you use the WPTODRAW Shell macro by selecting the *DrawPerfect* option on WordPerfect's Figure Edit screen.

Chapter 11

Presentations and Slides

In This Chapter

▶ How to create a DrawPerfect slide show
▶ How to view a slide show
▶ How to edit a slide show
▶ How to change the background colors and margins for your slides
▶ How to produce 35mm slides from your DrawPerfect files

What if the president of your corporation were coming to town and expected a thorough report and oral presentation about your division? You've used DrawPerfect to prepare handouts and overhead transparencies, but now you really want to make a big impression and feel you need something more. Why not rent a huge monitor, like the ones you see at the computer shows, and use it to display your graphics in DrawPerfect while you're making your presentation?

You can use the same graphics that you have already printed for your handouts, and present any number of charts or drawings right on the monitor. Since the effect is like viewing a series of slides, DrawPerfect's presentation feature is often called

Chapter 11

a *slide show*. You can present your slides in any order, for any length of time, and change them automatically or manually. To add some razzle-dazzle, you can use a variety of screen wipes for the transition between slides, such as fade and overlay. To further enhance your graphics, the Page Options menu provides several features you can use to create vivid backgrounds, including shading from top to bottom, top color, and bottom color.

If you have time to prepare a more traditional slide show using a slide projector, you can send your DrawPerfect files to a slide service bureau and receive your slides the very next day!

Creating and Viewing a Slide Show

While learning how to use the presentation feature, you can include any sequence of drawings or charts that you have created, or use some from DrawPerfect's Figure Library. The first step is to display the **File** menu and select the **Presentation** option, or press the Print key (Shift-F7) and then select the Presentation option. The Presentation menu appears, as shown in Figure 11.1.

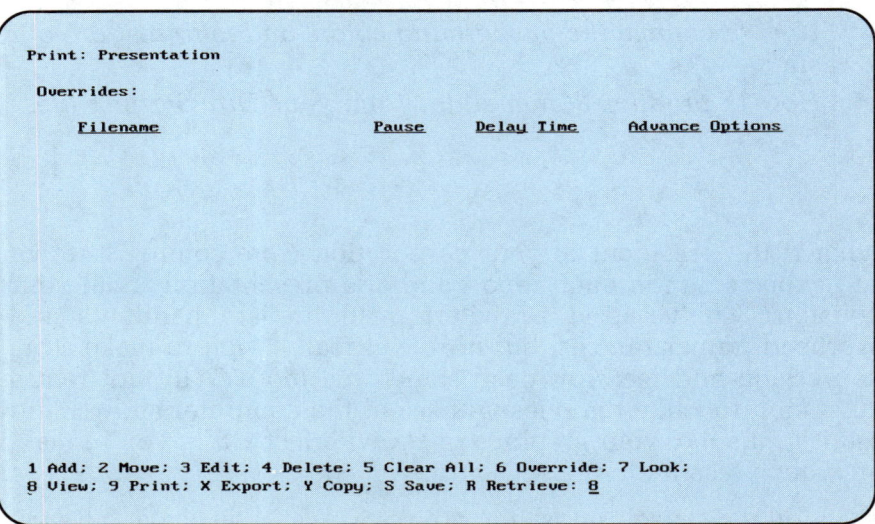

Figure 11.1 The Presentation menu

As you can see, the menu line at the bottom of the screen provides thirteen options. To begin creating your slide show, select **Add**. This will take you to the Presentation: Edit screen shown in Figure 11.2. We'll examine each of its four options in the next section.

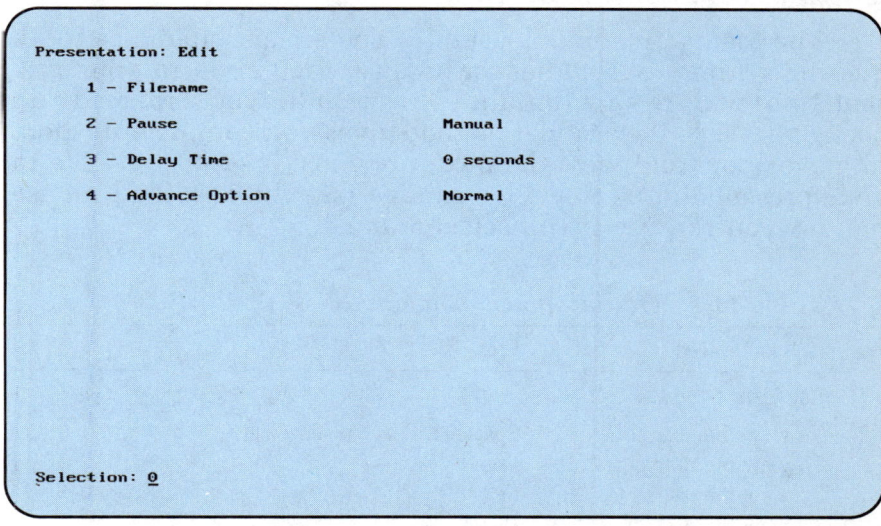

Figure 11.2   The Presentation: Edit screen

Using the Presentation: Edit Screen

Use this menu to select each chart or drawing that you want to include in your presentation. You can also use it to change the pause method and the advance option and, if you select the delay pause method, to specify the amount of time that a slide will be displayed.

To select the first chart or drawing for your presentation, choose the *Filename* option, type the file name, and press the Enter key. Alternatively, you can select a graphic from the List Files menu by selecting Filename, pressing F5 Enter, then moving the cursor onto the file and selecting the Retrieve option.

The next option on the Presentation: Edit screen is *Pause*. Use it to select a method for advancing to the next slide during your presentation: Manual or Delay. The *Delay* option advances each slide automatically after waiting a specific length of time, which you choose using the *Delay Time* option. The *Manual* option lets you advance each slide manually, by pressing Enter, Page Down, the Spacebar, or the right mouse button. Notice that DrawPerfect assumes you want to use the Manual pause method unless you change it to Delay.

The Manual method is useful if you are anticipating a lot of questions from your audience, because each slide in your presentation will remain on the screen until you are ready to change it. Also, the Manual method gives you complete freedom to move about and view the next, previous, first, or last slide in your presentation. Table 11.1 summarizes the keys and mouse buttons you can use if you select Manual.

Table 11.1 Manual pause commands

Action Desired	Press
Keyboard	
To view the next slide	Spacebar, Enter, or Page Down
To view the previous slide	Page Up
To view the last slide	End
To view the first slide	Home
To stop the presentation	F1
Mouse	
To view the next slide	Right button
To view the previous slide	Left Button

If you don't want to use the Manual option, just select the **Pause** option and choose **Delay** in response to the prompt that appears at the bottom of the screen:

```
1 Manual; 2 Delay: 0
```

If you select Delay, your next step is to choose the **Delay Time** option and indicate how long you want this particular slide displayed. This prompt appears:

```
Number of Seconds to Delay:
```

Type the number of seconds that you want this slide displayed (up to 60) and press Enter. Note that this option has no effect if you selected Manual for the pause method.

The last option on the Edit menu is *Advance Option.* You use an advance option to draw the curtain and open the next act, so to speak, erasing a slide from your screen to make way for the next one in the presentation. DrawPerfect provides fifteen different methods, often called *screen wipes,* including in, out, top-in, top-out, fade, and overlay. Normal is the default method, and it just removes the slide and replaces it with the next one. When you select Advance Option, the menu line shown in Figure 11.3 appears. A description of each method appears in Table 11.2.

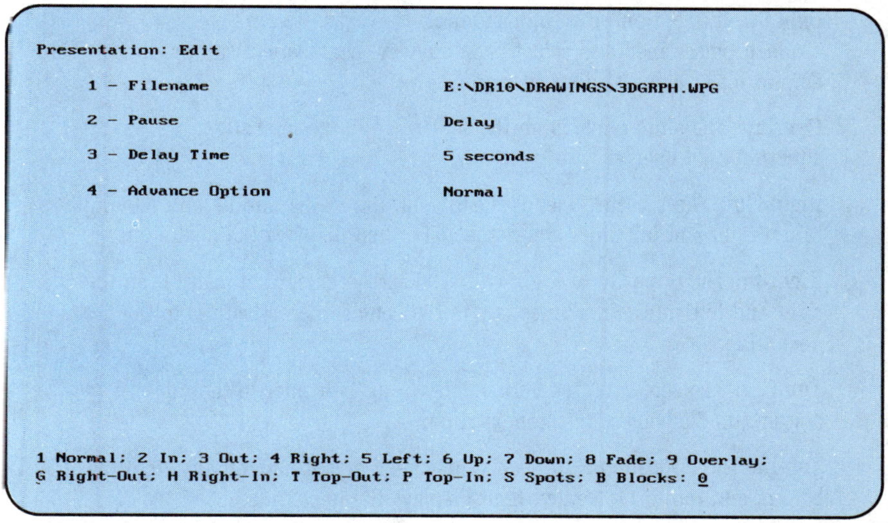

```
Presentation: Edit

    1 - Filename          E:\DR10\DRAWINGS\3DGRPH.WPG

    2 - Pause             Delay

    3 - Delay Time        5 seconds

    4 - Advance Option    Normal




1 Normal; 2 In; 3 Out; 4 Right; 5 Left; 6 Up; 7 Down; 8 Fade; 9 Overlay;
G Right-Out; H Right-In; T Top-Out; P Top-In; S Spots; B Blocks: 0
```

Figure 11.3 The Advance Options menu line

Table 11.2 Screen wipes

Normal: The most basic of transitions, it simply replaces the current slide with the next.

In: The screen erases from the outside inward, shrinking all four sides into a smaller and smaller box until the slide disappears completely and the next one appears.

Out: The reverse of *In.* The screen erases from the center to the outside perimeter, on all four sides. When the slide has completely disappeared, the next one appears.

Right: A vertical line erases the screen from left to right; then the next slide appears.

Continued

Table 11.2 (continued)

Left: The opposite of *Right*. A vertical line erases the screen from right to left; then the next slide appears.

Up: A horizontal line erases the screen from the bottom to the top; then the next slide appears.

Down: The opposite of *Up*. A horizontal line erases the screen from the top to the bottom; then the next slide appears.

Fade: The screen slowly dissolves; then the next slide appears. You can only use this option on a color monitor. However, if you have a monochrome screen and select Fade anyway, DrawPerfect can produce a similar effect using a different method.

Overlay: The slide remains on the screen while the next slide is superimposed over it.

Right-Out: The screen erases vertically starting in the middle and moving to the right and left sides simultaneously, then displays the next slide.

Right-In: The opposite of *Right-Out*. The screen erases vertically from the right and left sides simultaneously to the center, then advances to the next slide.

Top-Out: The screen erases horizontally from the center to the top and bottom, then advances to the next slide.

Top-In: The opposite of *Top-Out*. The screen erases horizontally from the bottom and top to the center, then displays the next slide.

Spots: The screen is dissolved by a spot pattern, then displays the next slide.

Blocks: The screen is dissolved by a series of squares, then displays the next slide.

As you can see, DrawPerfect provides an exciting variety of options that you can use to create a spectacular screen show. It's fun to experiment with them, and we encourage you to try them all.

Once you have completed all the necessary information for your first entry, press the Enter key to return to the Presentation menu. It should now resemble Figure 11.4. Notice that the information you typed for your first slide is displayed horizontally, under the headings *Filename, Pause, Delay Time,* and *Advance Options*. When you finish adding all your slides, this screen will serve as a script for your show, providing this information for each slide. Incidentally, when you run your presentation the slides will appear in the order shown in this list (provided you begin with the cursor at the top).

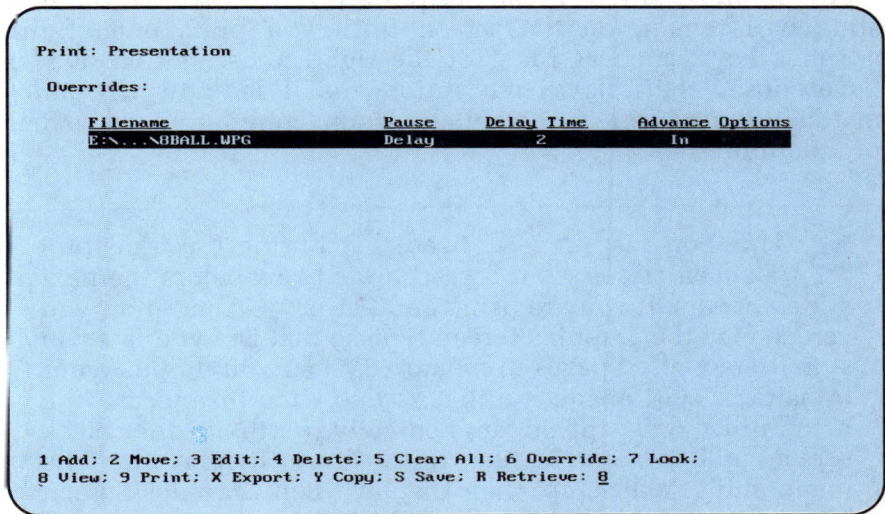

Figure 11.4 *The Presentation menu with first slide*

To add your next slide, select the **Add** option and repeat the steps you just studied. When you finish, use the **Save** option on the Presentation menu to save the whole list as a file. When you select Save, this prompt will appear:

`Presentation List to be Saved:`

Type a file name of one to eight characters and press Enter. DrawPerfect will add the three-character extension *DRP* to your file name. For example, if you save it under the name SALES89, the name will become SALES89.DRP. Once you've saved a presentation, you can bring it back anytime using the Retrieve option on this menu.

Viewing Your Slide Show

Once you have added the last slide to your list, you're all set to display your presentation. To do this, you'll use the View option. Since the first slide that appears will be the one the cursor is highlighting when you select View, be sure to move the cursor onto the first file in the list. Next, select **View**. Your presentation will begin, and the first graphic in the list will appear on the monitor. If the Advance Option is set to Manual, the first slide will remain on the screen until you press one of the advance keys, such as Enter or the right mouse button. If you have chosen the Delay Time option, the slide show will automatically run itself. Congratulations on completing your first production!

> **Tip:** You may have noticed that during the transition between slides, your screen turns black before the next slide appears. If you are using an EGA or VGA monitor, you can change the graphics screen type so that DrawPerfect can store two graphic pages in memory. When you do this, your transitions will change so that as one slide disappears, the next slide will appear immediately (without the black screen in between). To use this feature, display the File menu and select Setup, then Display, then Graphics Screen Type. Select IBM EGA (PRESENTATIONS) from the list of graphic screen drivers. Choose the Select option from the next menu, and then press F7 to exit the Setup: Display menu.

Creating a Slide Show Presentation

1. Display the File menu and select the Presentation option.

    The Presentation menu appears.

2. Select Add.

    The Presentation: Edit screen appears.

3. Select Filename, then type the file name for your first slide and press the Enter key. Alternatively, you can select a file from the List Files menu by selecting Filename, pressing F5 Enter, then moving the

cursor onto the file and selecting the Retrieve option.

4. If you want to use the Delay Time pause method so that your presentation moves from slide to slide without your intervention, select Pause. Change it to Delay, then select Delay Time and type the number of seconds you want this slide displayed.

5. Unless you want to use the Normal method to advance your slides, select Advance Option and choose one of the fourteen other screen wipe methods. When you finish, press Enter.

6. Repeat steps 2, 3, 4, and 5 for each graph you want to include in your presentation.

7. Select View to see the slide show.

This returns you to the Presentation screen.

Editing a Slide Show

After viewing the presentation, you'll probably find some changes you'd like to make. For example, maybe you'd like to rearrange the sequence, or remove a slide from the presentation. Does this mean you have to start all over again? Of course not! As you'll see, the Presentation menu includes several tools that you can use to make changes and corrections, including Move, Edit, Delete, and Override.

The *Move* option lets you rearrange the order of the files, and move one or more slides to another position in the list. To use it, place the cursor onto the file you want to reposition, then select Move. An asterisk will appear next to the file, and these instructions will appear on the prompt line:

```
Use the arrow keys or mouse to move to desired loca-
tion, then press Enter.
```

The next step is to move the cursor into the new position and then press Enter or the left mouse button. Note that DrawPerfect will insert the slide above the one the cursor is highlighting when you press Enter or the left mouse button.

The *Edit* option takes you back into the Presentation: Edit screen that you used to add a slide to your list and lets you change the file name, pause method, delay time, or advance option.

The *Delete* option does just what it says: deletes a slide from the show. It will not delete it from the disk, so don't be afraid to use it! When you select Delete, this prompt will appear at the bottom of the screen:

```
Delete Entry? No (Yes)
```

As you can see, DrawPerfect gives you a chance to change your mind and retain the slide. If you want to delete it from your list, select Yes. If not, select No.

The *Clear All* option is also self-explanatory. Use it to clear all the files from the Presentation screen, so you can start over and create a new presentation. Note that it erases the files from the screen, not from your disk. When you select Clear All, this prompt will appear:

```
Clear all Entries? No (Yes)
```

and you get a chance to change your mind. If you want to clear all the files, select Yes. If you decide against it, select No.

You can use the *Override* option: To change settings such as the pause method for all slides; to repeat the entire presentation again and again; to override the path in your file names; or to display a mouse pointer. When you select Override, the menu shown in Figure 11.5 appears. Notice that you can use it to override most of the options on the Presentation: Edit menu, including Pause, Delay Time, and Advance Option. If you select one of these three options, it changes the setting for all of the files in your list.

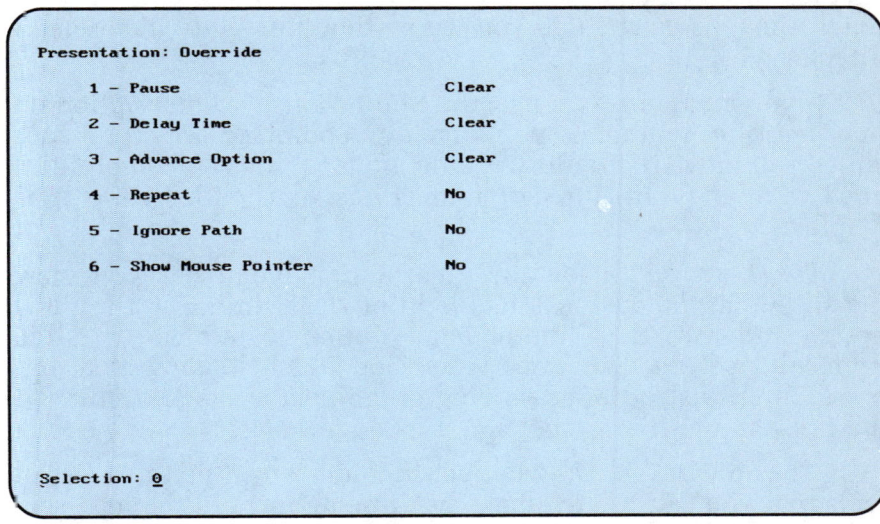

Figure 11.5 The Override menu

As an example, say that you have selected the Manual pause method for all your slides, but want to change it to automatic for one presentation. Select **Override**, then select **Pause** and change it to **Delay**. Press Enter to return to the Presentation menu, and you'll see the word *Delay* next to the Overrides: prompt near the top of the screen. Now select **View** to watch your presentation. It will run all by itself, and return to the Presentation menu after all the slides have been displayed. To turn off the override feature, select **Override** again, select **Pause** (or whichever option you changed), and then select **Clear**. Press Enter to return to the Presentation menu. Notice that the Overrides: line near the top of the screen is now blank, since none of the options are being overridden.

If you select the Repeat option on the Override menu and change it to Yes, the entire presentation will be repeated over and over until you stop it. In other words, after DrawPerfect displays the last slide in the list, it cycles back to the first one and displays them all again and continually repeats this procedure. To stop it, you can press Exit (F7) or Cancel (F1) or the equivalent mouse buttons (both simultaneously or the center button if you have one).

Use the *Ignore Path* option on the Override menu if you plan to run your presentation on a different computer. If you do, you won't have to edit the file names and type new paths and subdirectory names when you copy the files onto the other computer (just be sure that you copy the files into the default directory).

If you are using a mouse, the *Show Mouse Pointer* option on the Override menu lets you display a pointing arrow in your slides and move it around with the mouse. This can be helpful if you want to point out certain features in a slide while it is displayed.

The *Look* option on the Presentation menu lets you view the slide that the cursor is highlighting. It is similar to the View option and uses the same advance option to remove the slide from your screen. However, when you finish looking at it and press Enter, instead of advancing to the next slide you return to the Presentation list.

As you can see, DrawPerfect includes an impressive list of tools that you can use to edit your presentations. In the next section, you'll learn about a few other tools that you can use to enhance your presentations.

Page Options

DrawPerfect has several tools on the Setup menu that you can use to embellish your presentations, including Margins, Shading Top to Bottom in View, Top Color, and Bottom Color. They are found on the Page Options menu shown in Figure 11.6. To use this menu, display the **File** menu and select **Setup** (or press Shift-F1), then **Initial Settings**, then **Page Options**.

Margins

The margins are the blank space around the outside of your page. Unless you change them, the left, right, top, and bottom margins will be one inch each. To change one or more of them, select the **Margins** option on the Page Options menu. Type a

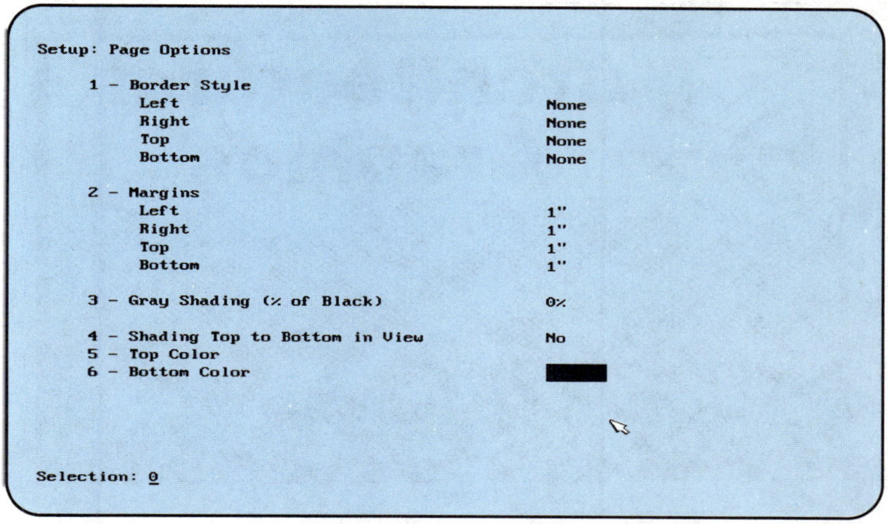

```
Setup: Page Options

    1 - Border Style
        Left                              None
        Right                             None
        Top                               None
        Bottom                            None

    2 - Margins
        Left                              1"
        Right                             1"
        Top                               1"
        Bottom                            1"

    3 - Gray Shading (% of Black)         0%

    4 - Shading Top to Bottom in View     No
    5 - Top Color
    6 - Bottom Color                      ████████


Selection: 0
```

Figure 11.6 The Page Options menu

number for the left margin and press Enter to move to the right margin setting (or just press Enter to accept the default of 1"). Repeat for the right, top, and bottom margin settings. Note that you don't have to type the inch mark because DrawPerfect will insert it automatically. Also, you can type numbers with decimals, such as 1.5 or .25. The margin settings affect the View option in the Presentation menu, the print preview option (View Drawing), and the printed version of the drawing.

Shading Top to Bottom in View

As the title implies, this feature works only in the View screens: View on the Presentation menu and View Drawing on the Print menu. It is used in conjunction with the next two options, *Top Color* and *Bottom Color,* which are the two background colors for your slides. The Top Color will appear in a horizontal band at the top of the screen, and the Bottom Color will appear in a band at the bottom. In between the two bands, the colors gradually change from the top to the bottom color. The Shading Top to Bottom option is especially effective in presentations.

Figure 11.7 shows how one of our drawings appeared in the View screen when we turned on this option. Although we used a color monitor to display it, we selected white for the top color and black for the bottom color.

Chapter 11

Figure 11.7 Using Top Color and Bottom Color

Selecting a Top Color and Bottom Color

Although the Top Color and Bottom Color options are much more dramatic on a color monitor, you can still use them on a monochrome monitor. The various shades will be interpreted as patterns.

To choose the top color in a shaded background, select **Top Color** from the Page Options screen. A menu of colors will appear at the bottom of the screen. To see more colors, select **Next**. To back up, select **Previous**. When you see the color you want to use, type the number appearing next to it and press Enter. The steps that you use to choose the bottom color are identical, except that you select **Bottom Color** from the Page Options screen.

When you finish using the Page Options menu, press Enter three times (or F7 twice).

Note that if you export a DrawPerfect file into Enhanced CGM format and send it to a slide service bureau (as described in the next section), the colors you select using the Top Color and Bottom Color options will be used as background colors for your slides.

Producing 35mm Slides from Your DrawPerfect Files

If you'd like to produce 35mm slides from your DrawPerfect files, you don't have to rush out and purchase an expensive film recorder, because there are many service bureaus that can create them for you. For example, we used a company called MAGICorp to produce slides and color laser prints from our DrawPerfect graphics, and were very pleased with the output. Since MAGICorp's production facility is located next to the distribution center of the Airborne Express delivery service, we were able to transmit our DrawPerfect files by modem at 3 p.m. and receive the finished slides the next morning. You can send your DrawPerfect files (by modem using a toll-free phone number) as late as 5 p.m. in your time zone, and still receive them the next morning. If you don't have a modem, you can mail the DrawPerfect files on disk.

In addition to 35mm slides with resolution of over 4000 lines, MAGICorp can produce color photographic prints, color overhead transparencies, and color laser prints. They can even replace the backgrounds in your slides with impressive photographic backgrounds, such as the U.S. flag, marble, granite, wood, velvet, fireworks, the earth, and the White House. MAGICorp provides the communications software (at no charge) that you use to transmit your DrawPerfect files by modem. Since it is entirely menu-driven, we found it easy to install and use. You can contact MAGICorp at 1-800-367-6244, or write them at this address:

MAGICorp Corporation
50 Executive Blvd.
Elmsford, NY 10523

MAGICorp Corporation and two other slide service bureaus, Beekman Group and Brilliant Image, are discussed in the DrawPerfect manual. For more information, look in the Reference section of your DrawPerfect manual, under the heading *Export*.

Preparing Your DrawPerfect Files for a Slide Service

To prepare your DrawPerfect files for a slide service bureau, you must export them to a special format called CGM. Fortunately, this is much easier than it sounds. With the chart or drawing on your screen, display the **File** menu and select **Export** (or press Ctrl-F5), then select **CGM**. You will see this prompt:

`Enter filename for CGM output:`

Either press Enter to accept the suggested name, or type a new one (from one to eight characters). DrawPerfect will automatically add the three-character extension *CGM* to your file name. Repeat this procedure for each DrawPerfect file that you want to translate into a slide. Be sure to send the CGM files—not the WPG files!—to the service bureau.

Some service bureaus, including MAGICorp, require that you use an enhanced version of the CGM format. DrawPerfect assumes you want to use the standard CGM format when you select Export, but you can change it to Enhanced using DrawPerfect's Setup menu. To do this, display the **File** menu and select **Setup** (or press Shift-F1), then **Environment**. Select the sixth option on the menu, **Export Enhanced CGM**, and change it to **Yes**. This is a one-time process that remains in effect indefinitely, or until you repeat the steps and change it back to No.

> ▶ **Tip:** You can use the Export option on the Presentation menu to automatically convert an entire presentation to CGM format (or to HPGL, SCODL, or VideoShow format). If you want to export a large number of files and they are already set up as a presentation, this is a much faster method than converting them individually.

What You Have Learned

In this chapter, you've learned how to use DrawPerfect's Presentation feature. You should now be familiar with the following:

▶ You can use the Presentation option to view a series of charts and drawings on your monitor. The graphics can appear in any order, for any length of time, and you can change them automatically or manually. To enhance the show, you can use a variety of screen wipe effects for the transition between graphics: normal, in, out, right, left, up, down, fade, overlay, right-out, right-in, top-out, top-in, spots, and block. The presentation feature is often called a *slide show*.

▶ To create a presentation, use the Presentation option on the Print menu.

▶ To select charts and drawings for your presentation, select the Add option from the Presentation menu and then select Filename from the Presentation: Edit menu that appears.

▶ DrawPerfect provides two methods that you can use to advance to the next slide during a presentation: Manual or Delay. The default is the Manual pause method, which lets you advance each slide manually by pressing Enter, Page Down, the Spacebar, or the right mouse button. You can use the Pause option on the Presentation: Edit menu to change it to Delay. This option advances each slide automatically, after a specific number of seconds that you have designated.

▶ You can use an Advance Option to select a screen wipe effect for each slide in your presentation. DrawPerfect will use it to erase the slide from your screen and advance to the next one. The default is Normal, but you can change it to in, out, right, left, up, down, fade, overlay, right-out, right-in, top-out, top-in, spots, or block. To change it, use the Advance Option selection on the Presentation: Edit screen.

- ▶ To display your presentation, move the cursor onto the first file in the list and then select the View option on the Presentation menu. If you are using the Manual Advance Option, when you finish viewing the first slide press Enter or the right mouse button to move to the next one. If you are using the Delay Time method, the slide show will automatically run itself.
- ▶ You can use the Move option on the Presentation menu to rearrange the order of the files in a presentation, moving one or more slides to another position in the list.
- ▶ You can use the Edit option on the Presentation menu to return to the Presentation: Edit screen for a specific slide and edit the file name, pause method, delay time, or advance option.
- ▶ You can use the Delete option on the Presentation menu to delete a file from the presentation.
- ▶ If you've just created and saved a presentation and want to create a new one, you can use the Clear All option on the Presentation menu to clear all the files from the list.
- ▶ You can use the Override option to change the pause method, delay time, or advance option for all slides simultaneously; to repeat the entire presentation again and again; to override the path in your file names; or to display a mouse pointer.
- ▶ Use the Look option on the Presentation menu when you want to view only the slide the cursor is highlighting. When you finish looking at it and press Enter, you return to the Presentation list.
- ▶ The Page Options menu includes several tools that you can use to change the background colors and margins for your slides: Margins, Shading Top to Bottom in View, Top Color, and Bottom Color. To use them, display the File menu and select Setup, then Initial Settings, then Page Options.
- ▶ You can create 35mm slides from your DrawPerfect graphics using a film recorder or by sending them to a slide service bureau, such as MAGICorp. Before sending your DrawPerfect graphics to a service bureau, you must translate them into a CGM format using the Export option on the File menu.

Chapter 12

An Introduction to Macros

In This Chapter

- What is a macro?
- How to create a simple macro
- How to edit a macro
- How to select a default directory for your macros
- How to use the macros that are included with DrawPerfect

A macro is a sequence of keystrokes that you record in a special file so that you can quickly replay them whenever you need them. Essentially, you can use them as shortcuts to any task that you perform frequently, such as retrieving a particular chart or drawing, turning on options such as Grid Display and Grid Snap, or selecting a drawing tool such as Box and changing its fill pattern before you begin drawing. To use a macro, you simply press a few keys and DrawPerfect replays all the keystrokes exactly as you originally typed them.

If you have used WordPerfect's macros, you already understand the basic concepts and procedures, which are identical. Even if you haven't, learning how to create, use, and edit DrawPerfect macros is fun and rewarding, so enjoy!

Creating Your First Macro

As you'll soon see, creating a macro to perform an everyday task such as turning on some of DrawPerfect's options or drawing a box is a simple process. You begin by pressing the Macro Define key (Ctrl-F10) and typing a name for your macro and a brief description of what the macro will do. The next step is to type the keystrokes for the macro, just as though you were performing that task in a real application. At this point it's as if a tape recorder is on and recording every key you press. When you finish recording the keystrokes, you press Macro Define again (Ctrl-F10). DrawPerfect then saves your new macro as a special file with the extension *.DRM*. As you can probably guess, the extension DRM stands for *DrawPerfect macro*.

There are two basic types of macros, differentiated by their names and the method you use to replay them. The file name for the first type can include between one and eight characters, such as OPTIONS, PRINTING, or GRID. The second type combines the Alt key with any letter A through Z, such as ALTO or ALTG. To replay an Alt key macro, you press Alt and the letter. To replay a named macro, you press Alt-F10, type the name, then press Enter. Since you only press two keys to use them, the Alt key macros are the real shortcuts!

As you type the macro, your keystrokes actually perform their normal functions in DrawPerfect, so it's a good idea to clear the screen (and save your work) before you begin creating your macro. After you finish recording the keystrokes for the macro, you'll want to clear the screen again.

> **Caution:** Never try to retrieve a macro using the List Files menu or the File menu's Retrieve option. To change a macro or view its contents, you must use the macro editor, which we'll discuss later.

Let's learn how to create a simple macro that will turn on the Grid Display and Grid Snap features on the Options menu. This task would normally require four keystrokes: *O* for Options, *G* for Grid Display, *O* for Options, and *R* for Grid Snap. By recording the keystrokes in a macro named ALTG, you can reduce this task to just two: Alt and G. Let's try it.

Your first step is to press the Macro Define key (Ctrl-F10) (sorry, mouse users, there is no mouse equivalent!). You should see this prompt in the lower left corner of the screen:

`Define macro:`

and it means that DrawPerfect is waiting for you to type a name for your new macro. Remember, macro names can include from one to eight characters, or you can name them using the Alt key in combination with any letter (A through Z). Let's name this macro *ALTG*. Press Alt and then type G (or just type AltG and press Enter). Next, this prompt appears:

`Description:`

A warning: If you see a prompt like this one instead of the `Description` prompt:

`ALTG.DRM Already Exists: 1 Replace; 2 Edit; 3 Description: 0`

it means there is already a macro on your disk that is using the same name. If this happens, press Cancel (F1) and begin again, using a different file name for this macro, such as ALTO or ALTR.

At this point, you may wish to type a brief description of your macro (up to 39 characters). This description will be visible when you edit the macro and can help you remember what it does. If you don't want a description, you can skip this step by pressing Enter once. Otherwise, type:

Turns on grid display and snap

then press Enter. Now you should see a new prompt in the lower left corner of the screen:

`Macro Define`

This prompt indicates that you have turned on the keystroke recorder, so be careful what you type! Select the Options menu, then select Grid Display by typing:

O G

Notice that the Grid Display is actually visible in your drawing window. Next, select the Options menu, then select Grid Snap by typing:

O R

Notice the `Snp` notation in the lower right corner of the screen, indicating that Grid Snap is now on.

> **Tip:** Mouse users: Although you can use the mouse while defining your macro, we recommend against it. Unlike keystrokes, you cannot change mouse movements using DrawPerfect's macro editor. Therefore, if you ever wanted to alter the macro in the future, the only way you could do it would be to redefine it. Another disadvantage to using the mouse is that it increases the size of your macro.

That completes your macro keystrokes, so your last step is to turn off macro definition and save the macro. To do this, press Macro Define (Ctrl-F10). The `Macro Define` prompt disappears, and DrawPerfect saves your file in the default directory using the name ALTG.DRM.

From now on, whenever you want to turn on DrawPerfect's Grid Display and Grid Snap options, just press Alt and G. However, it won't work correctly if you try it now, because both grid options are still on! Instead of turning the Grid Display and Grid Snap on, it will turn them off! As you just saw, when you define a macro, DrawPerfect actually uses the keystrokes. Before trying the macro, be sure to turn the two options off.

Display the Options menu and select Clear Options. This turns off the Grid Display and Grid Snap. Now try the macro by pressing Alt and G. If it worked properly, you will see the grid display and `Snp` notation almost immediately.

> **Tip:** To use an Alt key macro, press the Alt key first and hold it while pressing the letter key (such as G) just once, then release both keys.

An Introduction to Macros

 Creating and Using an Alt Key Macro

1. Press the Macro Define key (Ctrl-F10).

   This prompt appears in the lower left corner of the screen: `Define macro:`

2. Press Alt, then type a letter (such as B if you are naming the macro ALTB) and press Enter.

   This prompt appears: `Description:`

3. Type a brief description of your macro or press Enter to skip this step.

   This prompt appears: `Macro Define`

4. Type the keystrokes that you want to record in the macro and then press Ctrl-F10 to end macro definition.

   This ends the keystroke recording and saves the macro as a special type of file with the extension DRM.

5. To use the macro, press Alt and hold it down while pressing the letter once.

   ☐

A Drawing Macro

Let's try creating another simple macro, one that will draw a box using a specific fill pattern. This time, we will name it *BOX* (instead of using an Alt key combination). The keystrokes that you will record in the macro are:

    D (selects the Draw menu)
    B (selects Box)
    A (selects the Attributes menu)
    P (selects Fill Pattern)
    N (selects Next)
    29 Enter (selects pattern #29)
    Enter (sets corner, starts drawing box)
    Down Arrow 5 times, then Right Arrow 5 times (draws box)
    Enter (ends box drawing)

To create the box macro, begin by pressing the Macro Define key (Ctrl-F10). For the macro name, type:

box

then press Enter. For the description, type:

creates small box, uses fill pattern 29

then press Enter. Next, type the macro keystrokes:

d b a p n 29 Enter Enter

Press the Down Arrow key five times, press the Right Arrow key five times, and then press Enter. End macro definition by pressing Ctrl-F10.

Before using this macro, select File Clear to clear the screen. Next, run the macro by pressing Alt-F10, typing the macro name (Box), and pressing Enter. A small box should appear on the screen, as shown in Figure 12.1. Notice the fill pattern.

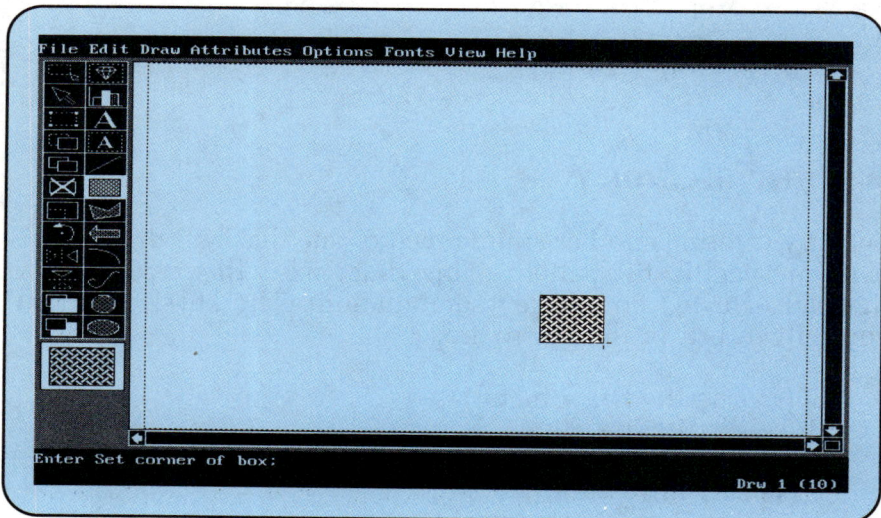

Figure 12.1   The main DrawPerfect screen after using the box macro

What if you had been using this macro for a few weeks and found that you really needed to create a much larger box? Don't feel like retyping the whole macro? No problem: Just use Draw-Perfect's macro editor to add the extra keystrokes to your macro. In the next section, we'll teach you how. Leave this box on the screen so you can compare the results after editing your macro.

Editing a Macro

The initial steps that you use to edit a macro are the same steps you use to create it: press Macro Define (Ctrl-F10), type the macro name, then press Enter. Next, you will see a prompt warning you that the macro already exists and asking if you want to replace it, edit it, or change the description. Let's try it.

Press Ctrl-F10 and type the macro name:

box

then press Enter. This prompt appears:

BOX.DRM Already Exists: 1 Replace; **2** Edit; **3** Description: ▯

Select the **Edit** option. Next, the macro editor appears, as shown in Figure 12.2. Don't feel intimidated—this screen is very logical and we'll explain it carefully!

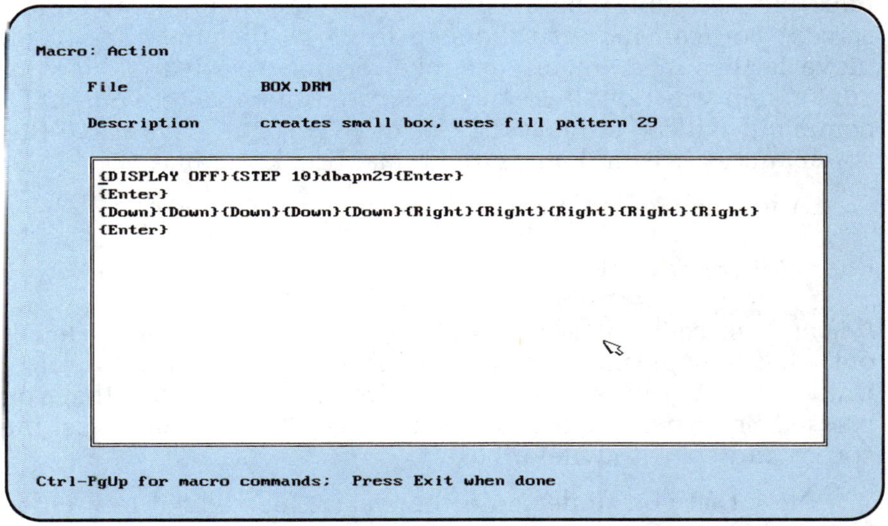

```
Macro: Action
     File           BOX.DRM
     Description    creates small box, uses fill pattern 29

     {DISPLAY OFF}{STEP 10}dbapn29{Enter}
     {Enter}
     {Down}{Down}{Down}{Down}{Down}{Right}{Right}{Right}{Right}{Right}
     {Enter}




Ctrl-PgUp for macro commands;   Press Exit when done
```

Figure 12.2   Using the macro editor

The macro file name appears at the top of the screen: *BOX.DRM*. Next, you see the description that you typed when

Chapter 12

you created the macro (assuming you did type one, an optional step). The macro keystrokes appear inside the large box. Notice that each keystroke is surrounded by braces. For example, {Down} means the Down Arrow key, {Right} means the Right Arrow key, and {Enter} means the Enter key.

You're probably wondering about {DISPLAY OFF} and {STEP 10} in the first line. These are commands that DrawPerfect automatically inserts into any new macro that you create. While the macro is running, {DISPLAY OFF} prevents you from seeing any prompts and menus that it is using. If you would prefer to see them, you can erase it by pressing the Delete key once (since your cursor should be on the command now). However, when you use the macro the menus go by so rapidly that you can hardly tell what is happening (although there is a Speed command that you can use to slow them down).

The second command, {STEP 10}, establishes how far the cursor will move each time you press an Arrow key. You may remember from Chapter 1 that the number that appears in parenthesis in the lower right corner of the main DrawPerfect screen is called the *Cursor Step*, and it is usually set to 10. This tells you how far the cursor will move when you press an Arrow key once. By pressing the Insert key (in the main DrawPerfect screen) you can increase the step to 25 so that the cursor will move farther in a single keystroke, or decrease it to 1. If your cursor step was not 10 when you created this macro, your STEP command will be either {STEP 1} or {STEP 25}. Let's leave this command as it is and study the remaining keystrokes.

After the step command, these characters appear:

```
dbapn29 {Enter} {Enter}
```

If you look back to the previous section, you can easily figure out what they mean. These are the keystrokes you used to select **D**raw, **B**ox, **A**ttributes, Fill **P**attern, **N**ext, and **29**. After that you pressed Enter twice, once to select pattern 29 and once to set the corner and start drawing a box.

Now that you understand the macro, let's edit it to include four additional Down Arrow and Right Arrow keystrokes so that the macro will create a slightly larger box. The cursor is already inside the edit box, but you need to move it down a few lines. To move the cursor, press the Down Arrow key twice. Let's insert a blank line for the new keystrokes so you will be able to see them more clearly as you type them. Press Enter once and then press the Up Arrow to move the cursor onto the new line.

We suspect you're wondering how to insert the {Down} keystroke into the editor, since pressing the Down Arrow key obviously does not work! Here's how: If you press Macro Define (Ctrl-F10), every keystroke you press after that will become part of the macro until you press Ctrl-F10 again.

To continue editing, press Macro Define (Ctrl-F10). Notice this prompt in the lower left corner of the screen, alerting you that Macro Define is on and any keystroke you press will now become part of the macro:

`Press` **`Macro Define`** `to enable editing`

Press the Down Arrow key four times and then the Right Arrow key four times. If you make a mistake, press Ctrl-F10, use the Delete key to erase the unwanted keystrokes (place the cursor on a keystroke that you want to erase and press Delete), then press Ctrl-F10 and begin again.

When you finish, you should see four more {Down} and {Right} keystrokes in the macro edit box, and your screen should resemble Figure 12.3. Since you are through making changes, your two last steps are to turn off Macro Define and exit from the macro edit screen by pressing Ctrl-F10, then Exit (F7).

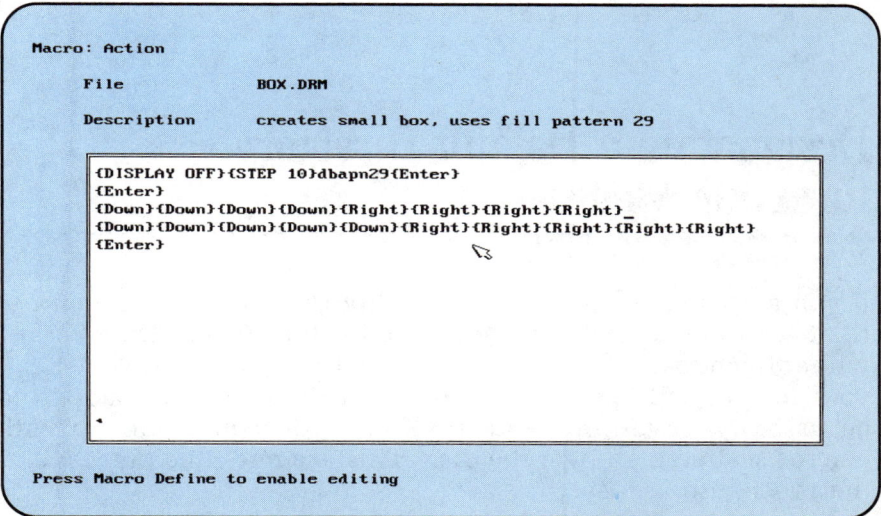

Figure 12.3 *The box macro after editing*

Now try the macro again. Begin by moving the cursor to the upper right corner of the screen. Next, press Alt-F10, type BOX, then press Enter. Is this box larger than the other one in the lower right corner?

◤ Editing a Macro

1. Press Ctrl-F10 and type the name of the macro that you want to edit.

    A prompt will appear asking if you want to replace, edit, or change the description.

2. Select the Edit option.

    The macro editor appears. All macro keystrokes are inside the box, and the cursor is at the top.

3. Edit the macro as necessary. To erase a keystroke, place the cursor on it and press Delete. To add keystrokes such as {Enter}, press Macro Define (Ctrl-F10), type the keystrokes, then press Ctrl-F10 again.

4. When you finish editing, press Exit (F7).

Designating a Default Directory for Your Macros

If you are using a hard disk, we highly recommend that you use the Setup menu to designate a subdirectory where DrawPerfect will automatically save each macro that you define. If you don't, your macros will be saved in whatever directory you happen to be using (your current directory), and you could end up with macros scattered all over the disk. This is a one-time process and the procedure is easy.

An Introduction to Macros

Begin by defining your macro subdirectory using the **Other Directory** option on the List Files menu (see Chapter 9 if you've forgotten how). Next, select **Setup** from the File menu (or press Shift-F1), select the **Location of Files** option, then select the **Keyboard/Macro Files** option. Type the name of the disk drive and the path to the subdirectory. For example, to store all of your macros in a subdirectory named MACROS (which itself is a subdirectory of the DR10 directory on drive C), you would type:

C:\DR10\MACROS

 Caution: DrawPerfect won't let you type a subdirectory name if you have not yet created it.

When you finish typing it, press Enter and Exit (F7). That's all there is to it! From now on, all of your macros will automatically be saved in this subdirectory, and you'll always know exactly where they are!

Using the Macros That Are Included with DrawPerfect

DrawPerfect includes several built-in macros that you can try, and even edit and modify as you please. However, before you can use them you have to select a keyboard layout. DrawPerfect's *Keyboard Layout* feature lets you customize your keyboard, changing the meaning of any key and/or assigning macros to key combinations such as Alt and any letter or Ctrl and any letter. Creating a keyboard layout is beyond the scope of this book, but using an existing one is easy. DrawPerfect comes with two ready-made keyboards, ALTRNAT and MACROS. Let's learn how to use the MACROS keyboard.

Display the **File** menu, then select **Setup** (or press the Setup key, Shift-F1). Select **Keyboard Layout**. A list of available keyboard definitions appears, similar to Figure 12.4. The cursor should be highlighting the ALTRNAT keyboard layout. If you do not see these definitions, you will have to install the keyboard definitions before continuing (see Appendix A for more information).

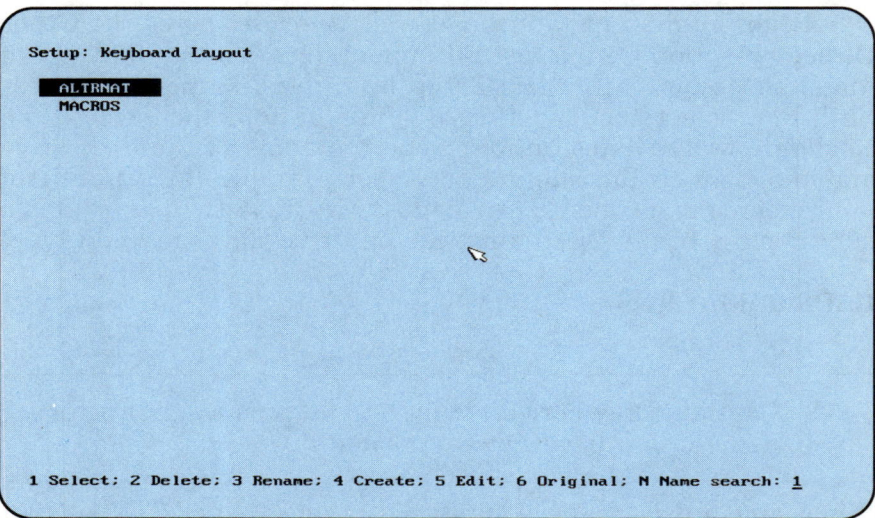

Figure 12.4   Selecting a keyboard definition

Place the cursor on *MACROS,* then select it (by typing 1 or S or clicking the left mouse button). Next, you return to the main Setup screen. Notice the name of the keyboard definition file you just selected, MACROS.DRK, next to the Keyboard Layout option. To return to the main DrawPerfect screen, press Enter or click the right mouse button.

Now that you have selected the MACROS keyboard, let's try a few of the macros. Two of the most useful macros are ALTL and ALTP. ALTP changes the paper size to portrait, and ALTL changes it to landscape (the default). Landscape is DrawPerfect's default, and it prints your drawing across a sheet of paper that is 11 inches wide and 8.5 inches long. Portrait is the opposite. It switches the orientation so that the drawings are printed on paper that is 8.5 inches wide and 11 inches long. Changing the paper size usually requires six keystrokes: *F* for File, *T* for Setup, *I* for Initial settings, *S* for Paper Size, either *1* for Standard Portrait or *2* for Standard Landscape, then F7 to return to the drawing window. When you use the macro, you save four keystrokes and you don't have to remember how to get to the Paper Size option (it's not very obvious). Instead, just remember ALTL and ALTP!

To try these macros, press ALTP to select portrait. The dashed border that surrounds your drawing changes to represent the portrait style. Press ALTL to change it back to landscape. If you try these macros after retrieving one of your charts or drawings, the change will be more dramatic because the figure will shrink when you select portrait (assuming it was created in landscape).

Several of the built-in macros are designed to help you format text lines. For instance, after selecting the Draw menu's Text Line option and pressing Enter to begin typing, you can press CTRLI to turn on italics, CTRLO to turn on outline, or CTRLD to turn on double underline. Try using the italics macro. Begin by displaying the Draw menu, selecting Text Line, then pressing Enter. Next, press Ctrl and I. Type a line of text, and you will see that it is italicized. Press Enter when you finish.

Three of the macros help you to change line drawing Attributes such as line color, style, or width. (These are used with Draw Line, not Draw Text Line.) For instance, you can use CTRLW to display the Line Width menu and select another width, CTRLC, to display the Line Color menu, and CTRLS to display the Line Style menu. Try using CTRLW to draw a thick line. Begin by pressing Ctrl and W, then select a thick line width, such as 16, by typing the number and pressing Enter. Next, display the Draw menu, select Line, then move the cursor to the starting position for your line and press Enter. Use the Arrow keys or mouse to draw the line.

The CTRLP and CTRLF macros are helpful when you are using one of these tools from the Draw menu: Box, Polygon, Circle, or Ellipse. You can use CTRLP to select the Fill Pattern menu or CTRLF to display the Fill Color menu. Be sure to use the macros to select a new color or pattern before you start drawing. If you are drawing an arrow, you can use CTRLA to change the arrow width.

Chapter 12

What You Have Learned

In this chapter, you've learned how to create macros and use them as shortcuts for any task that you perform frequently. You should now be familiar with the following:

▶ Macros are special files that you can create to run a sequence of DrawPerfect keystrokes that you use on a regular basis. Macros are saved on disk but cannot be retrieved like a regular DrawPerfect file.

▶ To create a macro, you press the Macro Define key (Ctrl-F10), type a name for your macro and a brief description of what it does, then type the keystrokes for the macro just as though you were performing the task in a real application. When you finish recording the keystrokes, you press Macro Define again (Ctrl-F10). DrawPerfect then saves your new macro as a special file with the extension .DRM.

▶ Macro file names can include from one to eight characters, or you can name them using the Alt key in combination with any letter (A through Z). To use an Alt key macro, you just press Alt and the letter. To use a named macro, you press Alt-F10, type the name, then press Enter.

▶ When you create a macro, DrawPerfect saves it in your current directory. If you change directories frequently, you can avoid having macros scattered all over your disk by using the Setup menu to designate a subdirectory for your macros. This forces DrawPerfect to automatically save all your macros in that subdirectory.

▶ To change a macro or view its contents, you can use Draw-Perfect's macro editor. The initial steps are just like creating the macro: You press Macro Define (Ctrl-F10), type the macro name, then press Enter. A prompt will then appear warning you that the macro already exists and asking if you want to replace it, edit it, or change the description. Selecting the Edit option takes you to the macro editor screen.

▶ DrawPerfect comes with several built-in macros, which you can use by selecting the MACROS keyboard layout on the Setup menu.

Appendix A
Installation

Introduction

Since the original DrawPerfect files are compressed and cannot be copied directly from the original disks, you must use the automatic installation program to install DrawPerfect. All the instructions in this appendix assume that you are installing DrawPerfect on a hard disk.

Program Installation on a Hard Disk

To install DrawPerfect on a hard disk, place the disk labelled *Install/Program 1* in drive A and close the drive door. Type:

A:

then press Enter to change the current directory to A. Next, start the installation program by typing:

Install

Appendix A

then pressing Enter. You will see this prompt in a box at the bottom of the screen:

```
Welcome to the DrawPerfect 1.0 Installation Program.
Continue? Yes (No)
```

Type **Y**. Next, this prompt appears:

```
Installing to a Hard Disk? Yes (No)
```

Type **Y**. The main Installation menu shown in Figure A.1 appears. To install DrawPerfect, select the first option, Program Files. Next, the DrawPerfect Program Installation menu appears providing four options: Basic, Custom, Network, and Exit. The Basic option assumes you want to install DrawPerfect on drive C in a subdirectory called *DR10* (the installation program will create the subdirectory automatically if DR10 is not found). If so, select it by typing **1** or **B**. If you want to install it on a different drive or subdirectory, select the second option, Custom, and then skip to the Custom section.

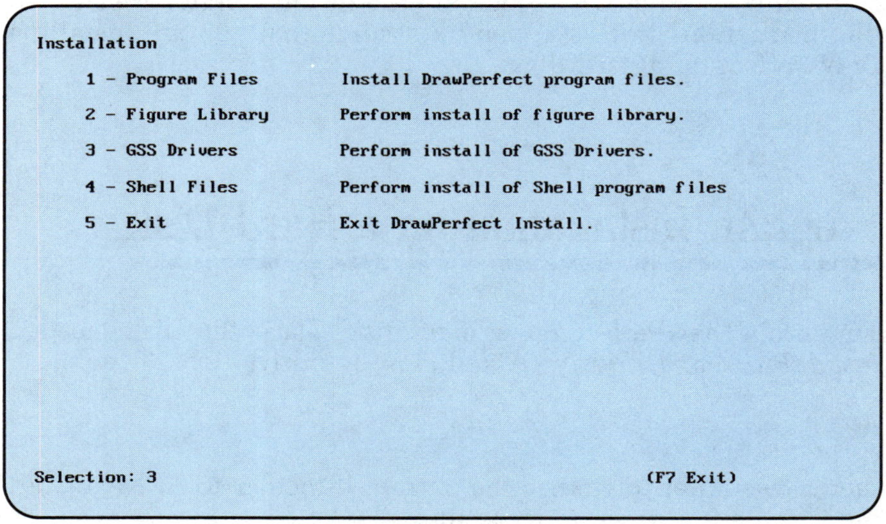

```
Installation
    1 - Program Files      Install DrawPerfect program files.
    2 - Figure Library     Perform install of figure library.
    3 - GSS Drivers        Perform install of GSS Drivers.
    4 - Shell Files        Perform install of Shell program files
    5 - Exit               Exit DrawPerfect Install.




Selection: 3                                        (F7 Exit)
```

Figure A.1 The main Installation menu

Basic Installation

If you select Basic Installation, this prompt appears:

`Do you want to install the `**`DrawPerfect Program`**`? Yes (`**`No`**`)`

    You will also see a prompt in a box near the bottom of the screen telling you that these files are necessary to run DrawPerfect. Since you must install them, select Yes by typing **Y** or pressing Enter. Next, this prompt appears:

`Insert the `**`Program 1`**` master diskette into A:\`

Note the prompt in the lower right corner:

`(`**`Enter`**` = Continue   `**`F1`**` = Cancel)`

This means that you can either cancel the installation process by pressing F1, or proceed with it by pressing Enter. To continue, press Enter.

    The installation program takes over and begins copying files from the floppy disk in drive A onto your hard disk. As it is working, you will see a box in the middle of the screen telling you which files are being installed, such as:

`Installing: `**`DR.EXE`**

As soon as all of the files on the first disk have been copied, you will see this prompt in the lower left corner of the screen:

`Insert the `**`Program 2`**` master diskette into A:\`

Remove the Install/Program 1 disk from drive A and replace it with the Program 2 disk, then close the drive door, and press the Enter key. You will again see a box with a prompt naming the files as they are installed, such as `Installing: `**`DR.FIL`**`.` After a minute or so you will hear a beep and this prompt will appear:

`Do you want to install the `**`Keyboard Files`**`? Yes (`**`No`**`)`

At the bottom of the screen a box will appear explaining what the keyboard files are.

Appendix A

```
The Keyboard Files provide different keyboard layouts
and specialized macros.
```

Since you will be using the keyboard files in Chapter 12, *An Introduction to Macros,* we recommend that you install them. Type **Y** or press Enter, and the two keyboard files will be copied. Next, you will hear a beep and see this prompt:

```
Do you want to install the Help Files? Yes (No)
```

Another box will appear near the bottom of the screen explaining what the Help files are for: They provide on-line help within DrawPerfect. We recommend that you install them, since the on-line help is excellent. We teach you how to use it in the first chapter. Type **Y** or press Enter, and the small box will reappear naming the help files as they are copied. Next, this prompt appears:

```
Do you want to install the Graphic Drivers? Yes (No)
```

Answer Yes to this question if your computer system includes any of the following video interface cards for your monitor: Hercules InColor, Paradise AutoSwitch EGA, Paradise VGA Plus, Video 7 VGA, IBM 8514 Adapter, ATI VIP VGA, ATI EGA Wonder, or MDA Genius 1 or 2. If you are unsure, just type **Y**. When you start DrawPerfect, it will automatically detect the card in your computer and choose the correct graphic driver (also called a video resource file, or VRS file) for it. If you need one of these files and do not install it in this step, DrawPerfect will not run at all!

The next prompt asks:

```
Do you want to install the Font File? Yes (No)
```

As the message in the box tells you, this file is necessary to run DrawPerfect, so type **Y** or press Enter to install it. You will then see this prompt:

```
Insert the Fonts/Utilities 1 master diskette into
drive A:\
```

Remove the Program 2 disk from drive A and replace it with the Fonts/Utilities 1 disk; then close the drive door and press the

Enter key. The box in the middle of the screen will appear again, naming the files as they are installed. After all the files are copied from the first Font/Utilities 1 disk, this prompt will appear:

```
Insert the Fonts/Utilities 2 master diskette into
drive A:\
```

Remove the Fonts/Utilities 1 disk from drive A and replace it with the Fonts/Utilities 2 disk; then close the drive door and press the Enter key. After a few files are copied, you will see this prompt:

```
Do you want to install the Utility Files? Yes (No)
```

As the message box tells you, these are special programs like GRAB, DRINFO, and GRAPHCNV. Although you won't be using them as you read this book, you may need them in the future. The DRINFO file is especially helpful if you are having trouble and need to call customer support. It provides information about what type of computer you are using, how much memory it has, the monitor and interface type, the DOS version, and much more. We recommend that you type **Y** to install these files (unless you are very low on disk space). The next prompt asks:

```
Do you want to install the Template Files? Yes (No)
```

The Template files are sample charts that you can retrieve and fill in with your own data. Since you will be working with these in Chapter 3, we recommend that you install them. Type **Y** or press Enter, and the templates will be copied.

    The next prompt asks:

```
Do you want to install the Learning Files? Yes (No)
```

If you plan to study the lessons in the DrawPerfect manual, go ahead and type **Y** to install these files. Note that the installation program will create a new subdirectory to install them in, naming it C:\DR10\LEARN.

    The installation program will then check the CONFIG.SYS file in your root directory to make sure it allows for 20 files, the number required to use DrawPerfect. You should see a prompt like this at the top of the screen:

```
Check C:\CONFIG.SYS file
```

followed by information telling you how many files yours will allow. If it is set for 20 or more, you will see this message:

```
No changes are necessary
```

and a prompt telling you to press any key to continue, so press Enter. If your CONFIG.SYS file does not allow for at least 20 files, you will be asked if you would like to have it changed. Since this is necessary to run DrawPerfect, type **Y**. If the program does not find a CONFIG.SYS file at all, you will be asked if you want to create it. Type **Y** in response to this and the prompt that follows it.

The installation program then checks the AUTOEXEC.BAT file in the root directory, if there is one. This prompt appears at the top of the screen:

Check C:\AUTOEXEC.BAT file

As the message below it tells you, this file contains a "batch" of commands that are automatically run each time you start your computer. One of these commands is a path command, which tells DOS where to look for the special command files that you type to start a program such as DrawPerfect or the Shell. If you add the name of the DrawPerfect directory to the path command inside this file, you can start DrawPerfect or the Shell from any subdirectory.

If an AUTOEXEC.BAT file is found, you are either asked if you want to add the DrawPerfect subdirectory to the path or, if no path command exists inside your AUTOEXEC.BAT file, if you want to create one. We do not recommend changing the AUTOEXEC.BAT file, and suggest that you type **N** in response to either of these prompts. The AUTOEXEC.BAT file is a very important one because it sets up your system. If something goes wrong, you may really regret changing it. Besides, this procedure is not required to run DrawPerfect.

However, if you see a message telling you that the AUTO-EXEC.BAT file was not found and asking if you want to create it, no harm can be done by creating one. In that case, type **Y** in response to this and the prompt that follows.

Printer Installation

The logical time to install your printer is when you install DrawPerfect. However, you can return to the Install program anytime to perform this task, or if you want to add another printer to your list. Since there are several ways to get to the printer installation section, we'll describe them all.

1. If you have been performing a basic or custom DrawPerfect installation, you will see this prompt:

   `Insert the `**`Printer`**` diskette into A:\`

   For the remaining instructions, skip to the paragraph following numbers 2 and 3.

3. If you have already installed and used DrawPerfect and are now ready to install your printer (or an additional one), begin by exiting to DOS so that you have a DOS prompt such as C> on your screen. Next, use the CD command to change to the subdirectory that contains your DrawPerfect files. For instance, if they are in DR10 you would type **CD\DR10**. Type **Install** and press Enter. Type **Y** in response to the prompt asking if you want to continue. The main Installation menu appears. Select Program Files, then select Custom from the next menu. The DrawPerfect Program Custom Installation menu appears. Select the fifth option, Select Printer. You should now see this prompt:

   `Insert the `**`Printer`**` diskette into A:\`

   Now skip to the paragraph following number 3.

3. If you have already installed and used DrawPerfect and are now ready to install your printer (or an additional one), begin by exiting to DOS so that you have a DOS prompt such as C> on your screen. Next, use the CD command to change to the subdirectory that contains your DrawPerfect files. For instance, if they are in DR10 you would type **CD\DR10**. Type **Install** and press Enter. Type **Y** in response to the prompt asking if you want to continue. The main Installation menu appears. Select Program Files, then select Custom from the next menu. The DrawPerfect Program Custom Installation menu appears. Select the fifth option, Select Printer. You should now see this prompt:

   `Insert the `**`Printer`**` diskette into A:\`

The next step (for everyone) is to place the Printer disk in drive A, close the drive door, and press the Enter key. You will then see an alphabetical list of printers. Notice that the first screen lists only printers whose names begin with A. To see the next screen, press the Page Down key. As of this writing there were 18 screens, so if you don't see your printer right away, keep trying. Alternatively, you can type **N** to use the Name search option, then type the first letter of your printer's name, such as **H** for Hewlett-Packard or **E** for Epson. This will move you instantly to the screen listing printers that begin with this letter. When you get there, press the Enter key. If your printer is not on the list, try calling WordPerfect Corporation to see if they have another disk to send you. The phone number is listed on the last screen.

To select your printer, type the number that appears to the left of it and press Enter. A prompt will appear asking if you want to select the printer. For instance, if you select HP LaserJet Series II, this prompt appears:

`Select printer HP LaserJet Series II? Yes (No)`

If you type **N**, you return to the printer list and can choose a different printer. If you type **Y**, the screen will change and this prompt will appear:

`Do you want to install the Printer (.ALL) File? Yes (No)`

As the message box tells you, this file is necessary to create the printer file for your printer, so you must type **Y** or press Enter. You will then see the small box telling you the name of the printer file that is being installed. After the file has been copied, this prompt will appear at the bottom of the screen:

`Do you want to install another printer? No (Yes)`

Notice that the assumption is No this time. If you do wish to install a second printer, just type **Y** and repeat the steps to select the printer name from the list. If not, just type **N** or press Enter.

You will then be returned to the main Installation screen (shown in Figure A.1) or the DrawPerfect Program Custom Installation screen (depending on how you got here). If you are in the Custom Installation screen, select Exit to return to the main Installation screen. Notice that you can also use it to install Figure Library files, GSS Drivers, or Shell Files. Since we will be asking you to use the Figure Library files and Shell files, we recommend that you install them. If you plan to use a plotter, film recorder, or color printer, you should also use the GSS Drivers option to install the file corresponding to your device.

If you want to exit from the installation program, type **E** or **5** to select the Exit option on the main Installation menu. The opening screen for DrawPerfect will appear. If you were performing a basic or custom DrawPerfect installation, you will be asked to enter your customer registration number. This is your DrawPerfect license number, and it should be on the registration card that came with your DrawPerfect package. We recommend that you type it, but if you don't have it available just press Enter. After a few minutes you will see a prompt asking you to press any key to exit. As soon as you press a key such as Enter or the Spacebar, you will exit the installation program and return to the DOS prompt.

Custom Installation

If you select Custom from the DrawPerfect Program Installation menu, the DrawPerfect Program Custom Installation menu appears. It should resemble Figure A.2. Select the first option, Install Files From; then type the name of the drive containing the original DrawPerfect disks that you will be copying from. For example, if your original disks will be in drive A, type:

A:

and press Enter. Next, select the second option, Install Files To. The screen changes and the Location of Files menu appears. Use it to type the name of the subdirectory (or subdirectories) where you want to install your DrawPerfect program files, printer files, keyboard/macro files, Figure Library files, learning files, and (optionally) backup files and drawing files.

Begin by selecting the first option, DrawPerfect Program. You will see a prompt asking you where you want to install the program files. Type the drive and directory name and press Enter. If you type the name of a directory that does not exist, you will see a prompt asking if you want to create it, such as this one that appeared when we asked to use a DR10 directory on drive D:

`D:\DR10\ doesn't exist, create? Yes (No)`

If this happens, type **Y** to create it. Notice that the subdirectory names appearing after the remaining options on this menu are either the same as the DrawPerfect directory, or are subdirectories of it. In our example, the Figure Library files will be copied into D:\DR10\FIGURES, and the Learn files will be in D:\DR10\LEARN. If you want to change any of the suggested subdirectories, select the option and type the subdirectory name. If not, just select Exit (and skip the next paragraph).

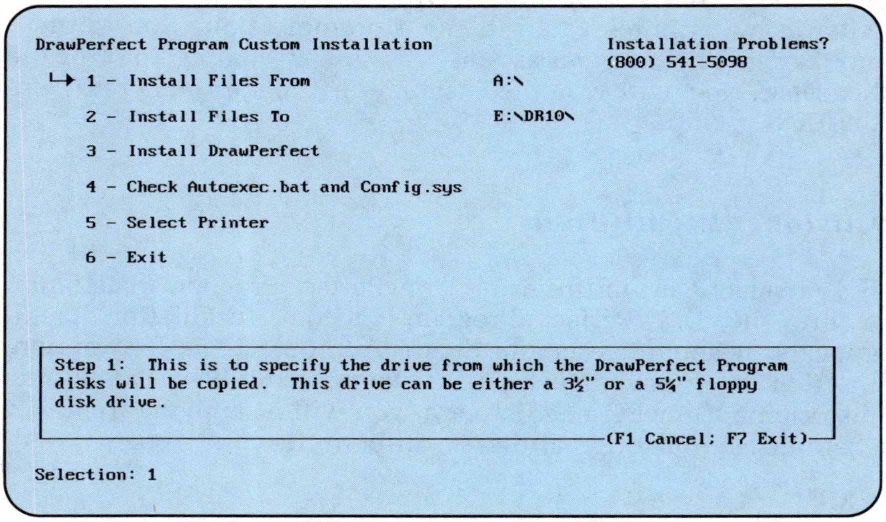

```
DrawPerfect Program Custom Installation          Installation Problems?
                                                 (800) 541-5098
↪ 1 - Install Files From              A:\

  2 - Install Files To                E:\DR10\

  3 - Install DrawPerfect

  4 - Check Autoexec.bat and Config.sys

  5 - Select Printer

  6 - Exit


  ┌──────────────────────────────────────────────────────────────────┐
  │ Step 1:  This is to specify the drive from which the DrawPerfect Program │
  │ disks will be copied.  This drive can be either a 3½" or a 5¼" floppy │
  │ disk drive.                                                      │
  │                                              ─(F1 Cancel; F7 Exit)─│
  └──────────────────────────────────────────────────────────────────┘

Selection: 1
```

Figure A.2   The DrawPerfect Program Custom Installation menu

If you select option 4, Figure Library Files, another screen will appear. Select the first option and enter a name for the directory where you want to install the DrawPerfect Figure Library, or press Enter to accept the suggested name. If the directory does not exist, you will be asked if you want to create it, so type **Y**. Repeat for the remaining selections on this screen, either pressing Enter to accept the suggested names or typing new directory names. Note that the installation program will assume you want all the figure files in the same subdirectory, FIGURES, unless you press F5 to select separate subdirectories for each category. For example, if you do this, animal pictures will be stored in \DR10\FIGURES\ANIMALS, business pictures will be stored in \DR10\FIGURES\BUSINESS, etc. You can override them, if you wish, by typing your own subdirectory names. When you finish, press F7 to return to the Location of Files menu.

Once you have specified a location for each type of file (except Backup and Drawing files, which are optional selections), select the Exit option. You return to the DrawPerfect Program Custom Installation menu. Select the third option, Install DrawPerfect. The remaining steps are almost identical to the ones described in the *Basic Installation* section, so we'll skip the details and describe the steps very succinctly. For more information, you can refer back to that section.

Type **Y** in response to the prompt asking if you want to install the DrawPerfect program and then press Enter (and if the Install/Program 1 disk is not in drive A, insert it, close the door, and press Enter). After a few minutes you will see a prompt asking you to insert the Program 2 disk. Remove the Install/Program 1 disk from drive A, insert the Program 2 disk, and press Enter. When you see the prompt asking if you want to install the keyboard files, type **Y**. Next, you will be asked if you want to install the Help files. We recommend that you type **Y**. The next prompt asks if you want to install the Graphic Drivers. Type **Y**. After those files are copied, this prompt will appear:

`Do you want to install the `**`Large or Small .DRS file`**`?`

Since you have a hard disk, select Large.

Next you will be asked to insert the Font/Utilities 1 master diskette into drive A. Remove the Program 2 disk, insert the Font/Utilities 1 disk, and press Enter. After the files are copied from that disk, you will see a prompt asking you to insert the Font/Utilities 2 master diskette. Remove the Font/Utilities 1 disk from A, insert the Font/Utilities 2 disk, and press Enter.

When you see the prompt asking if you want to install the utility files, type **Y**. The next prompt asks if you want to install the template files. Type **Y**. After they are copied, another prompt will appear asking if you want to install the Learning files. Select Y or N (you won't use them in this book). After that, you will return to the DrawPerfect Program Custom Installation screen. From this menu, select the fifth option, Select Printer.

You should see a prompt asking you to insert the Printer diskette into drive A. Remove the Font/Utilities 2 disk from drive A, insert the Printer disk, and press Enter. Select your printer from the list, as described in the Printer Installation section.

Installing the Shell Files

You can install the Shell when you install DrawPerfect, or anytime after that. If you just finished installing DrawPerfect, you will be in the main Installation program and can select the fourth option, Shell Files (then skip to the next paragraph). If not, start the program by exiting to DOS and changing to the subdirectory that contains your DrawPerfect files. (To change the subdirectory, type **CD** followed by the name of the subdirectory containing your Shell files, such as CD\DR10.) Next, type:

Install

and press Enter. In response to the prompt asking if you want to continue with the DrawPerfect Installation Program, type **Y** or press Enter. The main Installation menu appears. Select option 4, Shell Files.

The Shell Custom Installation menu will appear. Select option 1, Install Files From, and you will see this prompt:

`Install from:`

Use it to tell the program where the Shell files are located (presumably they are on drive A). If the drive name appears next to the prompt, press Enter to accept it. If not, type the name of the disk drive where you've inserted your original Shell disk. For example, if it is in drive B, type:

b:

(it doesn't matter whether you use uppercase or lowercase) and press Enter. Next, select option 2, Install Files To, and this prompt will appear:

`Install to:`

Type the drive and directory where you want the Shell files, if they don't already appear after the prompt. For example, if you want them in the root directory, type:

C:

and press Enter. If you want them in the DrawPerfect subdirectory (and it is named DR10), type:

C:\DR10

and press Enter. The last step is to select option 3, Install Shell, by pressing Enter or typing **3** or **I**. This prompt appears:

`Do you want to install the` **Shell Program**`? Yes (No)`

Type **Y** or press Enter. Next, you will be prompted to insert the Shell Program master diskette into drive A. Remove the disk in drive A and replace it with the disk labelled *WordPerfect Shell 3.0*. Note the prompt in the lower right corner, reminding you that you can cancel the Shell installation process by pressing F1. To continue it, press Enter. A small box appears in the middle of the screen with this message:

`Installing: Shell Files`

After several files have been copied, you will see a prompt asking you to confirm the name of the directory that contains your WordPerfect 5.1 files. It will be similar to this:

`Directory of WordPerfect: C:\WP51`

If the name is correct, just press Enter. If it is not, type the correct name and press Enter.

When the program is finished installing the Shell, you will return to the Shell Custom Installation menu. Type **4** or **E** to exit back to the main Installation menu. To exit the main Installation menu, select the Exit option by typing **E** or **5**.

How to Set Up Your Computer So That the Shell Menu Appears As Soon As You Turn on Your Computer

Since the Shell menu can be used to start any of your programs, you may wish to have it appear automatically whenever you turn on your computer. To do this, you have to modify your AUTOEXEC.BAT file and add the startup instructions for the Shell menu. The easiest way to modify the AUTOEXEC.BAT file is to use the Text In/Out key in WordPerfect, and we are assuming you have either WordPerfect 5.0 or 5.1.

Start WordPerfect in the usual way. To retrieve your AUTOEXEC.BAT file, press the Text In/Out key (Ctrl-F5), select the DOS Text option, then select option 2, Retrieve (CR/LF to [HRt]). In response to the Document to be retrieved prompt, type:

c:\autoexec.bat

and press Enter. If you don't have an AUTOEXEC.BAT file, you'll see an error message telling you that the file is not found. If so, press F1 and create the file following the instructions in the next paragraph. If you do have an AUTOEXEC.BAT file, the contents should appear. Move the cursor to the end of the file and place it on a blank line.

If you copied the Shell files into a subdirectory such as DR10 when you installed them, your first step is to type the command that will switch to that subdirectory. For example, if you copied them into DR10 on the C drive, type:

CD\DR10

and press Enter. Next (for everyone), type the Shell startup command:

SHELL

and press Enter. The last step is to save the file, using the Text In/Out key. Press Ctrl-F5, select DOS Text, then select Save. If the name AUTOEXEC.BAT appears next to the Document to be saved prompt, press Enter to accept it and press **Y** in response to the Replace prompt. If it does not appear, just type **C:\AUTOEXEC.BAT** and press Enter. Now exit WordPerfect by pressing **F7 N Y** (be sure to answer No when asked if you want to save the document). Restart your computer by pressing Alt, Ctrl, and Delete, and the Shell menu should appear.

Installing the Keyboard Definition Files and/or Help Files

In various chapters throughout this book we've referred you to this section to learn how to install the help files and keyboard definition files. The initial procedure is the same for both. Begin by exiting to DOS so that you have a DOS prompt such as C> on your screen. Next, use the CD command to change to the subdirectory that contains your DrawPerfect files. For instance, if they are in DR10, you would type **CD\DR10**. Next, start the installation program by typing:

Install

then pressing Enter. Type **Y** in response to the prompt asking if you want to continue, and the main Installation menu will appear. Select Program Files, and then select Custom from the next menu. The DrawPerfect Program Custom Installation menu appears. Now follow the steps below to install the help files or keyboard definition files (or both).

    Select the third option on the DrawPerfect Program Custom Installation menu, Install DrawPerfect. You will then see a prompt asking if you want to install the DrawPerfect program. Type **N**. The next prompt asks:

Do you want to install the **Keyboard Files**? Yes (No)

If you want to install the keyboard files, type **Y**. If you only want to install the Help files, type **N** and skip to the next paragraph. If you are installing the keyboard files, you should now see a prompt in the lower left corner of the screen telling you to insert the Program 1 master diskette in A. Find the Install/Program 1 disk and place it in drive A, close the door, and press Enter. Soon you will see another prompt telling you to insert the Program 2 diskette. Remove the Install/Program 1 disk from drive A

Appendix A

and insert Program 2, close the door, and press Enter. After the files have been copied, a prompt appears asking if you want to install the Help files, so follow the instructions in the next paragraph to proceed.

This prompt appears:

`Do you want to install the` **`Help Files`**`? Yes (No)`

If you want to install them, type **Y**. If not, type **N** and continue with the instructions in the next paragraph. If you installed the keyboard files, the Help files will now be copied from the Program 2 disk in drive A and you can skip to the instructions in the next paragraph. If you did not install the keyboard files, you will see a prompt in the lower left corner of the screen telling you to insert the Program 1 master diskette into A. Find the Install/Program 1 disk and place it in drive A, close the door, and press Enter. Soon you will see another prompt telling you to insert the Program 2 diskette. Remove the Install/Program 1 disk from drive A, insert Program 2, close the door, and press Enter.

The next prompt asks if you want to install the graphic drivers. Type **N** in response to this and the next five prompts until you are back in the DrawPerfect Program Custom Installation screen. Select the Exit option and then return to the DOS prompt by selecting Exit from the main Installation menu.

Installing the Figure Library Files

Unlike the other DrawPerfect files, the original Figure Library files are not in condensed form. To install them, you can either use the installation program, or use the List Files menu to copy them from the floppy disks onto your hard disk. To use the List Files method, please refer to Chapter 9 (*File Management*) for information about how to copy files. To use the installation program, begin by exiting to DOS so that you have a DOS prompt such as C> on your screen. Next, use the CD command to change to the subdirectory that contains your DrawPerfect files. For instance, if they are in DR10, you would type **CD\DR10**. Next, start the installation program by typing:

Install

then pressing Enter. Type **Y** in response to the prompt asking if you want to continue, and the main Installation menu will appear. Select the second option, Figure Library. Next, you can either select the Basic option to install all the Figure Library files into a subdirectory called Figures (which will be a subdirectory of your main DrawPerfect subdirectory) or the Custom option to create individual subdirectories for each category of files.

Custom Figure Library Installation

If you select Custom, you'll see the Figure Library Custom Installation screen. Use the second option, Install Files To, to specify where you want to copy Figure Library files in each category. For instance, you may want to copy the animal pictures to a subdirectory named ANIMALS, the business pictures into a subdirectory named BUSINESS, etc. The installation program will assume you want all the figure files in the same subdirectory, FIGURES, unless you press F5. This selects different subdirectories for each category. You can also type your own names for each category. If you type a subdirectory name that does not exist, you will be asked if you want to create it, so type **Y**. When you finish, press F7 to return to the Figure Library Custom Installation menu.

To begin installation, select the third option, Install Library. You will then see a prompt asking if you want to install all, part, or none of the files. The remaining steps are the same as the ones in the next section, *Basic Figure Library Installation,* so read on for the rest of the instructions.

Basic Figure Library Installation

If you select Basic, the next prompt asks how much of the Figure Library you want to install. Since there are four disks of figure library files, you may not want to install all of them, especially if you are low on disk space. You'll have three choices: All, Part, or None. If you select None, you will return to the main Installation menu and can select Exit to return to DOS.

If you select All, a prompt will appear asking you to insert the Figure Library 1 master disk into drive A. Find the disk and place it in drive A, close the door, and press Enter. After all the files are copied, you will be asked to insert the Figure Library 2 master disk into drive A, so do that. You'll repeat these steps for the remaining two disks, Figure Library 3 and Figure Library 4. You should then return to the main Installation menu. Select Exit to return to DOS.

If you select Part (instead of All), you will see a succession of prompts asking if you want to install the various categories of pictures: arrow, computer, flow chart, graphic, object, etc. If you type **Y** in response to any of them, you will be asked to insert one of the Figure Library disks into drive A. Locate the disk named in the prompt (1, 2, 3, or 4), insert it and close the drive door, and press Enter to continue. Repeat until you are returned to the Figure Library Custom Installation program; then select Exit. This takes you back to the main Installation menu, and you can select Exit again to return to DOS.

Appendix B

Changing DrawPerfect's Defaults

Introduction

This appendix discusses the Setup menu, which you can use to change many of DrawPerfect's defaults. In several chapters of this book we have asked you to turn to this section to learn how to perform tasks like installing your mouse, changing default settings for the fonts and font colors, and changing the default directory. We will cover all of these features, and mention some of the other options that we think will be useful to you.

To use the Setup menu, either display the File menu and select the Setup option or press the Setup key, Shift-F1. The Setup menu will appear. It includes these options: Mouse, Display, Environment, Initial Settings, Keyboard Layout (refer to Chapter 12 for a discussion of this option), and Location of Files. Changes you make while using the Setup options are stored in a file called DR{DR}.SET. These changes remain in effect permanently, unless you change them again through the Setup menu.

Installing Your Mouse

To run DrawPerfect, you do not need a mouse unless you want to use the Freehand option for drawing. However, it is the fastest and most efficient way to move the cursor, and also makes drawing and editing much easier.

There are two basic steps you must perform to install your mouse. The first is to use the manufacturer's instructions that came with your mouse to install it. The second is to use Draw-Perfect's Setup menu to indicate which mouse you are using. Obviously, we can't help you with the first task, so we will limit this discussion to the second one.

Begin by displaying the File menu and selecting the Setup option, or pressing the Setup key (Shift-F1). Next, select the Mouse option and then the Type option. You should see a list of mouse types made by a variety of manufacturers, such as Micro-Soft Mouse, Logitech Mouse, and Mouse Systems Mouse. Since each one works a little differently, you must use this menu to select the correct file—called a *mouse driver*—for your mouse.

Move the cursor onto your mouse and select it by pressing Enter. If you do not see your mouse in the list, select Mouse Driver (MOUSE.COM) from the list. This should work with any mouse, provided that you have installed the MOUSE.COM software that came with your mouse. Another option suggested in the DrawPerfect manual is to call WordPerfect Corporation and ask if they have created a driver for your mouse since you purchased the program.

After you've selected your mouse, you are automatically returned to the Setup: Mouse menu. If you use a mouse that is connected through a serial interface on the back of your computer, be sure to check the Port option. If you use other devices that are connected serially, such as a modem, you may need to change this option from COM 1 (the default) to another interface: COM 2, COM 3, or COM 4.

If you use your left hand to operate the mouse, you'll want to select the last option on this menu, Left-Handed Mouse, and change it to Yes. This reverses the operations of the left and right mouse buttons. However, you'll have to remember to reverse the mouse instructions as you read this book or the DrawPerfect manual: Press the left button when told to push the right one, and the right one when asked to push the left one!

You can use the other options on the Setup: Mouse menu, Double-Click Interval, Sub-Menu Delay Time, and Acceleration Factor, to control the mouse more precisely. Pressing the mouse button twice in rapid succession is called *double clicking*. It is different from clicking the button twice. Double clicking the left button serves the same function as pressing the left button, then pressing Enter. Two separate clicks are differentiated from a double click by a time period called the *Double-Click Interval*. You can use the Double Click Interval option to change this time interval. It is measured in 100ths of a second, and the default is 35 (slightly more than one-third of a second). Increasing it makes the interval longer. For instance, if you select 100, the interval will be one second.

You can use the Sub-Menu Delay Time option on the Mouse menu to change the amount of time that the cursor remains on a pull-down menu item before its submenu appears (after you select the menu title by clicking the mouse button). This option also controls the amount of time that it takes the mouse to drag the cursor onto a submenu to select an item. It is measured in 100ths of a second, and the default is 15.

The fifth option on the Mouse menu is Acceleration Factor. This determines how fast the cursor responds to mouse movement. The default is 24. You can change it to any number up to 200. By increasing it, you can make the cursor more responsive.

Display

As the name implies, you can use the *Display* option on the main Setup menu to change the screen display. If you use a color monitor, you'll find many of these options to be helpful.

The *Colors* option lets you change the background and foreground color in DrawPerfect's menus; the background and foreground color in the drawing window; and the appearance of bold text in DrawPerfect's menus. None of these changes affect the printed version of your drawings.

The *Graphics Screen Type* option is useful if you have two monitors attached to your computer, or if you are having trouble displaying DrawPerfect. When you install DrawPerfect, the installation program is supposed to automatically select the correct file for your monitor (called the *graphics driver*). If it doesn't select the right one, you can use this menu to override it.

You can use the *Menu Letter Display* option to change the appearance of the letter that you type to select options. For instance, on the main DrawPerfect screen you can select F for File, D for Draw, or E for Edit and these letters appear in boldface. You can use this option to select Bold, Underline, or Normal.

We discussed the next option, *Text Quality While Editing*, in Chapter 3. To speed up your typing and editing, DrawPerfect displays text in medium quality. As a result, text appears as an outline of the selected font (but is always printed in high quality). You can use this option to change the text display to *High Quality* so it will appear filled in (solid black), or change it to *Draft* for faster viewing. As the name implies, *Text Quality While Editing* has no effect on the printed version of your drawings.

If you select the *View Drawing in Black and White* option and change it to Yes, when you use the View Drawing option on the Print key your drawing will appear in black and white instead of in color (on a color monitor).

You may remember learning about *Redraw* in Chapter 2. DrawPerfect displays a Redraw prompt whenever it senses a change that might affect other sections of the drawing. The prompt is a warning that you have to press F9 or select ReDraw from the View menu. You can use the *Automatic Redraw While Editing* option on the Display menu to force DrawPerfect to redraw the screen automatically, so that you'll never have to do it yourself. However, when you do this you may notice that drawing and editing takes a little longer. The *Display Cursor While Drawing* option does just what you think it would: lets you turn off the cursor display while drawing. This is useful if you find that the cursor interferes with your ability to see clearly while drawing small objects.

The *Start With Mini-object* option was covered in Chapter 4, so we'll just review it here. As soon as you press Enter to start drawing an object, the cursor will move from your starting position and automatically draw a small version of the object. For instance, when you select Box from the Draw menu and press Enter, a small box appears on the screen. The default for this option is Yes. If you change it to No, DrawPerfect won't automatically create a mini-object.

The last option on this menu is *Filename on the status line*. The default is Yes, which is why you always see the file name in the lower left corner of the screen when you save a file or retrieve one from the disk. You can use this option to change it to No.

Environment

You can use the *Environment* option on the Setup menu to:

1. Change DrawPerfect's automatic backup options, Timed and Original.
2. Have your computer make a beeping noise when error messages are displayed (in case you are not watching).
3. Permanently change the cursor speed, cursor step number, and acceleration delay.
4. Save drawings in WordPerfect 5.1 format instead of 5.0 format. If you use WordPerfect 5.1, we recommend that you change this option to No. When you do, your DrawPerfect WPG files won't be compatible with WordPerfect 5.0, but they will use less disk space. If you leave the default for this option set to Yes, your DrawPerfect files will be compatible with both version of WordPerfect, 5.0 and 5.1.
5. Change the *Save with Even Border Width* option to Yes. This removes the extra white space that is saved with a chart or drawing (if it does not occupy the whole page), and replaces it with an even border width of 1/4 inch on all four sides.
6. Change the CGM format to enhanced CGM (discussed in Chapter 11, *Presentations and Slides*).
7. Change the *Color Mapping When Converting* option to Yes so that when you retrieve a file whose colors match the background color of your drawing window, DrawPerfect will adjust the colors so they won't disappear into the background.
8. Change the *Units of Measure* option for Position Display from inch marks to centimeters, points, or 1200ths of an inch.

The Backup Options

The *Timed Drawing Backup* option forces DrawPerfect to automatically save the chart or drawing in your drawing window at specific time intervals, such as every 5 or 10 minutes; you specify the time interval when you select the option. By default, this option is set to Yes, and saves every 30 minutes. The files are saved in a special file called DR{DR}.BK1 (if you are using the second drawing window, Drw 2, the name will be DR{DR}.BK2). This backup file is erased if you exit the normal way, using Exit on the File menu or the Exit key. However, if the power fails or if for some other reason you shut off your computer without exiting from DrawPerfect, the backup file will not be erased and you can retrieve it after renaming it (use List Files to rename it). If you don't need it, be sure to erase it. If you forget to erase it, the next time you run DrawPerfect you will see a message asking if you want to rename or delete your old backup file. This happens when your backup time interval is reached and DrawPerfect tries to save the contents of your drawing window into the DR{DR}.BK1 or DR{DR}.BK2 file. Since there is already a file of the same name, it asks you to rename or delete it. To be on the safe side, always rename it and then check it later to see if you need it.

When you save a file (after editing) that you've already saved under the same name, DrawPerfect always asks if you want to replace the first version. You'll see a prompt like this:

```
Replace C:\DR10\PROFITS89.WPG? No (Yes)
```

PROFITS89.WPG is the original file name and corresponds to the disk file, which differs from the screen version if you've made any changes since last saving it. If you select Yes in response to the Replace prompt, DrawPerfect will erase the disk file and replace it with the version on your screen. However, if you change the *Original Drawing Backup* option to Yes, DrawPerfect will automatically save both versions. The version in the drawing window will be saved under the original name, and the previous version will be saved under the same name with the extension BK!. For example, if you save a chart using the name PROFITS89.WPG, then make some changes to it and save it again, the original version is renamed and becomes PROFITS89.BK! and the edited version is saved under the name PROFITS89.WPG.

Initial Settings

You can use the *Initial Settings* option on the main Setup menu to change predefined settings—often called the *defaults*—for many of DrawPerfect's features. You can change the defaults for paper size and type, margins, border style, drawing attributes such as line color, style, and width, and many more. Although you can change most of these options through other menus, such as the Attributes menu for line color, style, and width, doing so only changes the drawing you are working on. In contrast, when you use the Setup method, the change affects the current drawing and any new ones you create in the future. Remember, when you make a change through the Setup menu, the change remains in effect permanently, or until you return to the Setup menu and change it again.

We'll limit our discussion of the Initial Settings menu to the features we think are the most important, and those we promised to teach you in this book.

When you select the third option on the Setup menu, *Initial Drawing Settings,* a menu appears with six choices: Draw Command, Charts, Attributes, Options, Grid, and Font. You can use the first one, *Draw Command,* to change the initial drawing object. The default initial drawing object is line. When you start DrawPerfect, the program initially assumes you want to draw a line, and this prompt appears in the lower left corner of the screen: Enter Start line. You can use the *Draw Command* option to change that assumption so that you'll start with a Figure, Chart, Text Line, Window Text, or one of the other drawing tools: Box, Polygon, Arrow, Arc, Curve, Circle, or Ellipse.

You can use the second option on the Initial Drawing Settings menu, *Charts,* to change several default settings that are used when you create charts. You can use the *Chart Type* option to change the default Chart Type to bullet, simple, freeform, bar, line, pie, area, stacked bar, hilo, scatter, or mixed. We alluded to the second option on this menu, *Sample Data,* in Chapter 2. You may recall that DrawPerfect provides sample data and titles when you select one of the chart options (bar, line, etc.) and then enter the Graph Edit screen. If you do not want DrawPerfect to display this sample data, select the Sample Data option and change it to No. The *Font/Axis Color* option lets you change the default color for the X- and Y-axes and for their labels and titles.

The *Text Chart* option lets you change the following default settings that are in effect when you create a bullet, simple, or free-form text chart: title font and color, subtitle font and color, body font and color, and (for bullet charts) bullet character.

Attributes is the third option on the Initial Drawing Settings menu. You can use it to change the default settings for line color, style, and width, fill color and pattern, and arrow width.

Options, the fourth selection on the Initial Drawing Settings menu, lets you change the defaults for four drawing options: Freehand, Constrain, Stretch, and Position Display.

You may recall studying the Grid in Chapters 3 and 4. The Grid is a set of points that serve as a guide while you draw. You can use the *Grid* option on the Initial Drawing Settings menu to turn on Grid Display and Grid Snap permanently; to change the defaults for the spacing of points along the X- and Y-axes (*X Size and Y Size*); and change the default setting that regulates how often the points are actually displayed (*Display Interval*).

The last option on the Initial Drawing Settings menu is *Font.* You can use it to change the default settings for the font (size and type) and font color that DrawPerfect will use when you type text using the Text Line or Window Text features.

You can use *Print Options* on the Initial Setup menu to change the defaults for four print options: Binding Width, Number of Copies, Graphics Quality, and Text Prints Solid Black. In Chapter 7 you learned how to change these options through the File Print menu (or by pressing Shift-F7). However, when you use that method, the next time you use DrawPerfect, the options revert back to the defaults.

The *Paper Size* option on the Initial Setup menu lets you select a different paper size and type from the following list: Standard Portrait, Standard Landscape, Legal Portrait, Legal Landscape, Square, 35mm Format, US Government, A4 Portrait, A4 Landscape, and Other. Landscape means that your drawing will print sideways on the page. For example, the default of *Standard Landscape* prints your drawing across the width of a page that is 11 inches wide (and 8.5 inches long). Portrait is the opposite. Standard Portrait, for instance, prints across paper that is 8.5 inches wide and 11 inches long.

Use the *Other* option for a paper size that doesn't fit into one of the above categories. When you select it, you are prompted to type your own dimensions for paper width and length. After you select a new size and return to the drawing window, you'll notice a change: The dashed line inside the drawing window that represents the page borders matches the paper size you have selected.

We covered three of the selections on the Page Options menu in Chapter 11 (*Presentations and Slides*): Shading Top to Bottom in View, Top Color, and Bottom Color. The other options are Border Style, Margins, and Gray Shading (% of Black). You can use *Border Style* to select a style for the left, right, top, or bottom border of your printed drawing. The default is None. You can select from among the following styles: single, double, dashed, dotted, thick, and extra thick. The border appears at the margin, and only in the printed version of your drawings.

The margins are the blank space around the outside of your page. Unless you change them, the left, right, top, and bottom margins will be one inch each. To change one or more of them, select the *Margins* option and type a number for each margin. You can use whole numbers or decimals, such as 1.5 or .25, but you don't have to type the inch mark because DrawPerfect will insert it automatically. The margin settings appear in the printed version of your drawings and in both View options: in the Presentations menu and in the Print menu (View Drawing).

You can use the *Gray Shading* (% of Black) option to change the background of your printed drawings, varying the shading intensity that will appear as the background color. The default is 0% gray shading, which means the background will be white. You can change it to any level up to 100%. Choosing 100% will make the background completely black, while everything between 0 and 100% is a shade of gray. Remember, this feature only affects the printed page.

Location of Files

You can use the *Location of Files* option on the main Setup menu to tell DrawPerfect where to store the following files:

- ▶ Backup files
- ▶ Keyboard and macro files

▶ Printer files
▶ Figure Library files
▶ Drawing files

We discussed the last option, *Drawing Files,* in Chapter 9, *File Management.* You can use this option to permanently change the default directory. When you do, DrawPerfect will automatically use it for any new files that you save.

To use any of the Location of Files options, just select it and then type the directory name and path (and drive, if necessary) that you want to use. When you finish, press Enter three times to return to the drawing window. Incidentally, if the directory does not exist, you'll see an error message when you try to select it. If this happens, just exit from Setup and use List Files to create the directory and then try again.

INDEX

3-dimensional effect, pie chart, 191-193
8BALL.WFG file, 180
> (submenu) symbol, 5-6

A

advance command, Presentation option, 267
alphabetical features list, help function, 16-17, 22
Alt key macro, 282-283
    creating, 285
Alt-Shift-G (transfer data) key, 258-259
Alt-Shift-S (transfer data) key, 257
Arc option, 135
arcs, drawing, 134-135
Area, zoom, 142-143
area charts, 203-204
areas
    copying, 157-159
    deleting, 156-157
    moving, 159-161
    sizing, 161-163
Arrow tool, 130-132
arrows drawing, 130-132
asterisks (*) in file names, 214-215
Attributes
    menu, 114-116, 118-123
        Fill Pattern, 131
    option, 320
AUTOEXEC.BAT file, 300, 308-309
automatic backup, 318
Automatic Redraw While Editing, 316
Axes Format option, 198-199

B

Back option, Edit menu, 163-165
backing up files, 212, 226
    current file automatically, 318
backslash (\) symbol, 213
bar charts
    changing to line, 54-56
    creating, 31-39
        from WordPerfect tables, 257-259
basic installation, 297-300

binding option, 184-185
blocks, screen wipe, 268
Box
    option, Draw menu, 113-117, 120-123
    tool, 106-108
boxes, drawing, 107-108, 113-117, 120-123
buffers, printer, 183
bullet text chart, 71-80
    modifying, 89-94
BUTTERFLY.WPG file, 142

C

cancel all print jobs, 182-183
center text option, 73-74
CGM format option, 317
Chart options
    Area, 204
    Line, 194-197
    Pie, 189-191
    Stacked Bar, 201-202
Chart Type option, 319
charts
    area, 203-204
    bar, 31-39, 54-56, 257-259
    creating
        graph descriptions, 60-62
        spreadsheet data, 204-207
    editing, 47-53
    enhancing with drawings, 62-66
    labeling, 56-57
    line, 54-56, 194-201
    moving, 58-59
    pie, 188-193
    printing, 43-45
    retrieving, 46
    rotating, 58
    saving, 39-43, 59-60
    stacked bar, 201-202
    text, 70-101
Circle option, Draw menu, 123-124
clear all slides from show, 272-273
Clear option, File menu, 113
clear screen preserve options, 113
clearing the screen, 22-24

Clipboard, 249-252
Color Mapping When Converting, 317
colors, 315
commands, FORMAT (DOS), 214
CONE.WPG file, 180
CONFIG.SYS file, 299
constrain, 129
Constrain option, 129, 141-142
Control Printer option, 180-183
copying
    files
        multiple, 228-229
        single, 227-228
    selected items/areas, 157-159
creating
    new directories, 236-237
    slide shows, 264-271
    text charts, 71-80
Ctrl-Alt-D (switch to DrawPerfect) key, 243-247
Ctrl-Alt-W (switch to WordPerfect) key, 243-247
Ctrl-F10 (macro define) key, 282-286, 290
cupolas, drawing, 113-126
current directory, 217
cursor, 4
    movement, 10-11
        Graph Data screen, 38-39
    step, 8
Curve option, 136
curves, drawing, 136
custom installation, 303-306

D

data
    graph, entering, 34-39
    point markers, 200-201
default directory, changing, 237-238
defaults, changing, 313-317, 319-320
defining
    keyboard layout, 291-292
    macros, 283-286
delay command, Presentation option, 266
Delete tool, 110-112
deleting
    directories, 238
    files, 230-232
    objects, 110-111
    selected items/areas, 156-157
    slides from show, 272
designating macro directory, 290-291
Dir prompt, 212, 214-215
directories, 211-214
    copying files between, 227-229
    creating, 236-237

    current, 217
    default
        changing, 237-238
    deleting, 238
    designating macro, 290-291
    parent, 217
    viewing contents, 218-221
disk, installing DrawPerfect, 295-300
Display Cursor While Drawing, 316
Display Option
    Automatic Redraw While Editing, 316
    Colors, 315
    Display Cursor While Drawing, 316
    Filename on the status line, 316-317
    Graphics Screen Type, 315
    Menu Letter Display, 316
    Save with Even Border Width, 317
    Start With Mini-object, 316
    Text Quality While Editing, 316
    View Drawing in Black and White, 316
displaying lists of files in directory, 218
DOLLAR-3.WPG file, 137
double-clicking, 314-315
down
    screen wipe, 268
    pan, 146
Draw
    command, 319
    menu, 106-110, 113-126, 130-133, 137
        Arc, 135
        Arrow, 130-132
        Chart, 189-191, 194-197, 201-204
        Curve, 136
        Ellipse, 132-134
        Line, Freehand, 147-148
drawing, 9, 103
    arcs, 134-135
    arrows, 130-132
    boxes, 106-108, 113-117, 120-123
    circles, 123-124
    cupolas, 113-126
    curves, 136
    ellipse, 132-134
    enhancing charts, 62-66
    freehand, 147-148
    triangles, 108-110, 117-120
    wind vane, 122-123
    windows, 120-123
Drawing on Disk option, 178-180
drawing tools
    Arc tool, 130, 134-135
    Arrow tool, 130-132
    Box tool, 106-108
    Curve tool, 130
    Ellipse tool, 130, 132-134

Index

Line tool, 122-123
Polygon tool, 108-110
Size tool, 137-139
Stretch tool, 139-141
drawing window, 8
drawings
   moving (panning) on screen, 146
   previewing, 183-184
   printing specific areas, 146
   saving, 24
DrawPerfect
   defaults, changing, 313-317, 319-320
   exiting, 25-26
   Figure library, 62-66, 87-91
   function keys, 13-16
   keyboard, 10-11
   mouse, 10
   producing slides, 277-278
   starting, 2, 3
   switching to WordPerfect, 243-247
   transferring files to WordPerfect, 247-252
drivers
   graphics, 315
   mouse, 314-315
DRM file extension, 282
Drw 1, 8
DR{DR}.SET file, 313

E

Edit menu, 110-112, 153-170
   Size, 137-139
editing
   areas, 153-155
   charts
      modifying data, 52-53, 58-59
      move option, 47-52
   items, selecting objects, 152-153
   macros, 287-290
   slide shows, 271-274
   text, 167-168
      charts, 84
Ellipse option, 132, 133, 134
ellipses, drawing, 132-134
enhancing charts with drawings, 62-66
entering graph data, 34-39
Environment
   menu, 317-318
   option, 278
exiting
   help feature, 21-22
   DrawPerfect, 25-26
exploding pie charts, 193
extensions, file, 217

F

F3 (help) key, 14, 20-21
F5 (List Files) key, 212, 218
fade, screen wipe, 268
Figure library, 62-66, 137, 142
   files, 310-312
   retrieving figures, 87-91
Figure option, Draw menu, 124
figures, modifying, 169-170
file
   extensions, 217
      .DRM, 282
      .WPG, 42-43, 46, 59-60, 178-180, 217, 317
   list, 216
   management, 211-212
   names, 214-215, 217
File menu, 106, 113, 173
   List Files, 178-180, 212, 223-238
   Presentation, 264-274
   Print, 146, 174-180, 184-185
   Setup, 185, 274-276, 278, 291-292
Filename on the status line, 316-317
files
   8BALL.WPG, 180
   AUTOEXEC.BAT, 300, 308-309
   backing up, 226
   BUTTERFLY.WPG, 142
   CONE.WPG, 180
   CONFIG.SYS, 299
   copying, 227-229
   deleting, 230-232
   DOLLAR-3.WPG, 137
   DR{DR}.SET, 313
   Figure library, 310-312
   help, 309-310
   keyboard definition, 309
   marking, 230
   moving, 232-233
   printing, 235
   renaming, 234
   retrieving, 223-226
   searching, 222
   shell, installation, 306-307
   transferring between DrawPerfect/ WordPerfect, 247-252
   viewing contents, 220-221
Fill Color option, 119-120
Fill Pattern option, 114-116, 118, 131
fill patterns, selecting, 114-116, 118-120
Font/Axis Color option, 319
Fonts menu, 5, 85
formats, text charts, built-in, 99-100
formatting y-axis numbers, 198-199
freeform text chart, 71

freehand, drawing, 147-148
Freehand option, 130, 147-148
Front option, Edit menu, 163-165, 320
function keys, 13-16
    help feature, 18
    help function, 17
        template, 20-21

G

graph data, entering, 34-39
Graph Data options, 202
    screen, 54-58
Graph Data screen, 34-39, 188-191, 194-197
    cursor movement, 38-39
graph descriptions
    creating charts, 60-62
    replacing, 59-60
Graph Edit
    options, 202
    screen, 32-34, 59, 189-191, 194-197
Graph Options screen, 191-193
graphic images, transferring from WordPerfect to DrawPerfect, 253
graphics driver, 315
Graphics Screen Type, 315
graphs *see* charts
Gray Shading option, 321
Grid Display option, 104-105
Grid Lines option, 197-199
Grid Snap option, 104-105

H

hard disk, installing DrawPerfect, 295-300
header area, 216
help feature, 14-15, 20
    alphabetical features list, 16-17, 22
    exiting, 21-22
    function key template, 20-21
    function keys, 17-18
    topical guide, 18-20
help files, installing, 309-310
horizontal lines, creating, 94-96

I

icon menu, 6-7
Ignore Path option, 274
Import option, 204-207
importing spreadsheet data, 204
    for charting, 205-207
in
    screen wipe, 267
    zoom, 142-145
Initial Drawing Settings
    Attributes, 320
    Chart Type, 319
    Draw Command, 319
    Font, 320
    Options, 320
    Print Options, 320
    Text Chart, 320
Initial Setup menu, 320
installing DrawPerfect
    custom, 303-306
    Figure library files, 310-312
    hard disk, 295-300
    help files, 309-310
    keyboard definition files, 309
    printer, 301-302
    Shell files, 306-307
installing mouse, 313-315
items
    changing size, 138-139
    copying, 157-159
    deleting, 110-111, 156-157
    mirroring, 165-166
    modifying, 168-170
    moving, 159-161
    overlapping/positioning, 163-165
    presentation material, 265-267
    restoring, 112
    rotating, 165-166
    sizing, 161-163
    stretching, 140-141

J

job list, printer, 180-183

K

keyboard
    definition files, installing, 309
    layout definition, 291-292
    moving within menus, 12-14
    using with DrawPerfect, 10-11
keys
    Alt-Shift-G (transfer data), 258-259
    Alt-Shift-S (transfer data), 257
    Ctrl-Alt-D (switch to DrawPerfect), 243-247
    Ctrl-Alt-W (switch to WordPerfect), 243-247
    Ctrl-F10 (macro define), 282-283, 285-286, 290
    F3 (help), 14, 20-21
    F5 (List Files), 212, 218
    function, 13-16
    Shift-F7 (print)
    Shift-F10 (retrieve), 46

L

labeling charts, 56-57
left
   screen wipe, 268
   pan, 146
libraries, Figure, 137, 142
line charts, 194-201
   from bar charts, 54-56
Line Color option, 121-122, 123
Line option Draw menu, 123
Line Width option, 123
lines
   drawing, 123-126
   grid, 197-199
   horizontal, 94-96
List Files
   F5 key, 212, 218
   option, 178-180, 212, 223-238
   screen, 216-222
listing files in directory, 218
Location of Files option, 321-322
Look option, 218-221, 274

M

Macro Define (Ctrl-F10 key), 282-283, 285-286, 290
macros, 281
   creating, 282-286
   DrawPerfect provided, 291-293
   editing, 287-290
   keyboard layout, 291-292
MAGICorp Corporation, 277
Manual pause method, 265-266
margins, 274-275, 321
Margins option, 321
markers, data point, 200-201
marking files, 230
Menu Letter Display, 316
menus
   Attributes, 114-116, 118-123, 131
   Draw, 106-110, 113-126, 130-137, 147-148, 189-191, 194-197, 201-202, 204
   Edit, 110-112, 137-139, 153-170
   File, 106, 113, 146, 173-180, 184-185, 212, 223-238, 264-276, 278, 291-292
   Fonts, 5, 85
   Help, 14-22
   icon, 6-7
   Initial Setup, 320
   keyboard, 12-14
   mouse, 12, 315
   movement within, 12-14
   Options, 104-105, 139-141, 197-201
   Page Options, 274-276

   Print, 180-183
   pull-down, 5-6
   Setup, 315-322
   Shell, 308-309
   View, 142-146
mirroring objects, 165-166
Modify option, Edit menu, 167-170
modifying
   bullets, 89-94
   chart data, 52-53, 58-59
   figures, 169-170
   objects, 168-170
   text, 167-168
      charts, titles, 84-86
mouse
   driver, 314-315
   installing, 313-315
   moving within menus, 12
   using with DrawPerfect, 10
Mouse menu, 315
movement, cursor, 10-11, 38-39
moving
   charts, 58-59
   objects, 47-52, 58-59
   files, 232-233
   selected items/areas, 159-161
   drawings, 146

N

name search, 222
named macros, 282
   creating, 285-286
names, files, 214-215
normal, screen wipe, 267
Number of Copies option, 185
numbers, formatting, 198-199

O

objects, selecting for action, 152-153
Options, 320
   restricting use, 141-142
Options menu, 104-105, 197-201
   Constrain, 141-142
   Graph options, 191-193
   Stretch, 139-141
Other Directories option, 236-238
out
   screen wipe, 267
   zoom, 142-145
overlapping items, positioning, 163-165
overlay, screen wipe, 268
Override option, Presentation menu, 272-274
   Ignore Path option, 274
   Look option, 274
   Show Mouse Pointer, 274

P

Page Options menu, 274-276
pan, 129, 146
Pan option, 129, 142-146
Paper size option, 320
parent directory, 217
path, 213
pause command, Presentation option, 265-266
pie charts, 188-193
    exploding, 193
Polygon
    option, Draw menu, 117-120
    tool, 108-110
positioning overlapping objects, 163-165
presentation, preparing, 263
Presentation option, 264-274
Presentation: Edit Screen, 265-273
previewing
    drawings, 183-184
    text charts, 82-84
Print Drawing option, 174-177
print jobs, canceling, 182-183
Print
    menu, Control Printer, 180-183
    options, 146, 320
        changing, 184-185
Print Window option, 176-180
printer
    buffer, 183
    installation, 301-302
    job list, 180-183
printing
    charts, 43-45
    drawings, 173
    files, without retrieving, 235
    from drawing window, 174-180
    specific areas of drawings, 146
    text charts, 82-84
    without retrieving files, 178-180
programs, Shell, 241
prompt line, 8
pull-down menus, 5-6

R

rearranging slide shows, 271-272
redraw prompt, 156-157
renaming files, 234
Representation option, 200-201
restoring objects/areas, 112, 157
restricting the use of tools/options, 141-142
retrieving
    charts, 46
    figures from Figure library, 87-91
    files, 223-226
    WordPerfect text into DrawPerfect, 254-255
reversing images, 165-166
right
    screen wipe, 267
    pan, 146
right-in, screen wipe, 268
right-out, screen wipe, 268
root directory, 213
Rotate options, Edit menu, 165-166
rotating
    charts, 58
    objects, 165-166

S

Sample Data option, 319
saving
    charts, 39-43
        replacing graph description, 59-60
    drawings, 24
    text charts, 81
screen, clearing, 22-24
screen wipes
    blocks, 268
    down, 268
    fade, 268
    in, 267
    left, 268
    normal, 267
    out, 267
    overlay, 268
    right, 267
    right-in, 268
    right-out, 268
    spots, 268
    top-in, 268
    top-out, 268
    up, 268
screens
    Graph Data, 34-39
        Options, 54-58
    Graph Edit, 32-34, 59
    View 275-276
searching for a file by name, 222
Select Area, 152-153
Select Item, 153-156
selecting
    areas to edit, 153-155
    objects for action, 152-153
    presentation material, 265-267
Setup menu, 321-322
    Display, 315-317
    Environment, 317-318
    Initial Settings, 319-320
    Location of Files, 321-322

Setup option, 185, 274-276, 291-292
shading objects, top to bottom, 275-276
Shell
    Clipboard, 249-252
    files installation, 306-307
    menu, starting DrawPerfect, 308-309
    starting, 242
    utility program, 241
Shift-F7 (print) key, 45
Shift-F10 (retrieve) key, 46
Show Mouse Pointer option, 274
simple text chart, 71
size, changing object, 138-139
Size option, 130, 137-139
sizing items/areas, 161-163
slide production service bureaus, 277-278
slide show
    clear all slides, 272-273
    creating, 264-271
    deleting slides, 272
    editing, 271-274
    rearranging, 271-272
    viewing, 269-270
slides, preparing, 263, 277-278
spell checking DrawPerfect text, 256-257
spots, screen wipe, 268
spreadsheet data in charts, 204-207
stacked bar charts, 201-202
standard landscape default, 320
Start with Mini-object option, 105-106, 315
starting
    DrawPerfect, 2-3
        with Shell menu, 308-309
    Shell, 242
status line, 8
stretch 139
Stretch option, 130, 139-141
stretching objects, 140-141
subdirectories, 213-214
subdirectory path, 213
subtitles, 56-57, 96-99
switching between WordPerfect and DrawPerfect, 243-247

T

Table feature, WordPerfect, 257-259
templates, text chart, 99-101
text
    editing, 167-168
    retrieving into DrawPerfect, 254-255
    spell checking in WordPerfect, 256-257
Text Chart option, 320
text charts
    built-in formats, 99-101

bullet, 70-80
    creating, 71-80
    editing, 84
freeform, 70-71
lines, creating, 95-96
modifying
    bullets, 89-94
    titles, 84-86
previewing, 82-84
printing, 82-84
saving, 81
simple, 70-71
titles, 96-99
Text Quality While Editing, 316
Timed Drawing Backup, 318
titles, text chart, 96-99
    modifying, 84-86
tools, drawing, 106-108
top-in, screen wipe, 268
top-out, screen wipe, 268
topical guide, help feature, 18-20
transferring
    files between DrawPerfect/WordPerfect, 247-252
    graphic images from WordPerfect to DrawPerfect, 253-255
triangles, drawing, 108-110, 117-120

U

Units of Measure option, 317
up, screen wipe, 268
Up, pan, 146

V

View Drawing in Black and White, 316
View Drawing option, 184-185
View
    menu
        Pan, 146
        Zoom, 142-145
    option, 269-270
    screen, 275-276
viewing
    directory contents, 218-221
    file contents, 220-221

W

wind vane, drawing, 122-123
windows, drawing, 120-123
WordPerfect
    switching to DrawPerfect, 243-247
    tables, creating a bar chart, 257-259
    transferring files to DrawPerfect, 247-252

WPG file extension, 42-43, 46, 59-60,
    178-180, 317

X–Y–Z

X Mirror option, Edit menu, 165-166
x-axis position, 114

Y Mirror option, Edit menu, 165-166
y-axis
    numbers, formatting, 198-199
    position, 114

zoom, 129
    feature, 176-180
    option, 129, 142-145